HEINEMANN COORDINATED SCIENCE · HIGHER

CHEMISTRY

Martin Stirrup

Heinemann

Contents

Heinemann Educational Publishers
Halley Court, Jordan Hill, Oxford, OX2 8EJ
a division of Reed Educational & Professional Publishing Ltd

OXFORD PORTSMOUTH NH (USA) CHICAGO
MELBOURNE AUCKLAND IBADAN
GABORONE JOHANNESBURG BLANTYRE

© Martin Stirrup, 1996

First published 1996

ISBN 0 435 58002 7

02 01
10 9 8 7 6 5

Designed and typeset by Ken Vail Graphic Design

Edited by Sarah Ware

Illustrated by: Simon Girling and Associates (Mike Lacey
Peter Wilks), Nick Hawken, Sylvie Poggio Artist Agency
(Samantha Rugen), John Plumb, Squires Graphics, Ken Vail
Graphic Design (Jennie Grove, Graeme Morris, Sam Vail).

Cover design by Ken Vail Graphic Design

Cover photo by SPL/J. Schad (Inset: SPL/R. Ressmeyer)

Printed in Great Britain by Bath Press Colourbooks, Glasgow

Acknowledgements

The authors and publishers would like to thank the
following for permission to use photographs:

p 2 *T:* Tony Gudgeon. p 2 *L:* J.Allan Cash. p 2 *M:* Tony Gudgeon. p 2 *R:* Tony
Gudgeon. p 8: Tony Gudgeon. p 9: Peter Gould. p 12: Peter Gould. p 13 *T:* Silvestris,
Frank Lane Picture Agency. p 13 *B:* Tony Gudgeon. p 14 *T:* David Nunuk/Science
Photo Library. p 14 *L:* Courtesy of De Beers. p 14 *B:* Peter Gould. p 15 (2): Peter
Gould. p 16 *T* (2): Roger Scruton. p 16 *B:* Sinclair Stammers/Science Photo Library.
p 17: J.Allan Cash. p 21 *T:* Peter Gould. p 21 *B:* Tony Gudgeon. p 22: Peter Gould.
p 26: Mary Evans Picture Library. p 27: Peter Gould. p 30 *T:* Roger Scruton. p 30 *B* (3):
Peter Gould. p 31 (3): Peter Gould. p 38: Peter Gould. p 39 *T:* Courtesy of De Beers.
p 39 *B:* Peter Gould. p 41 (2): Peter Gould. p 46: Meg Sullivan. p 47: Courtesy of
Lever Brothers. p 48 *T* (2): Roger Scruton. p 48 *B* (3): Peter Gould. p 49 *T:* William
Harnick, Holt Studios. p 49 *BT:* Nigel Cattlin, Holt Studios. p 49 *B:* Geo Science
Features. p 51: Peter Gould. p 52: Peter Gould. p 53 (2): Peter Gould. p 54 *T:* J.Allan
Cash. p 54 *L:* J.Allan Cash. p 54 *B:* Zefa. p 55 *T:* Adam Woolfitt/Robert Harding.
p 55 *L:* Harvey Pincis, Science Photo Library. p 56: Geo Science Features. p 58 (2):
Peter Gould. p 59: Peter Gould. p 60 *T* (2): Geo Science Features. p 60 *TL:* Roger
Scruton. p 60 *B:* Peter Gould. p 61 *T* (2): Geo Science Features. p 61 *B:* Photo Library
International/Science Photo Library. p 62 *T:* J.Allan Cash. p 62 *B:* Topham Picture
Point. p 64: Wm. Canning Ltd. p 66: Alex Bartel/Science Photo Library. p 67: Ancient
Art & Architecture. p 68 *T:* Tony Gudgeon. p 68 *B:* Roger Scruton. p 69 *T:* Michael
Rosenfeld/Tony Stone. p 69 *L:* Julia Kamlish/Science Photo Library. p 69 *B:* Beyen of
Cowes. p 70 *T:* J.Allan Cash. p 70 *L:* Nigel Friaias/Robert Harding. p 70 *B:* Bruce
Henry/Frank Lane Picture Agency. p 71 *T:* Mark Edwards/Still Pictures. p 71 *B:*
NASA/Science Photo Library. p 72 *T:* Roger Wilmhurst/Frank Lane Picture Agency.
p 72 *B:* Martin Bond/Environmental Picture Library. p 73 *L:* J.Allan Cash. p 73 *R:*
Mark Newman/Frank Lane Picture Agency. p 74: Peter Gould. p 76 *R:* NASA/
Science Photo Library. p 76 *L:* Solid Fuel Association. p 76 *B:* British Gas. p 77: British
Gas. p 78: Tony Gudgeon. p 79: Peter Gould. p 81: Tony Gudgeon. p 82 *T:* Amanda
Gazidis/Environmental Picture Agency. p 82 *B:* Tony Gudgeon. p 83 (2): Tony
Gudgeon. p 84 *L:* S.Whitehorn/Environmental Picture Agency. p 84 *B:* David
Townend/Environmental Picture Agency. p 85: Guy Van Raaij/Environmental Picture
Agency. p 86: Earth Satellite Corporation/Science Photo Library. p 87: John
Shaw/Natural History Picture Agency. p 90 *T:* US GeoSurvey/Science Photo Library.
p 90 *M:* NASA/Science Photo Library. p 90 *B:* Jim Greenfield/Planet Earth Pictures.
p 91: J.Allan Cash. p 92: Action Plus. p 93: Philip Carr/Environmental Picture Agency.
p 94: Planet Earth Pictures. p 96 *T:* Vanessa Miles/Environmental Picture Agency. p 96
L: Sue Cunningham/Environmental Picture Agency. p 96 *BR:* Hulton Deutsch. p 97:
EPL/Christa Stadtler. p 98 *T:* J.Allan Cash. p 98 (top inset): Geo Science Features. p 98
L: M.J.Thomas/Frank Lane Picture Agency. p 98 (bottom inset): Claude Wurldsan,
Marie Perenna/Science Photo Library. p 98 *BR* (2): Peter Gould. p 99: R.David/Zefa
Pictures. p 100: Geo Science Features. p 101 *TL:* Geo Science Features/M. Hobbs. *TR:*
Geo Science Features/Dr B. Booth. p 101 *L:* Martin Stirrup. p 102 *T:* NASA/Science
Photo Library. p 102 *B:* David Hosking/Frank Lane Photo Agency. p 103 *T:* Geo
Science Features. p 103 *M:* Martin Stirrup. p 103 *B:* Natural History Museum. p 104
T: Geo Science Features. p 104 *L:* Martin Stirrup. p 105 *T:* Geo Science Features. p 105
B: Natural History Museum. p 106 *TL & TR:* Natural History Museum. p 106 *BT,
BM, & B:* Geo Science Features. p 107 *TL & TR:* Geo Science Features. p 108: Geo
Science Features. p 109: Martin Stirrup. p 110: Associated Press/Topham. p 111:
J.Allan Cash. p 113: John S.Shelton. p 114: D.Cavagnaro, Panda/Frank Lane Picture
Agency. p 122: Mary Evans Picture Library. p 123: Peter Gould. p 126 *TL:* Geo
Science Features. p 126 *TR:* Natural History Museum. p 126 *T:* Geo Science
Features/Dr B. Booth. p 126 *TM:* The Natural History Museum. p 126 *BM:* The
Natural History Museum. p 126 *B:* Peter Gould. *B:* p 127: Peter Gould. p 128: Peter
Gould. p 129: Peter Gould. p 130: Peter Gould. p 132 (2): Peter Gould. p 142 *T:*
Martin Stirrup. p 142 *L:* Peter Gould. p 143: Mary Evans. p 146: B.O.C. Gases. p 148
(3): Peter Gould. p 149: Peter Gould. p 150: Peter Gould. p 151: Tony Gudgeon.
p 152 (2): J.Allan Cash. p 154 *T:* Peter Gould. p 155 *T* (2): Peter Gould. p 155 *R:*
Tony Gudgeon. p 155 *B* (2): Peter Gould. p 157 *T:* Topham/Picturepoint. p 160 (5):
Peter Gould. p 161: Tony Gudgeon. p 163: Peter Gould. p 164: Tony Gudgeon.
p 165: Courtesy of Johnson Matthey. p 167 (2): Tony Gudgeon. p 168 *T:* Topham/
Picturepoint. p 168 *B:* Courtesy of British Petroleum. p 169: J.Allan Cash. p 170 (2):
Peter Gould. p 171 *T:* Peter Gould. p 171 *TR:* Tony Gudgeon. p 171 *BR:*
L.Campbell/Natural History Picture Agency. p 172 *T:* Peter Gould. p 172 *TL:* Tony
Gudgeon. p 172 *BL:* Peter Gould. p 178 *TL:* Oscar Barriel/Latin Stock, Science Photo
Library. p 178 *TR:* Peter Gould. p 178 *B:* Peter Gould. p 179: Robert Harding Picture
Library. p 181: J. Allan Cash. p 182: Mary Evans.

The publishers have made every effort to trace the
copyright holders, but if they have inadvertently
overlooked any, they will be pleased to make the necessary
arrangements at the first opportunity.

How to use this book

Heinemann Coordinated Science:Chemistry has been written for your GCSE course and contains all the information you will need over the next two years for your exam syllabus.

This book has five sections. Each section matches one of the major themes in the National Curriculum.

What is in a section?

The sections are organised into double-page spreads. Each spread has:

Colour coded sections so you can quickly find the one you want.

Clear text and pictures to explain the science.

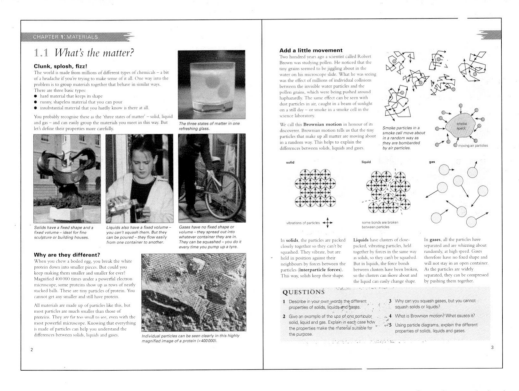

Questions to help check your understanding of the important ideas on the spread.

At the end of each section, there are double-page spreads of longer questions. These are to help you find out if you understand the key ideas in that section. They can also help you revise.

Assessment and resource pack

All the answers for questions in this student book are in the *Heinemann Coordinated Science: Higher Chemistry Assessment and resource pack.*

1

1.1 *What's the matter?*

Clunk, splosh, fizz!

The world is made from millions of different types of chemicals – a bit of a headache if you're trying to make sense of it all. One way into the problem is to group materials together that behave in similar ways. There are three basic types:

- hard material that keeps its shape
- runny, shapeless material that you can pour
- insubstantial material that you hardly know is there at all.

You probably recognise these as the 'three states of matter' – solid, liquid and gas – and can easily group the materials you meet in this way. But let's define their properties more carefully.

The three states of matter in one refreshing glass.

Solids have a fixed shape and a fixed volume – ideal for fine sculpture or building houses.

Liquids also have a fixed volume – you can't squash them. But they can be poured – they flow easily from one container to another.

Gases have no fixed shape or volume – they spread out into whatever container they are in. They can be squashed – you do it every time you pump up a tyre.

Why are they different?

When you chew a boiled egg, you break the white protein down into smaller pieces. But could you keep making them smaller and smaller for ever? Magnified 400 000 times under a powerful electron microscope, some proteins show up as rows of neatly stacked balls. These are tiny particles of protein. You cannot get any smaller and still have protein.

All materials are made up of particles like this, but most particles are much smaller than those of proteins. They are far too small to see, even with the most powerful microscope. Knowing that everything is made of particles can help you understand the differences between solids, liquids and gases.

Individual particles can be seen clearly in this highly magnified image of a protein (×400 000).

Add a little movement

Two hundred years ago a scientist called Robert Brown was studying pollen. He noticed that the tiny grains seemed to be jiggling about in the water on his microscope slide. What he was seeing was the effect of millions of individual collisions between the invisible water particles and the pollen grains, which were being pushed around haphazardly. The same effect can be seen with dust particles in air, caught in a beam of sunlight on a still day – or smoke in a smoke cell in the science laboratory.

We call this **Brownian motion** in honour of its discoverer. Brownian motion tells us that the tiny particles that make up all matter are moving about in a random way. This helps to explain the differences between solids, liquids and gases.

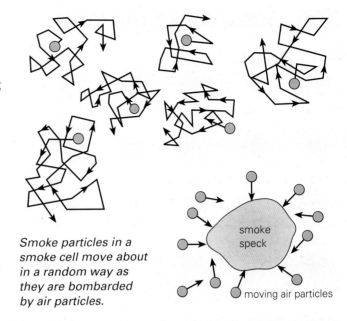

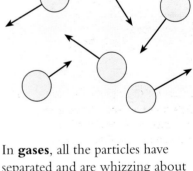

Smoke particles in a smoke cell move about in a random way as they are bombarded by air particles.

smoke speck

moving air particles

solid

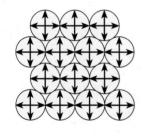

vibrations of particles

liquid

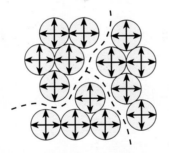

some bonds are broken between particles

gas

In **solids**, the particles are packed closely together so they can't be squashed. They vibrate, but are held in position against their neighbours by forces between the particles (**interparticle forces**). This way, solids keep their shape.

Liquids have clusters of close-packed, vibrating particles, held together by forces in the same way as solids, so they can't be squashed. But in liquids, the force bonds between clusters have been broken, so the clusters can move about and the liquid can easily change shape.

In **gases**, all the particles have separated and are whizzing about randomly, at high speed. Gases therefore have no fixed shape and will not stay in an open container. As the particles are widely separated, they can be compressed by pushing them together.

QUESTIONS

1 Describe in your own words the different properties of solids, liquids and gases.

2 Give an example of the use of one particular solid, liquid and gas. Explain in each case how the properties make the material suitable for the purpose.

3 Why can you squash gases, but you cannot squash solids or liquids?

4 What is Brownian motion? What causes it?

5 Using particle diagrams, explain the different properties of solids, liquids and gases.

1.2 *The way they move*

The heat connection

The link between solids, liquids and gases is that one form can be turned into another. Raising the temperature makes solid ice melt to give liquid water, which boils to give gaseous steam. What is more, if things cool off the process is **reversible** – steam condenses back to water, water freezes to ice. To understand this, you need to think about what happens to the particles as the temperature rises and falls.

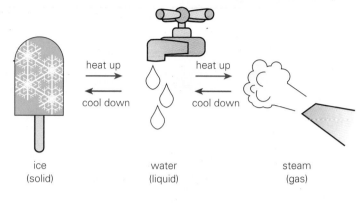

ice
(solid)

heat up
cool down

water
(liquid)

heat up
cool down

steam
(gas)

If you want to see why particles move apart when they move faster, get a group of your friends to stand close together, and then tell them to start dancing!

Expansion and contraction

All the particles that make up matter are moving. The hotter they are, the faster they move. When you heat something, you are transferring energy to the particles which makes them move more quickly.

In solids, the particles are vibrating about a fixed position, held in place by the interparticle forces. If the solid is heated, however, they will vibrate faster and will move further from this position before moving back to it. This has the effect of nudging the particles apart a little – the solid **expands**. When solids cool, the particles slow down again, the forces pull them back closer together and **contraction** occurs.

Melting and boiling

Imagine the particles were balls held together by elastic (to represent the interparticle force). Now start to shake the balls faster and faster to simulate heating. Eventually, the elastic will snap.

In a similar way, the interparticle forces that hold particles together act like elastic bonds. When a solid is heated, the particles move faster and faster until they break free from the bonds that held them in place. At first just a few bonds break and the solid **melts**. But if heating continues, all the bonds will break and the liquid will **boil** as all the particles break free.

Unlike the elastic in your model, however, breaking the interparticle bonds is a reversible process. If you cool things down, the particles slow down again and are pulled back together when they collide – the gas condenses and the liquid freezes.

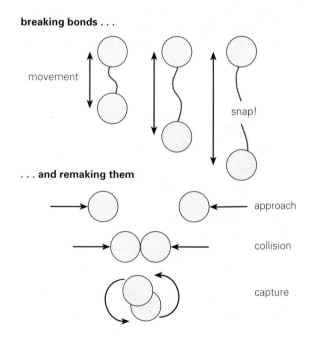

breaking bonds . . .

movement

snap!

. . . and remaking them

approach

collision

capture

Changing state

When you switch on a kettle, the temperature rises steadily as energy from the electricity is put into the water. The more energy that goes in, the faster the water particles move. Temperature is a measure of how fast the particles are moving.

At 100°C, the water starts to boil and an automatic kettle will switch itself off. But what would happen if it didn't? Would the temperature continue to rise as more and more energy came in? The answer is no. Boiling water stays at 100°C no matter for how long it has been boiling. So where does all the energy go? It goes into breaking the bonds that held the particles together, and so making steam.

In the same way, ice stays at 0°C when it is melting. The temperature will start to rise again only when all the ice has turned to water.

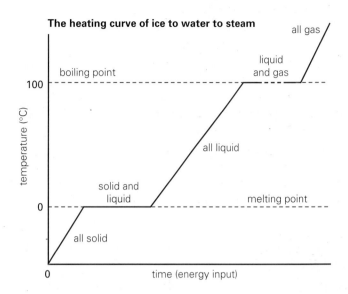

This graph shows what happens if you melt ice and then boil the water. The horizontal parts of the graph show how the temperature remains constant during melting and boiling.

Cooling curves

It is important to realise that these effects are reversible. When a liquid solidifies, the heat energy that was needed to melt it in the first place is given out again as the bonds snap together. The temperature stays constant even though energy is still being lost to the cooler surroundings.

You can use this idea to find the melting point of a substance. Stearic acid (a kind of wax) melts in boiling water. If you measure the temperature of the stearic acid as it cools down, you get a graph like this. Its temperature drops steeply at first, but then 'sticks' at about 69°C, as the liquid starts to turn to a solid. The temperature 'sticks' at the melting point of the stearic acid.

Different chemicals have different melting and boiling points. Scientists often use the melting point of an unknown substance to help identify it.

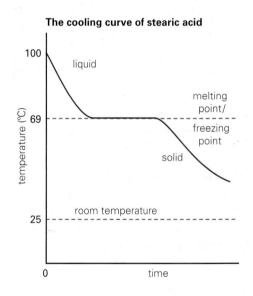

QUESTIONS

1 Describe in your own words why most solids expand when heated.

2 Describe the three states of matter in terms of a battle between the interparticle forces and the movement of the particles. Which wins in each case – the forces or the movement?

3 Explain why the temperature of boiling water stays at 100°C.

4 Ethanol boils at 79°C and freezes at −117°C. Draw an annotated temperature/time graph like the one above for the heating of ethanol from −150 to +100°C.

5 Liquids can also turn to gases without being heated – by evaporation, when particles break free and escape from the surface. Why does the liquid cool when this happens?

1.3 *Mixing it*

Chaotic air

Gases like air are in a state of total chaos. They are made up of countless billions of tiny particles whizzing around at high speed in all directions. They are constantly crashing into each other or anything else that gets in the way – including you!

This idea explains **air pressure**. The constant bombardment of particles pushes against you from all directions. That's just as well, as air pressure is equivalent to 10 tonnes on every square metre. If it did not act in all directions it would squash you flat!

Fortunately for us, gas pressure acts equally in all directions

Try making pinholes in a bag of water to prove it!

The sky is falling . . . ? If it were solid, you would be in trouble!

What's that smell?

This chaotic movement can also help to explain how smells travel through the air. Smelly substances such as perfumes release particles into the air. When they reach your nose, they are detected by special cells.

But how do they get to your nose? You might think that they have to be carried on a breeze, but smells still spread, even in a completely draught-free room.

Diffusion

If you've ever been jostled in a crowd, you will easily understand what happens. Perfume particles get caught up in the mad dance of the air particles. They are battered and bounced around until they are spread evenly through the air. Gases always mix themselves up like this. The process is called **diffusion.**

Naturally, the faster the particles are moving, the sooner this mixing occurs – so increasing the temperature speeds up diffusion.

Diffusion is easily demonstrated with the brown gas nitrogen dioxide.

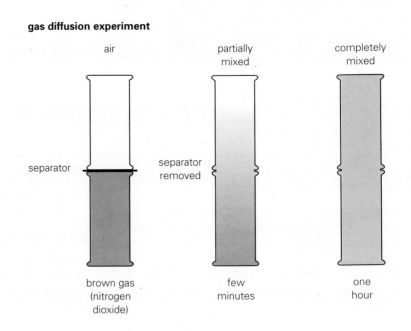

gas diffusion experiment

air

partially mixed

completely mixed

separator

separator removed

brown gas (nitrogen dioxide)

few minutes

one hour

Watching diffusion

If you hold a piece of damp blue litmus paper above a beaker of strong hydrochloric acid, it will gradually turn red (see 5.1). This is because some hydrogen chloride gas evaporates from the acid and diffuses through the air.

If you hold a piece of damp red litmus paper above a beaker of strong ammonia solution, it will turn blue. This is because some ammonia gas evaporates from the solution and diffuses through the air.

The ammonia reaction occurs faster than the acid reaction because ammonia particles have only half the mass of hydrogen chloride particles, so they diffuse much faster.

If hydrogen chloride and ammonia gases meet, they react to form white clouds of ammonium chloride. If you place a few drops of concentrated hydrochloric acid at one end of a glass tube and a few drops of ammonia solution at the other end, white clouds start to form close to the acid. This again shows that the ammonia gas is diffusing faster then the hydrogen chloride.

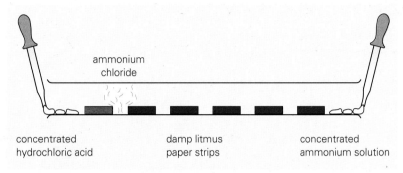

Ammonia diffuses faster than hydrogen chloride, so the white ammonium chloride forms closest to the acid.

In liquids, too

Diffusion occurs in liquids, although much more slowly than in gases, because the particles are not moving as fast. So you don't have to stir the milk and sugar into your coffee – if you're prepared to wait!

Lead nitrate and potassium iodide solutions react to give 'clouds' of solid yellow lead iodide. If you drop crystals of lead nitrate and potassium iodide at either side of a beaker of distilled water, you can again watch diffusion occurring, as the yellow solid slowly forms between the two crystals.

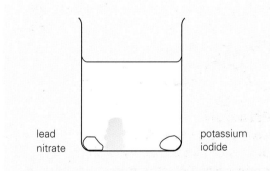

QUESTIONS

1a What causes air pressure?
  b How big a force does it exert on every square metre?
  c Why doesn't this squash you?

2 Your friend thinks smells spread through the air because of draughts. Explain why draughts help, but are not necessary.

3a Why does ammonium chloride form closer to the acid than the ammonia in the experiment shown above?

b Explain how the relative mass of the particles causes this effect.

4 With crystals of lead nitrate and potassium iodide in water, the yellow solid forms closer to the lead nitrate crystal. Which reactant is diffusing faster?

5 If you drop a potassium permanganate crystal in water it dissolves and the purple colour slowly spreads out. Why is this so slow compared to diffusion in gases?

1.4 Solutions

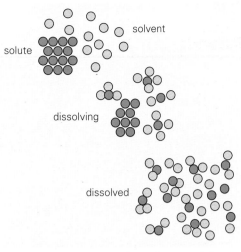

The solvent captures the solute particles and jostles them away.

What's the solution?

You know that sugar dissolves in water – but what exactly does that mean? The sugar seems to disappear, yet you know that it's still there. You can still taste it in sweet drinks. Also, if you let the water evaporate away, you get the sugar back.

This is another example of 'self-mixing', like diffusion. Particles in solids and liquids are held in place by interparticle forces – but even when particles are different, there may still be forces of attraction between them.

This is true of salt and water. When solid salt (the **solute**) dissolves in liquid water (the **solvent**), the water particles surround and 'capture' the salt particles at the edges. These then diffuse off though the liquid until thorough mixing occurs.

Speeding up solution

You can increase the speed at which something dissolves by raising the temperature (which makes the particles move faster) or stirring (which helps the mixing process).

Crushing the solid also helps. This works because solution can occur only at the surface of a solid, and breaking it up into smaller pieces increases the surface area. This relationship between size and relative surface area is very important.

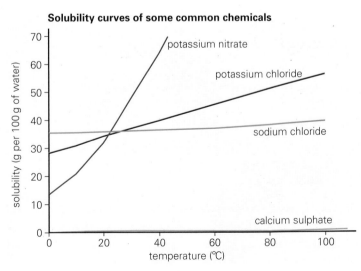

Same volume – different surface area.

Which solvent?

Many common chemicals, such as salt, dissolve in water. Others, such as grease, do not dissolve at all in water – though they may well be soluble in other solvents such as tetrachloroethene (dry cleaning fluid), methylated spirit or turpentine.

Beach tar doesn't come off with water – but methylated spirit will dissolve it away.

Solubility

Even the most soluble substance will not keep on dissolving indefinitely. Eventually the solution can take no more, and is said to be **saturated**. The degree of solubility of a chemical is defined as the number of grams of solute that dissolve in 100 g of solvent. This usually varies with temperature. For solids, warming the mixture not only speeds up the process but usually allows more solute to dissolve.

Solubility curves of some common chemicals

Saturation

If solute particles in solution collide, they may well stick together. When a solute first starts to dissolve, its concentration in the solvent is low, so the number of such collisions is relatively low. As more is dissolved, however, the number of collisions increases. Eventually, the number of new particles breaking free from the solid is matched by the number colliding, clumping together and falling back out of solution. This is saturation.

If water evaporates from a saturated solution (or if a warm one is cooled), more particles clump together than split apart and the solute begins to crystallise out of the solution.

More about crystals

So why do we get the beautiful shapes of crystals? As the particles fall out of solution, they stack up into regular, geometrical shapes. Some, such as common salt, form simple cubes. Others stack in a more complex way, giving more complex shapes, particularly if the particles are not simple spheres. Different chemicals stack to give different shapes, and this can often help to identify a substance.

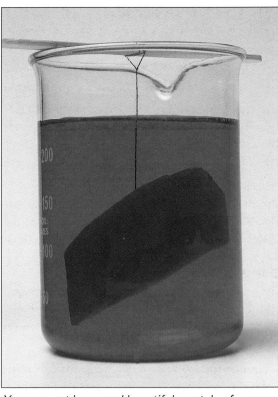

You can get large and beautiful crystals of copper sulphate by letting the water slowly evaporate from saturated copper sulphate solution.

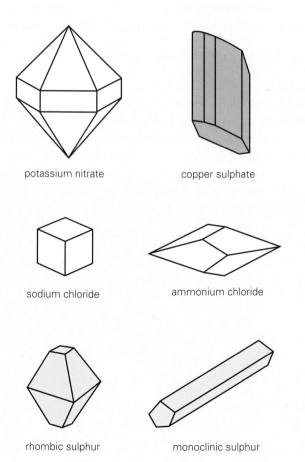

potassium nitrate

copper sulphate

sodium chloride

ammonium chloride

rhombic sulphur

monoclinic sulphur

QUESTIONS

1a Describe what happens to sugar particles when you put sugar in your tea.

b You don't need to stir the sugar into your tea, as long as you are patient. Explain this statement.

2a Give three ways in which the speed of solution may be increased.

b Explain how each method works.

3 From the solubility graph:

a How hot would water need to be to dissolve 60 g of potassium nitrate per 100 g of water?

b What effect does raising the temperature have on the solubility of common salt?

c Calcium sulphate is often said to be insoluble in water. Is this strictly true?

4 Explain what would happen if a hot, saturated solution of potassium chloride was allowed to cool down.

2.1 *The material for the job*

Why use that?

Why are windows made of glass? Part of the answer is obvious – you can see through glass, it is **transparent**. You could in fact use any transparent material that can be formed into sheets in the same way. It is the **physical properties** of glass that are important, not the material itself.

The same principle applies to everything we use. The material that is used has the properties needed for the job.

Here are some important physical properties.

Why not use steel for windows?

Which is easier to carry?

Density

How heavy something is depends on how big it is – but it also depends on what material it is made from. Some materials such as lead are often said to be 'heavy', while others such as balsa wood are said to be 'light'. But to make this a fair comment, the mass of the same volume of each material must be compared. This *relative* mass is called the **density**. The standard unit for density is the **kilogram per cubic metre** (kg/m^3) though grams per cubic centimetre (g/cm^3) are usually used instead.

Density is a very important property, as the heavier an object is, the more energy will be needed to lift, carry or push it. Would you rather lift a 20 kg aluminium ladder or the old-style 30 kg wooden one? Or push a child in a 3 kg aluminium buggy, or the 9 kg steel version?

Strength

Materials that can withstand the effects of large forces are said to be **strong**. Steel is a good example – which is why we build large, 'heavy duty' structures such as bridges or machines out of it. Bricks also have to be strong, if they are not to be crushed by the weight of the bricks above them in a tall building. This type of strength is called **compressive strength**. And don't worry, a household brick could support another 40 000 above it – many times the height of the tallest sky scraper.

Lift cables need another kind of strength, however, because they are being stretched not squeezed. This is called **tensile strength**. Strength is measured in **newtons per square metre** – force/area – so a thicker rope will support a bigger load than a thinner one, for example. One of the strongest materials known is spiders' silk – a strand 200 times as thick would support a car.

Bricks are easily strong enough for the foundations of tall buildings.

A particular explanation

Differences in density and strength are caused by the arrangement of particles.

For a given type of particle, the more closely they are packed, the denser the material. Different materials are made from different particles, however, and particles vary in both size and mass. This obviously affects the overall density of the material.

different materials – different particles

different forces – different strengths

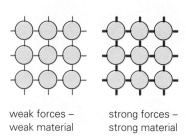

weak forces – weak material   strong forces – strong material

Strength depends on the forces between the particles.

With strength, it is the size of the forces *between* the particles that matter, as these forces hold the particles together. In some materials, such as steel, these forces are very large, so the particles are tightly bonded and the material is strong. In others, such as wax, they are small, so both bonds and material are weak. In liquids, some of these force bonds are broken, so liquids cannot be strong. Neither can gases.

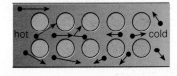

low density   high density

The density of a solid depends on the arrangement of the particles, but also on the mass of the particles themselves.

Conductors and insulators

Materials which allow energy to pass along them easily are called **conductors**, while those which do not are called **insulators**. Materials which are good conductors of electricity are often good conductors of heat energy too. But the two processes, though linked, are different – try not to confuse them!

Electricity

When electricity flows, tiny charged particles called **electrons** move through the material (see 3.4). All materials have electrons, but in conductors *some* of these electrons are only loosely attached to the particles and may move freely. In insulators *all* the electrons are firmly held.

Heat

These 'loose' electrons are also responsible for the transfer of heat energy in metals. As the metal is heated, these electrons move faster, spreading out through the metal and carrying the energy with them.

metals conduct electricity

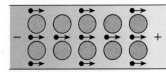

metals conduct heat

 moving electrons

metal particles

The conduction of heat and electricity in metals depends on the movement of electrons.

QUESTIONS

1 If you were to push a steel rather than an aluminium pushchair, how many times as much energy would you need to use?

2a List five situations where high compressive strength is needed.

 b List five situations where high tensile strength is needed.

3 You can brush through a spider's web easily – explain how it is still one of the strongest materials known.

4 The particles of iron and aluminium are packed together in a similar way. Why is iron so much denser than aluminium?

5 Explain, in particle terms, what happens when a solid conducts **a** heat and **b** electricity.

2.2 Metals

The problem with classifying materials as solids, liquids or gases is that any substance can, in theory, exist in all three states. It's just a matter of temperature. Another way of looking at materials splits them into metals and non-metals. You are probably quite good at deciding which materials are metals, but could you explain why?

Metals are shiny

One obvious feature of metals is the way they reflect light. Their characteristic shiny appearance is called a **metallic lustre**. Many metals have a silvery appearance, though some are golden or brown. Some metals, such as lead, may appear dull, but that is because the surface has reacted with the air. If this corroded layer is scraped off, the true lustre reappears.

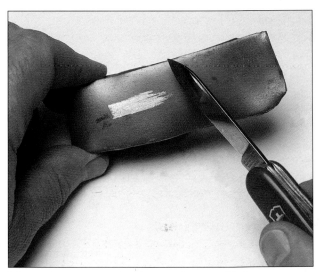

You need to scrape lead to see its metallic lustre.

Most metals are solids

Most metals have high melting points, so they are solids at room temperature. The one exception is mercury, the liquid metal that is used in thermometers. At the other extreme, tungsten has such a high melting point that it can be used in light bulbs, where it glows 'white hot' without melting.

Most metals are dense

Most metal objects feel heavy for their size. Iron is nearly eight times as dense as water, for example. Lead is famous for its 'heaviness', and so can be used to weigh things down, but gold is almost twice as dense.

Aluminium is much less dense, which is why it is used to build aeroplanes – an 'iron' aeroplane would weigh three times as much, and so would need three times as much energy to get it off the ground!

A few metals, such as sodium, have even lower densities and will float on water.

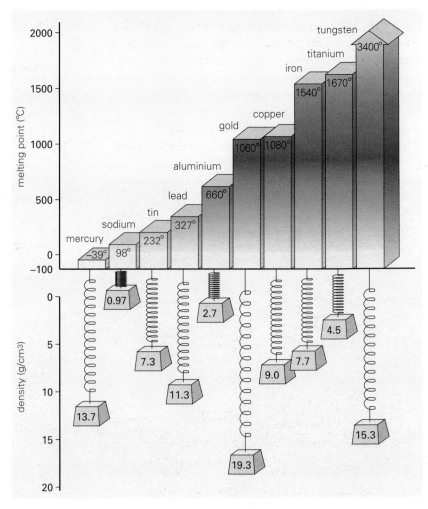

Melting points and densities influence the use of many metals.

12

Metals are strong and hard...

Iron is a very strong metal. It is often used to build structures such as bridges or the girder framework for skyscrapers. Many other metals are strong like this.

Iron can also be very **hard**. The metal teeth of a saw or file can cut through softer materials such as wood.

...but they can be shaped easily

Metals can be beaten or stretched into shape – especially if they are hot. This makes them easy to shape – they are said to be **malleable**. In the past, blacksmiths heated iron in the forge and beat it into shape with hammers. Now gigantic rollers squeeze hot iron out into sheets for car body panels or cans. Girders are made by forcing hot iron out through shaped holes, like toothpaste from a tube.

Metals conduct heat

Heat is transferred from the flame to the eggs by **conduction** through the metal of the frying pan. The handle is not made of metal, as heat would conduct along this too and burn your hands.

Top quality saucepans and frying pans often have thick copper bottoms. This is because copper is a very good conductor of heat.

Metals conduct electricity

Metals also conduct electricity. 'Mains' electricity is carried along thick copper wires. They are covered by an insulating layer of plastic to stop the electricity escaping and giving you a shock.

The hot iron is flattened out between the hammer and the anvil.

Copper is used to conduct both heat and electricity.

QUESTIONS

1 Why do some metals seem dull until you scratch them?

2 Rearrange the metals shown in the diagram in order of increasing density.

3 A con-man tried to pass off gold-coated lead bars as solid gold. How could you tell they were not gold?

4 Describe how girders are made.

5 Silver is a better conductor of electricity than copper. Why do you think copper is used rather than silver for the electrical wiring in houses?

6 Copper is a good conductor of electricity, but is very dense and not very strong. Aluminium is a good conductor of electricity, and has a low density but is not very strong. Steel is not a very good conductor of electricity, but even thin steel cables are very strong.
The cables that are hung on electricity pylons to carry electricity for the National Grid are made of aluminium threaded with steel. Explain why.

2.3 *Non-metals*

It is quite easy to make a list of the properties you would expect a 'typical' metal to show. Non-metals are not so straightforward. Their properties vary widely – and can be quite different to those of metals. Here are some examples.

Sulphur

Sulphur is a bright yellow solid. Its crystals have a glassy lustre. It melts at 120°C and is about twice as dense as water. It is quite soft and shatters if you hit it. It is a poor conductor of both heat and electricity.

Sulphur – definitely not a metal!

Diamond

Diamond is a colourless, crystalline form of carbon (which also makes up most of coal and soot). Its lustre is even more sparkly than glass and well-cut crystals are used in the most expensive jewellery.

Diamond has a very high melting point (over 3500°C) and is nearly four times as dense as water. It is very hard – the hardest of all materials. Diamond-studded drill bits are used to cut through the rock in oil wells. But it is brittle. If struck with a hammer it would shatter.

Diamonds are excellent conductors of heat but do not conduct electricity.

A common non-industrial use of diamond.

Graphite

Graphite is a grey-black crystalline form of carbon. It has a dull appearance. Like diamond, it has a very high melting point (over 3500°C), but it is only twice as dense as water.

Unlike diamond, graphite is very soft. Your pencil 'lead' is made of graphite, and pieces break off as you rub it on the paper. Also unlike diamond, graphite conducts electricity to some extent but is a poor conductor of heat. It is used to make electrical resistors and is added to some lubricating oils.

Nitrogen and oxygen

Nitrogen and oxygen are the two main gases in the air. Nitrogen boils at minus 196°C, oxygen at minus 183°C. Like most gases, they do not conduct heat or electricity.

It's hard to believe that graphite and diamond are both forms of carbon – their physical properties are so different!

Bromine

Bromine melts at minus 7°C and boils at 59°C, so it is a liquid at room temperature. It is a brown liquid that is three times as dense as water. It does not conduct electricity.

Non-metal summary

- Non-metals can be solids, liquid or gases.
- Solid non-metals can be dull or have a sparkly, glassy lustre.
- Solid non-metals usually have lower densities than 'typical' metals such as iron.
- Some non-metals are strong, others are weak.
- Some are soft, but others are very hard.
- Most solid non-metals cannot be squashed or stretched into shape. They tend to shatter or crumble.
- Non-metals are usually poor conductors of both heat and electricity.

Bromine is a brown liquid that easily turns into a brown vapour.

Check out the chemistry!

To look for a more reliable definition of non-metals, you need to look at their chemical reactions, not just their physical properties.

When non-metals burn in oxygen, they turn into oxides which are **acids**. The oxides of metals are always **bases.** (See chapter 5.)

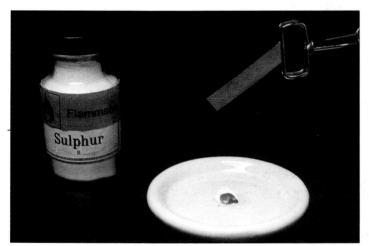

The oxide fumes from burning sulphur turn damp blue litmus paper red, showing that they are acidic.

QUESTIONS

1 List the reasons why you would not class sulphur as a metal.

2a Draw up a table with three columns, headed **property**, **diamond** and **graphite**.
  b Fill in the properties for diamond and graphite.
  c Which properties are the same, which are different?
  d Which property of graphite is very unusual for a non-metal?

3 Bromine and mercury are both liquids. How could you tell equal volumes of them apart if you were given them in two sealed flasks while wearing a blindfold?

4 For each of the following, decide whether it is a metal or a non-metal. Give reasons for your answers.
A is a shiny brown solid. Its density is 9 g/cm³. It melts at 1080°C, conducts heat and electricity and can be beaten into shape with a hammer.
B is a grey solid. Its density is 2.4 g/cm³. It melts at 1420°C. It shatters if beaten with a hammer.
C is a silvery-white solid. Its density is 0.86 g/cm³. It melts at 62°C, conducts heat and electricity and can be cut with a knife.
D is a very hard, yellow or brown solid that melts at 2300°C. It does not conduct heat or electricity.

5 The fumes from burning element X turn blue litmus paper red. Is X a metal or a non-metal?

2.4 Separating mixtures 1

Most natural materials are mixtures, so a lot of initial processing has to take place, in order to separate out the things you want from the things you don't. In order to be able to do this, you need to exploit the differences in the physical properties of the materials involved.

From the rocks to your chips – it takes a lot of processing.

Dissolve

In Cheshire, rock salt is mined from underground beds, where it forms layers in the rocks. As salt is soluble in water but rock is not, one way to get it out is to pump down fresh water – and pump the salt solution (brine) back to the surface.

Settle and decant...

The brine obtained in this way is, of course, muddy with solid particles in suspension in the water. These solid particles will settle out in time, and the clear brine may then be **decanted** off. Drinking water is often left to stand in 'settling tanks' to get rid of suspended sand and mud like this.

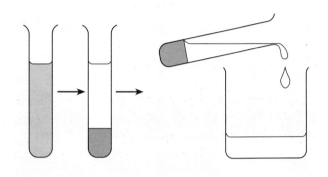

Suspended solids will settle out in time.

...or centrifuge and decant

Settling can take a long time, but there is a way to speed up the process in the laboratory, by using a **centrifuge**. This spinning device slings the solid material to the bottom of the tube in the same way as a fairground spinner pins you to the wall or a spin drier dries your clothes. (For a more detailed explanation, ask your physics teacher!)

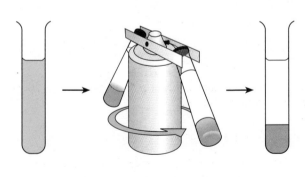

This centrifuge looks like a small spin drier and works in a similar way. It makes the solid settle out in just a few seconds.

Filtration

Another way to remove suspended solids is to **filter** the liquid. The fibres in the filter paper act as a fine sieve, trapping the solid particles but letting the water through. This can be a slow process – but don't be tempted to poke the solid **residue** with a glass rod – you will only break the filter paper and have to start all over again.

A **Buchner funnel** speeds up the process by lowering the pressure in the flask, so that air pressure pushes the **filtrate** through.

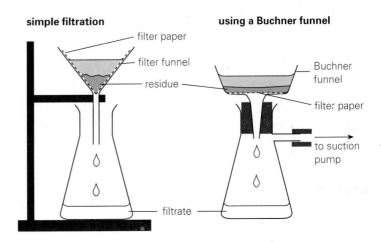

Getting back the solute

Once you have a clear filtrate, you can get the dissolved salt back by evaporating the water. In many parts of the world, sea salt is obtained by trapping sea water in shallow 'pans' and allowing the sun to do the work.

In the laboratory, you may wish to speed up the process by boiling some of the liquid away first, to increase the concentration.

If this is done in an evaporating basin over a Bunsen burner, the heat should be turned off before the last water has gone or else it will start to spit and you will lose a lot of material.

A safer way is to heat the solution over a **water bath**. As this is being heated by boiling water, the temperature will never rise above 100°C (see 1.2).

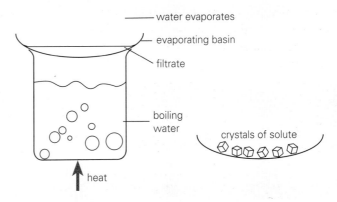

In hot climates, salt can be obtained by evaporating sea water.

Water will evaporate from a solution rapidly but safely if heated over a beaker of boiling water. The solute crystallises out.

QUESTIONS

1 Sugar cane is boiled with water to extract the sugar. Explain why this process works.

2 Why is drinking water that is taken from rivers often left to stand in large tanks before it is carefully run off for further processing?

3 Describe how you could obtain a clear solution of copper sulphate from a mixture of copper sulphate crystals and sand.

4 Copper sulphate crystals start to break down if heated directly. How could copper sulphate crystals be obtained from the solution in question 3?

2.5 *Separating mixtures 2*

Chromatography

In mixed solutions, you may need to separate out the different solutes so that you can identify them. If a spot of mixed ink or food colour is put on a filter paper and water is soaked up through it, the different dyes move up the paper at different rates. The dyes that are best at dissolving (the most soluble) move the fastest.

You can use this method to compare the dye used in sweets, for example, and compare them to known dyes. Or you could compare the black inks used in different parts of a letter or cheque, to see if they were written by the same pen – a good way to check for forgeries!

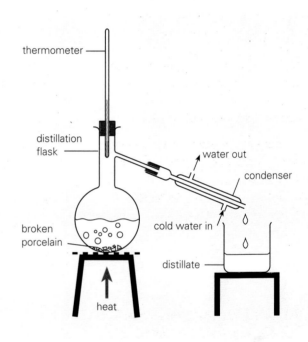

Tartrazine can be harmful to some children. Do any of these sweets contain it?

Getting the liquid back

Sometimes it's the liquid you want to get back from solution. In the Persian Gulf, it's not the salt they want from the sea but the water for drinking. They use their cheap oil to boil the water, but then collect and **condense** the vapour back again into pure, **distilled** water.

In the science laboratory, you will probably use this apparatus to distil liquids. When the liquid boils in the flask, the gas passes out of the side arm into the condenser. The central tube in the condenser is surrounded by a jacket of cold water. This cools the vapours down and so makes the vapours condense. The pure liquid drips out into the collecting flask.

If the liquid being distilled is flammable, you should use an electric heater or a water bath rather than a Bunsen burner.

Laboratory distillation apparatus. The pieces of porcelain in the flask help the liquid to boil smoothly and so reduce the risk of it 'bubbling over' into the condenser.

Oil and water

Liquids such as oil and water do not mix – they are **immiscible**. The juice formed in the pan when roasting meat is a mixture like this – the oil (molten fat) floats on the surface as it is less dense than the watery gravy. This oil can be scooped off with a spoon, but a better method uses a separating jug, which allows the gravy to be poured off from underneath the oil.

The **separating funnel** used to separate immiscible liquids in the laboratory works on the same principle. The denser liquid is run off from below.

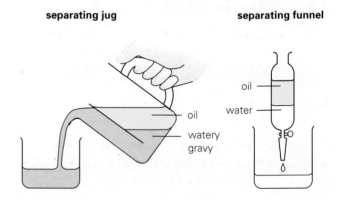

Fractional distillation

If the liquids do mix (they are **miscible**), such as water and alcohol in beer or wine, separation is more difficult. Even though alcohol boils at 79°C, a clean separation is not possible using the simple apparatus, as boiling occurs over the 79–100°C temperature range. At the start, the distillate is almost pure alcohol. But as the temperature rises, the proportion of water increases and the initial alcohol-rich mixture is steadily replaced by a water-rich one.

This problem may be overcome using a **fractionating column**. Here, the vapours rise up a tower and may condense back to liquid over and over again and drip back into the flask. As boiling continues, the temperature at the top of the column rises until it reaches 79°C at the escape outlet – the alcohol vapour then pours over to be condensed and collected in the flask. Once all the alcohol has gone from the mixture, the temperature starts to rise again, and the flask must be changed before water starts to collect at 100°C.

More complex mixtures may also be separated in this way, several different **fractions** being collected. One important mixture that is separated like this is crude oil (see 7.2).

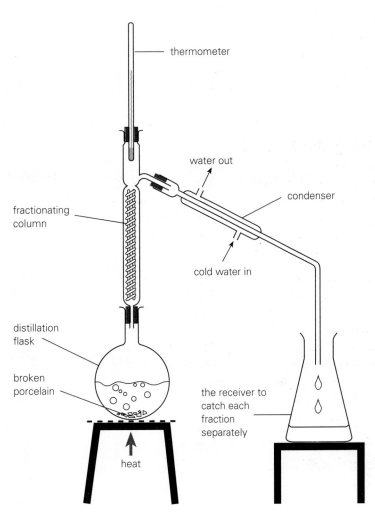

When the top of the tower reaches 79°C, the alcohol vapour passes into the condenser. But any water vapour condenses out in the tower and drips back into the flask, as the tower is still below the boiling point of water.

QUESTIONS

1 For the following, state how you would separate the mixture, explaining your choice of method. What difference in property are you exploiting?
  a water from ink
  b oil from vinegar
  c pure alcohol from wine or beer.

2 Describe how chromatography may be used to compare the colourings used in 'real' and imitation Smarties.

3 Scientists suggest that too much fat in our food is bad for the heart – but many people think that meat stock makes delicious gravy. How could you reduce the fat content of the juices from roasted meat?

4 Wine is approximately 10% alcohol in water. Brandy is 40% alcohol. Describe, step by step, how brandy could be made from wine.

3.1 *Atoms and molecules*

Naming the pieces

Everything is made up of particles. For most materials, these particles are themselves built from smaller particles called **atoms**. Groups of two or more atoms joined together are called **molecules**. When different elements combine like this they form **compounds**. There are 92 different kinds of atoms that occur naturally on Earth. These can combine to give an enormous number of different compounds.

The particles in any one **pure** substance are all made in the same way. In a few cases, like helium gas, the particles are just single atoms. In others, such as sulphur, they are molecules containing just one type of atom. Substances made from one type of atom only are called **elements**. As there are 92 different types of atom, there are 92 different elements on Earth.

All other substances are made from two or more different types of atoms, combined in different ways.

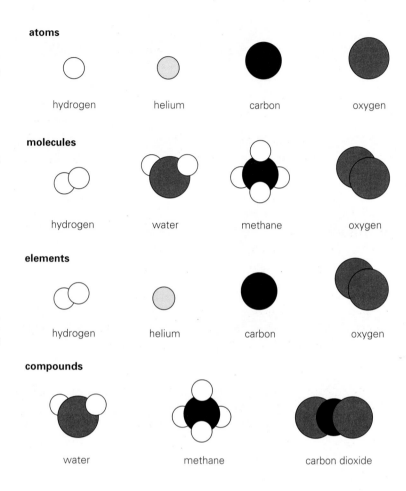

atoms

hydrogen   helium   carbon   oxygen

molecules

hydrogen   water   methane   oxygen

elements

hydrogen   helium   carbon   oxygen

compounds

water   methane   carbon dioxide

Using symbols

Each of the 92 elements has a unique, internationally recognised symbol of one or two letters. Most of these are obvious from the name of the element, but some seem odd because they refer to older names no longer used.

Some elements and their symbols		
Single letters (always capital)	**Double letters (first letter capital)**	**Some 'oddities'**
H hydrogen	He helium	Na sodium – from the Latin name *natrium*
C carbon	Mg magnesium	K potassium
N nitrogen	Al aluminium	Fe iron – iron and steel are the ferrous metals
O oxygen	Si silicon	Cu copper
S sulphur	Cl chlorine	Pb lead – plumbers used to work with lead pipes
I iodine	Br bromine	Ag silver – argent is French for coins –(silver)
	Ca calcium	Au gold
	Zn zinc	Hg mercury

Symbols for compounds

The symbols for molecules are simply a list of the elements they contain. The symbols for these elements are written in a particular order. If there is more than one atom of a particular element in a compound, this is shown by a small number (a subscript) after its symbol, as shown:

hydrochloric acid is written as HCl
(one atom of hydrogen, one of chlorine)

sulphuric acid is written as H_2SO_4
(two hydrogen, one sulphur, four oxygen)

nitric acid is written as HNO_3
(one hydrogen, one nitrogen, three oxygen)

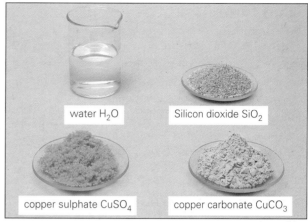

water H_2O
Silicon dioxide SiO_2
copper sulphate $CuSO_4$
copper carbonate $CuCO_3$

How many of each type of atom are there in these four compounds?

Spelling it out

It's easy to get confused when thinking about these different types of particle. Here is a model that might help.

Atoms are like the letters of the alphabet, while compounds are like words. If you think how many words are possible from just 26 letters, each with its own specific meaning, you will realise just how many different types of material could be made from 92 atoms.

Fortunately, there are rules you can learn that will help you to understand which combinations of atoms are possible, and what the likely properties of those compounds might be. The history of chemistry is like a great detective story, following the search for the patterns in nature that led to an understanding of these rules.

A whole dictionary from 26 letters, the whole world from 92 elements!

QUESTIONS

1   The diagram shows four sets of particles, **A**, **B**, **C** and **D**. Which show **a** elements, **b** compounds, **c** solo atoms, **d** molecules. You will use the letters more than once.

2   Write your own definitions for the terms *molecule*, *element* and *compound*.

3   Are the following molecules of elements or compounds?
   a iron oxide, Fe_2O_3
   b iodine, I_2
   c ethane gas, C_2H_6

4   How many atoms are there altogether in a molecule of glucose, $C_6H_{12}O_6$?
   How many of each type of atom are there within this?

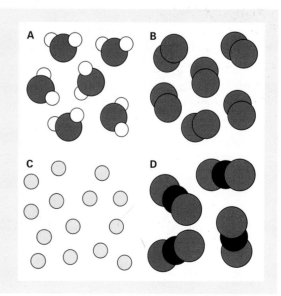

3.2 *Chemical formulae*

Using formulae

The combination of symbols used to show the make-up of a chemical compound is called its **chemical formula**. Using chemical symbols and formulae is a convenient shorthand that you will find more and more useful as you study chemistry. But have you wondered why the proportions of different atoms varies from substance to substance?

For example, why is:

hydrochloric acid   H Cl

but water .... H_2O ?

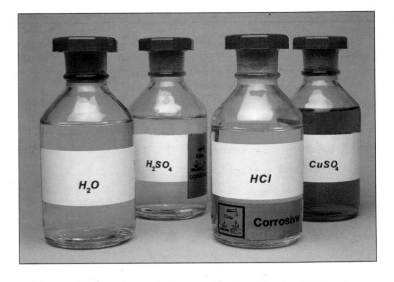

How many arms?

The answer lies in the number of **chemical bonds** that different types of atoms can make. This will be explained in chapter 4, but for the moment you can think about the number of 'arms' each type of atom has.

Hydrogen atoms and chlorine atoms both have only one arm each. So the simplest molecule that they can make has one atom of hydrogen attached to one atom of chlorine.
Hence H—Cl or HCl.

But oxygen has two arms, so every oxygen atom can grab hold of two hydrogen atoms.
Hence H—O—H or H_2O

More non-metal compounds

You can extend this idea to explain the formulae of a lot of simple compounds of non-metals. For example, nitrogen has three arms while carbon has four.

Usually every arm has to be used. With 'one-armed' hydrogen, you can predict the formulae of:

ammonia:

$$\begin{array}{ccc} H & & H \\ & \diagdown \; \diagup & \\ & N & \\ & | & \\ & H & \end{array}$$

and methane:

$$\begin{array}{c} H \\ | \\ H-C-H \\ | \\ H \end{array}$$

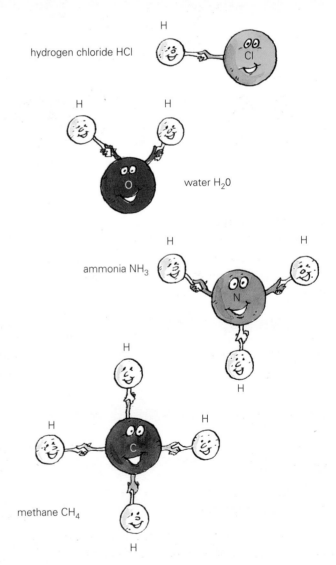

To work out the formulae of simple compounds, think of 'cartoon molecules' if it helps.

Double and triple bonds

Atoms with more than one arm can make 'double handshake' **double bonds**. A carbon atom can 'grab' two oxygen atoms like this, to make carbon dioxide.

Many non-metal elements form molecules from two of their own atoms. Hydrogen forms an H—H single bond, while oxygen forms an O=O double bond.

Nitrogen has three arms so it has to have a **triple bond** in its N_2 molecule.

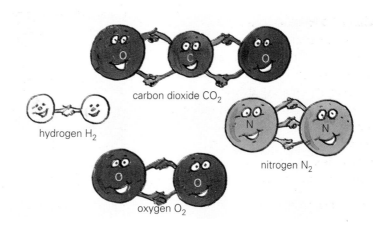

carbon dioxide CO_2

hydrogen H_2

nitrogen N_2

oxygen O_2

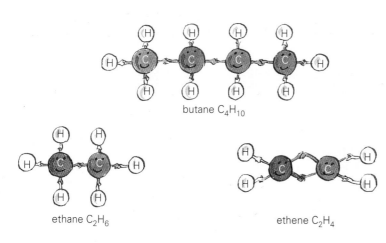

butane C_4H_{10}

ethane C_2H_6

ethene C_2H_4

Carbon chains

Carbon atoms can join together in simple chains. The 'spare' arms usually grab hold of hydrogen atoms to complete the compound. Sometimes, two carbon atoms join together with a double bond, which leaves two fewer arms free to grab hold of hydrogen atoms.

Beware of 'oddities'

The 'use every arm' rule works for many compounds, but non-metals can also make other compounds that do not fit this simple rule. For example, carbon monoxide has just one oxygen atom joined to one carbon atom.

When you see a chemical formula for a compound in a reference book, the proportions of the different atoms have always been confirmed by experiment.

carbon monoxide CO

Carbon monoxide does not follow the simple rule. Why do you think it is more reactive than carbon dioxide?

QUESTIONS

1 Why does H_2O have two hydrogens, but HCl have only one?

2 Why does CH_4 have four hydrogens, but CO_2 have only two oxygens?

3 Chlorine has only one 'arm'. What is the formula of the simplest possible compound of carbon and chlorine? Draw a cartoon of it.

4 Prop<u>a</u>ne has the formula C_3H_8, but prop<u>e</u>ne is C_3H_6.
   a How must two of the carbon atoms be joined in prop<u>e</u>ne?
   b Draw a cartoon of this molecule.

5 What is unusual about the compound carbon monoxide, CO?

3.3 Metal salts

Metal salts

When metals and non-metals combine they form salts such as common salt, sodium chloride NaCl. Although the chemical bond in salts is a different type, you can still use the 'number of arms' idea to work out their formulae. This is often called the **valency**.

Sodium and chlorine both have a valency of 1, so NaCl is the simplest combination. But calcium has a valency of 2, so calcium can grab hold of two chlorine atoms in calcium chloride $CaCl_2$.

Calcium and oxygen both have a valency of 2, so they can make the simple compound calcium oxide CaO, with a 'double handshake' double bond.

But sodium oxide is Na_2O, because sodium has a valency of 1, so one oxygen atom grabs two 'single-armed' sodium atoms.

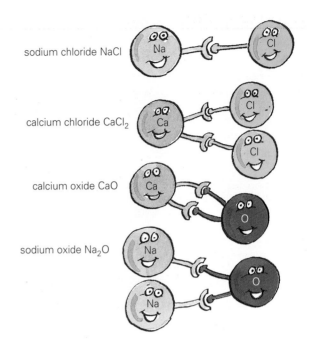

sodium chloride NaCl

calcium chloride $CaCl_2$

calcium oxide CaO

sodium oxide Na_2O

Getting radical

Some salts combine metals with clusters of atoms that always hang around together. These clusters can be found combined with hydrogen in acids, and have names that come from their acids. They are called **radicals**. For example:

nitric acid HNO_3 $\longrightarrow$ nitrates NO_3
sulphuric acid H_2SO_4 $\longrightarrow$ sulphate SO_4
carbonic acid H_2CO_3 $\longrightarrow$ carbonate CO_3

Radicals have one or more free arms, so they too can be given a valency number. As hydrogen has a valency of 1, you can work out the radical's valency from the number of hydrogen atoms in the acid molecule. So, NO_3 has a valency of 1 but SO_4 and CO_3 have valencies of 2.

In acids, hydrogen behaves as if it was a metal. There is also a radical that does this, that forms when ammonia dissolves in water.

It is called the ammonium radical NH_4.

It can form salts such as ammonium chloride NH_4Cl.

Metal valencies			Non-metal and radical valencies		
1	2	3	1	2	3
sodium (Na)	magnesium (Mg)	aluminium (Al)	chloride (Cl)	oxide (O)	phosphate (PO_4)
potassium (K)	calcium (Ca)	iron(III) (Fe)	bromide (Br)	sulphide (S)	
copper(I) (Cu)	copper(II) (Cu)		iodide (I)	sulphate (SO_4)	
silver (Ag)	iron(II) (Fe)		hydroxide (OH)	carbonate (CO_3)	
[hydrogen (H)]	lead (Pb)		nitrate (NO_3)		
[ammonium (NH_4)]	zinc (Zn)		hydrogencarbonate (HCO_3)		
Some metals, such as iron and copper, can take on different valencies. This is shown in brackets after the name. So iron(III) has a valency of 3, and so on.					

Working it out

To work out the formula for a salt, you have to match the number of valency arms for the metal and non-metal parts in the simplest way possible. If the valency number is the same for both parts, then this is easy:

potassium(I) and nitrate(I) $\longrightarrow$ KNO_3 (single bond)

calcium(II) and sulphate(II) $\longrightarrow$ $CaSO_4$ (double bond)

If the valencies are not the same, you need to balance the arms. If more than one radical is needed, the group is put in brackets.

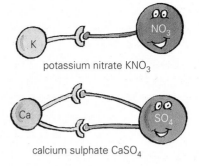

potassium nitrate KNO_3

calcium sulphate $CaSO_4$

Cartoon models for salts can help you to see what is going on.

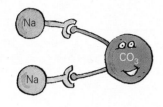

sodium(I) and carbonate(II) $\longrightarrow$ sodium carbonate Na_2CO_3

calcium(II) and nitrate(I) $\longrightarrow$ calcium nitrate $Ca(NO_3)_2$

Some get tricky

It can get tricky to work out the formulae of some compounds, but drawing arm diagrams can help. If you try to combine aluminium(III) and oxygen(II) to make aluminium oxide, you can build up the compound as shown.

1 one aluminium arm free – add another oxygen

2 now one oxygen arm free – add another aluminium

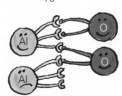

3 now two aluminium arms free – add another oxygen

4 all arms used – aluminium oxide is Al_2O_3

QUESTIONS

1 Phosphoric acid has the formula H_3PO_4. What is the valency of the phosphate radical PO_4?

2 Work out the formulae for the following salts:
 a sodium nitrate   e lead nitrate
 b magnesium carbonate   f iron(III) chloride
 c calcium bromide   g aluminium phosphate
 d potassium sulphate   h iron(III) oxide

3 Are the following formulae correct or incorrect? If they are incorrect, what should they be?
 a AgI_2 c $PbOH$ e KO
 b NH_4Br d $MgOH$ f $Zn(PO_4)_2$

3.4 *Inside an atom*

There are 92 different types of atoms, giving 92 different elements with different properties. To understand why the elements are different, you will need to know what the atoms themselves are made from.

What's inside an atom?

The simple answer is a lot of empty space! But how was this discovered? In 1911 a physicist called Rutherford bombarded some very thin gold leaf with **alpha particles** from a radioactive source. To his surprise, most passed straight through as if the gold was not there.

He concluded that most of the matter was concentrated in a central region he called the **nucleus**. Most particles simply missed this and passed right through the gold. He also decided from other experiments that this nucleus must have a positive electrical charge.

As atoms are neutral, the charge on the nucleus is balanced by an equal and opposite negative charge on **electrons** which whizz around the nucleus, rather like a 3D solar system.

Rutherford calculated the size of the nucleus compared to the whole atom. It is just one hundred thousandth of the atomic diameter – that's like a 1 cm marble within a 1 km diameter sphere!

Naming the parts

Later work was done to find out what made up the nucleus. It consists of two types of particles of almost identical mass. **Protons**, which carry a positive charge, and **neutrons** which have no charge. Neutrons are, if you like, the packaging which stops the like charges on the protons pushing the nucleus apart.

Rather than give these **sub-atomic particles** their real, very tiny mass in kilograms, they are given a relative mass compared roughly to a hydrogen atom (hydrogen = 1). The mass of an electron is, by comparison, so small that it is usually ignored. Charges also come in relative values, +1 on a proton and −1 on an electron particle. In an atom, the number of electrons is equal to the number of protons, so the charges cancel out.

Rutherford won the Nobel prize for physics, for his work on atomic structure.

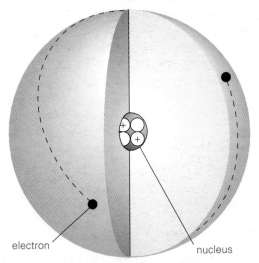

An atom is like a 3D solar system, with electrons whizzing around the tiny nucleus at the centre. A helium atom has two electrons, two protons and two neutrons.

The properties of the sub-atomic particles		
Particle	Relative mass	Relative charge
proton	1	+1
neutron	1	0
electron	$\frac{1}{1864}$	−1

Building atoms

The atoms of different elements have different numbers of protons in them. Hydrogen, the simplest element, always has just one proton, while uranium always has 92. All the atoms in an element have the same number of protons. This defines the element. The number of protons is called the **atomic number** (Z) of the element. (This is sometimes called its **proton number**.)

Another important number is the **relative atomic mass** (A_r) of the atoms. This is found by adding the number of neutrons to the number of protons in the nucleus – electrons have too small a mass to worry about. (This is sometimes called its **mass number**.)

Elements are often shown by their symbols with these two important numbers alongside them. The smaller number is the atomic number (Z), while the larger number is the relative atomic mass (A_r) – that is, the total number of both protons and neutrons. The difference between these two numbers therefore gives you the number of neutrons in the nucleus.

relative atomic mass ... A_r X
atomic number .... Z

For example:

$^{4}_{2}He$ 2 protons + 2 neutrons

$^{7}_{3}Li$ 3 protons + 4 neutrons

You can work out what is in the nucleus from the two numbers.

A variable nucleus

Most elements are given a whole-number figure for their relative atomic mass for general usage. This reflects the 'billiard ball' model of the nucleus, made from equal sized particles. Chlorine, however, is always given a relative atomic mass of 35.5. What does this mean? Do we have 'half a neutron'?

The answer is that it is possible to have different versions of the same element which have different numbers of neutrons and therefore different relative atomic masses. These are called **isotopes**. Most elements have one particular version that is the most common, but chlorine has two, ^{35}Cl and ^{37}Cl. The relative atomic mass given is the average of the two isotopes as found in nature; ^{35}Cl is the commoner of the two.

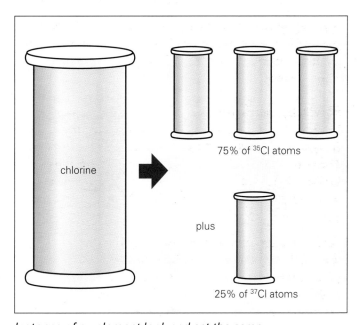

Isotopes of an element look and act the same.

QUESTIONS

1 Why did Rutherford conclude that most of an atom was empty space?

2 Describe the mass, charge and location of the three main sub-atomic particles.

3 How many protons and neutrons are there in the nuclei of:

  a $^{16}_{8}O$ **b** $^{24}_{12}Mg$ **c** $^{56}_{26}Fe$ **d** $^{238}_{92}U$?

4 Carbon[12] and carbon[14] are isotopes of carbon. Describe what is meant by this.

5 Explain why the relative atomic mass of chlorine is 35.5.

6 There are forces of attraction between protons and neutrons, but like charges repel. How do neutrons help to keep the nucleus stable?

3.5 The first 20 elements

Lining them up

The elements are usually arranged in order by their atomic number. When you do this, the relative atomic mass also goes up. In general, the more protons there are, the more neutrons are needed in the nucleus to keep it stable.

What about the electrons?

Since atoms are neutral, there must be as many negatively charged electrons orbiting the nucleus as there are positively charge protons inside it. These electrons whizz around at very high speed. Because they travel so fast, they seem to be everywhere at once. This gives the atom its spherical shape – a kind of electron cloud. (This is like your TV picture, which you see complete, yet is made from a tiny dot of light scanning rapidly across and down the screen.)

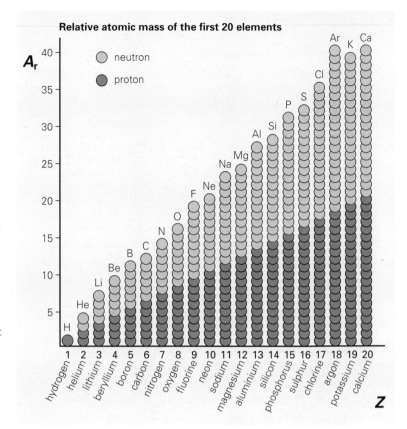

In general, the number of neutrons in the nucleus goes up with the number of protons, but in a less regular way.

Electron shells

An important feature, however, is that these clouds form **electron shells** around the nucleus. Each shell can take only a set number of electrons. Elements with low atomic numbers, and hence low numbers of electrons, fill the inner shells first under normal conditions. Elements with more electrons use the outer shells, as the inner shells become full. For the first 20 elements, the simple rule is that the innermost shell can take only two electrons, but each shell after that can take eight. Shells are also known as **energy levels**. The innermost shell, closest to the nucleus is the lowest energy level. The outermost shell is always the highest energy level.

The arrangement of electrons in these shells is called the **electron configuration**, and it is this which determines the chemistry of the element, as you will see in the next section.

The number of electrons in each shell can be written in turn, separated by commas. For example, potassium has 19 electrons: 2, 8, 8, 1.

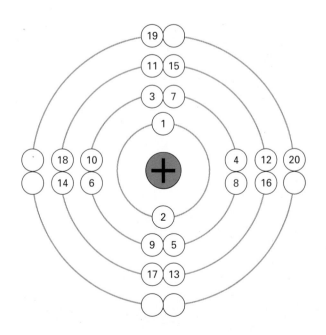

Electron shells and possible electron positions.

The electron configuration of the first 20 elements

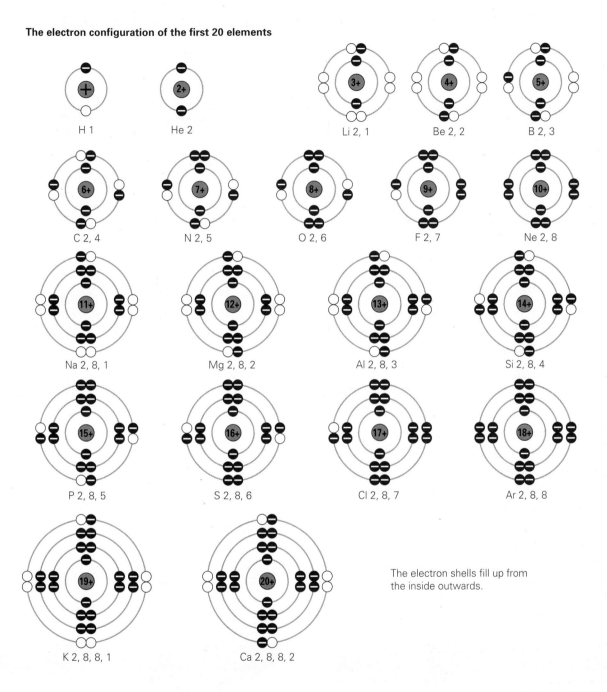

H 1   He 2   Li 2, 1   Be 2, 2   B 2, 3

C 2, 4   N 2, 5   O 2, 6   F 2, 7   Ne 2, 8

Na 2, 8, 1   Mg 2, 8, 2   Al 2, 8, 3   Si 2, 8, 4

P 2, 8, 5   S 2, 8, 6   Cl 2, 8, 7   Ar 2, 8, 8

K 2, 8, 8, 1   Ca 2, 8, 8, 2

The electron shells fill up from the inside outwards.

QUESTIONS

1 Write a list of the names of the first 20 elements in order of atomic number.
Next to each element write its: **a** symbol **b** number of protons **c** relative atomic mass **d** number of neutrons **e** number of electrons and **f** electron configuration (numbers separated by commas).

2a How many electrons can be fitted into each of the first three electron shells?

b In which order are the shells filled?

c Look at the electron configuration diagrams shown above for a few minutes.

d Close this book and draw the electron configuration for elements number 1 to 10, working them out from the simple rules.

29

4.1 *Chemical changes*

Physical or chemical?

When something melts or boils, the particles stay the same – they are just arranged differently. Changes like this are called **physical changes**. They are easily reversible. In **chemical changes**, however, the make-up of the particles themselves changes. Compounds may be broken up or elements joined together, and completely new substances are formed. These changes are not easily reversed, and heat or light are often given out (or taken in) as the change occurs.

For example, if you heat candle wax, it will melt as the wax particles vibrate more and some of the bonds between them are broken. This is a physical change. If you cool the molten wax down, it will return to solid wax. But if you burn a candle, the wax particles react with the oxygen in the air, forming new particles. This is a chemical change, as you cannot get the wax back. New substances are formed (the waste gases), and heat and light are given out.

A burning candle shows both physical and chemical changes.

Breaking up a compound

For a chemical reaction to occur, any existing compounds have to be broken up. How can this happen?

Bunsen burners can reach a maximum temperature of only 1000°C or so. That's hot enough to melt or boil many substances, but not usually enough to affect the strong **chemical bonds** that hold the atoms together within a compound. So the compounds themselves are not affected. But what if the temperature kept rising... to 10000, or even 100000°C? Just as the interparticle bonds in a solid snap when the particles vibrate faster as melting point is approached so, eventually, the chemical bonds *within* a compound will reach breaking point if the temperature gets high enough.

All compounds could in theory be split into atoms this way – but in practice only certain compounds can be heated sufficiently in the laboratory to be destroyed like this. Mercury oxide has weak chemical bonds holding it together. If you heat it gently over a Bunsen burner, the compound is split up into metallic mercury and oxygen.

mercury oxide   heat →   mercury + oxygen

Heat energy alone can break up mercury oxide.

Coming together

Iron and sulphur are elements. If you mix iron filings and flowers of sulphur together you get a dirty, yellow-grey mess that contains both sulphur and iron atoms. But the atoms have not combined, and so the two materials still keep their individual properties. They may easily be separated again, by pulling out the iron with a magnet, for example. This, then, is simply a **mixture**.

But if you give this mixture a kick of energy by heating it in a tube, a change will take place. Part of the mixture will suddenly start to glow brightly, and this glow will spread throughout the material – even if the Bunsen burner is turned off. If you remove it from the tube – once it has cooled down – you will see that it is now a uniformly grey, hard but brittle solid. It is no longer magnetic. It is a new **chemical compound**, iron sulphide.

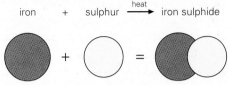

Heating a mixture of iron and sulphur results in a chemical reaction.

To make this compound, new chemical bonds have been formed between the iron and sulphur atoms. They cannot easily be broken, so the reaction is not reversible.

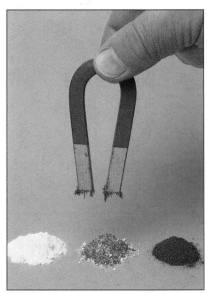

A mixture of iron and sulphur can easily be separated.

The chemical reaction between iron and sulphur gives off heat and light.

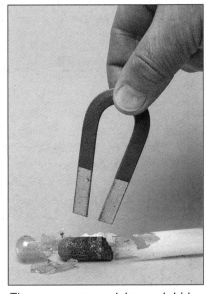

The new compound, iron sulphide, has new properties.

QUESTIONS

1 Describe the physical and chemical changes that occur when a candle burns.

2 Use what happens during melting to help you explain, in your own words, how heat energy might eventually break up a chemical compound.

3 Iron oxide is not changed by being heated in a Bunsen flame. Are the chemical bonds in iron oxide stronger or weaker than those in mercury oxide?

4a How can you tell that no new compounds have been made when iron and sulphur are simply mixed together?

b Once the iron and sulphur mixture has been heated, how do you know that a chemical reaction has occurred?

31

4.2 *Ions and bonding*

What is it that makes atoms join together to form compounds? To understand chemical bonding, you need to look closely at the electrons.

Atomic heaven?

Helium, neon and argon are all unreactive gases. They are called the noble gases because they don't join with the riff-raff in chemical reactions! But why are they like this?

If you look at their electron configuration, you will see that their highest energy levels (outer shells) are full. This makes them very stable, since this is the most efficient way to balance out the forces within the atom. As a consequence, they do not easily take part in chemical reactions which upset this stability.

A rather less scientific model is that, as far as atoms go, 'happiness is a full outer electron shell'. This is what all atoms aim for and once they have got it they won't give it up easily.

One over the eight ...

Sodium is a very reactive metal. If you look at its electron configuration, you will see that it has one electron too many for this state of atomic bliss. This electron is left on its own in the outermost shell, and is less firmly held than the others. As a result, this electron is easily lost, and it is this that leads to the chemical reactivity of sodium.

But if sodium loses an electron, it will no longer be electrically neutral. It will have one more proton than electron, giving it a net positive charge. Charged particles like this are called **ions**. Positively charged ions are called **cations**.

All metals have one or more 'loose' electrons like this, and so tend to form positive ions. This is also why metals conduct electricity.

... and one under!

Chlorine is a green gas that has the opposite problem – it is one electron short of atomic bliss! Like sodium, this state of electron imbalance leads to chlorine's reactivity, as it will try to gain an extra electron to fill the outer shell. When chlorine gains an electron, it also becomes an ion. But this time there is one extra electron, giving a net negative charge. Negative ions are called **anions**. Many non-metals form anions like this.

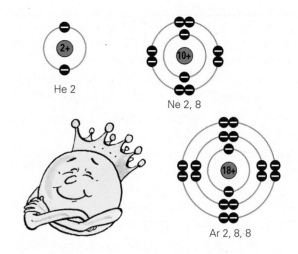

Atomic bliss – not to be lost! The noble gases have full outer shells.

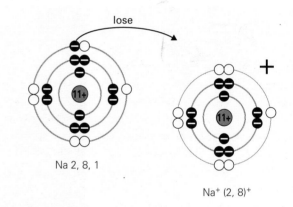

Metals like sodium form positive cations. These have a full outer shell, like a noble gas.

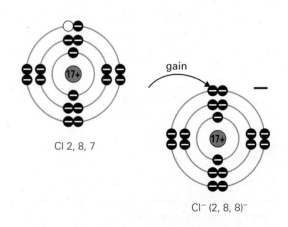

Non-metals like chlorine need to gain electrons to form anions. These also have a full outer shell, like a noble gas.

Atomic dating

You may already have guessed what is coming next. If sodium desperately wants to lose an electron and chlorine desperately wants to gain one ... they are made for each other! An atom of sodium will readily give its spare electron to an atom of chlorine and, when this has happened, both will achieve a full outer shell.

But in doing this, they have upset their electrical balance, based on equal numbers of protons and electrons. They both become charged particles – ions. Sodium now has one more proton than it has electrons, so it has a net single positive charge. Chlorine gains the net single negative charge from its extra electron. These oppositely charged ions are then attracted to each other, giving rise to an **electrostatic** chemical bond. This is called an **ionic bond**, and is very strong. So from two reactive elements you get a very stable compound which is difficult to break apart. A sodium cation and a chloride anion form sodium chloride.

Other ionic arrangements

All metals have electrons to lose and most non-metals want to gain them – indeed, that is a good working definition of metals and non-metals. But the number of electrons involved does vary. Magnesium and calcium have two electrons to lose so they form double-charged cations. These two electrons could go to two separate chlorine atoms, forming *two* chloride anions (Cl^-). So one calcium atom, for example, could form **single ionic bonds** with two chlorine atoms. Alternatively, both of the electrons could be given to one oxygen atom because this needs two electrons to fill its outer shell. This would form a double charged anion. So magnesium, for example, could form one **double ionic bond** with oxygen.

The number of electrons available for loss or gain is the same as the element's valency (see 3.3).

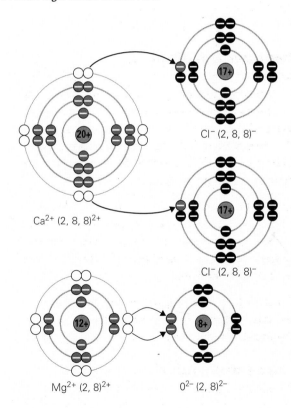

A marriage made in heaven?

QUESTIONS

1   Using the model of your choice, explain why potassium tends to lose an electron, while chlorine tends to gain one.

2   Explain the stages in the formation of an ionic bond between sodium and chlorine.

3   Sulphur has a configuration 2, 8, 6.
   a Draw its electron shells.
   b What ion will it form? (Draw it.)
   c How many sodium atoms would be needed to help it form this ion?
   d Draw a diagram of the ionic compound sodium sulphide that could form in this way.

4.3 *More about ions*

Common salt

You have seen how compounds form between metals such as sodium and non-metals such as chlorine by ionic bonding. The bond diagrams given for these are very useful, but do not give a true picture. There is no such thing, for example, as a single sodium chloride (common salt) molecule – NaCl. This simply represents the proportion of the different ions present in a salt crystal. In fact, every Na^+ ion is surrounded by and attracted to six Cl^- ions, and vice versa. This regular stacking pattern gives rise to the typical cubic shape of salt crystals. This **giant structure** of ions is known as an **ionic lattice**.

Ionic solids

As electrostatic bonds are strong, so is the whole ionic lattice. This makes many **ionic solids** very hard. It also means that they have high melting points. It takes a lot of energy to break ionic bonds.

Because the ions are held firmly in place, ionic solids do not conduct electricity. But the presence of ions does make them brittle. If they are struck sharply, rows of ions may be displaced sufficiently to bring *like* ions together. If this happens, repulsion replaces attraction and the crystal splits apart along a mirror-smooth **cleavage plane**.

Water soluble

Ionic solids also tend to dissolve in solvents such as water. Water molecules surround the ions in the ionic crystal and weaken the electrostatic bonds. The ions break loose and are 'carried' away by the water molecules.

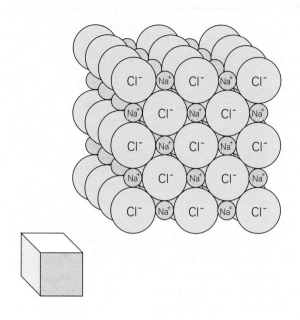

Common salt is a typical ionic material.

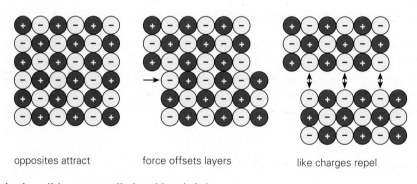

opposites attract   force offsets layers   like charges repel

Ionic solids are usually hard but brittle.

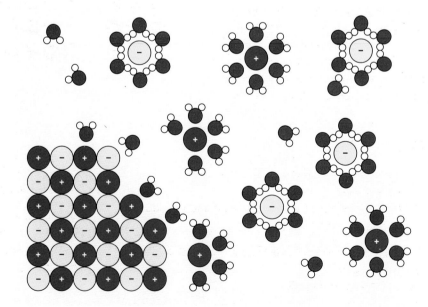

Water molecules can capture ions.

Electrolysis

Once in solution, of course, the ions are free to move, and this is also true if the ionic solid melts. So ionic materials do conduct electricity in solution or when molten.

They can also be torn apart by electricity. If terminals are put into molten salt, the positive sodium ions are attracted to the negative **cathode**, while the negative chloride anions are attracted to the positive **anode**. Tearing ionic compounds apart like this is called **electrolysis**.

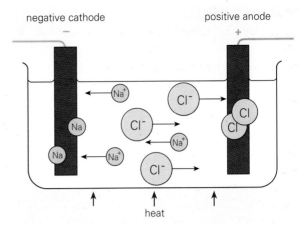

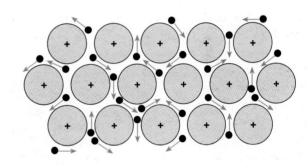

The electrolysis of molten salt produces sodium metal at the cathode and chlorine gas at the anode.

Metals

Metals all have 'loose' outer electrons that they easily shed to leave stable, positive ions. In a solid metal, the atoms are stacked closely together and these 'loose' electrons break away and wander freely through the material. They form a 'sea' or 'cloud' of electrons around and between the positive ions in the **metallic lattice**. It is these electrons that move when a metal conducts electricity or heat (see 2.1).

The strong electrostatic force of attraction between the negative electron 'sea' and the positive ions binds the whole solid together, making metals, in general, strong materials with relatively high melting points that do not dissolve in solvents.

Metal cations are tightly held in a 'sea' of electrons.

Metals are easy to shape

The 'sea' of electrons that binds the metal lattice together can move and change shape. This means that rows of metal ions can move over one another if a force is applied to them – but still 'stick' in the new positions when the force is removed. This is why it is easy to beat or stretch metals into shape.

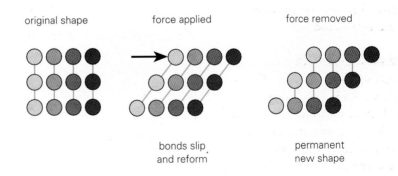

QUESTIONS

1a Explain what happens when molten salt is electrolysed.

  b What would you get if molten aluminium oxide was electrolysed like this?

2 Use your understanding of ionic solid structure to explain why:

  a salt crystals are brittle

  b salt melts at a high temperature

  c salt dissolves in water.

3 Metals conduct electricity, have high melting points and can be beaten or stretched into shape. Explain these properties in terms of the structure of a metal.

4.4 *Share and share alike*

Do it yourself!

Metals and non-metals can help each other to get full shells in an ionic bond, but non-metals can get close to this on their own – by sharing electrons.

Chlorine atoms are just one electron short of having a complete electron shell. If two atoms get together, they can share a pair of electrons, which then go around both atoms. This holds the two atoms together in what is called a **covalent bond**. Chlorine therefore forms Cl_2 molecules – it is as if the two atoms had 'popped' together like two bubbles.

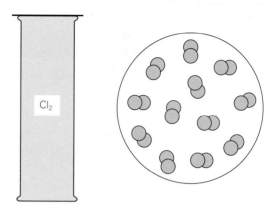

Chlorine has molecules with two atoms joined together by a covalent bond.

Showing covalent bonds

The symbol for a chlorine molecule is Cl_2, but the single covalent bond can be shown by a linking bar in the **structural formula** Cl–Cl (see 3.2).

The bonding can also be shown in **dot and cross** diagrams of the electron shells. The electrons are shown as pairs in their orbits, using dots in one atom and crosses in the other. The shared pair of electrons appears as one dot and one cross.

Only the outer shell of electrons takes part in covalent bonds, so these diagrams are sometimes simplified to show the outer electrons only. Other covalent bonds can be shown in this way, just looking at the four pairs of electrons that are needed to fill the outer shell. In the case of hydrogen, however, the shell can take only one pair of electrons.

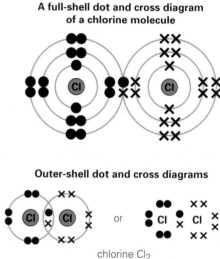

A full-shell dot and cross diagram of a chlorine molecule

Outer-shell dot and cross diagrams

or

chlorine Cl_2

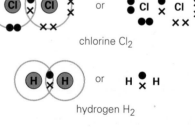

or

hydrogen H_2

Covalent bonds can be shown in different ways.

Outer-shell dot and cross diagrams

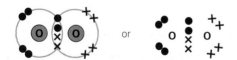

or

Structural formula

$$O = O$$

Oxygen (O_2) shares two pairs of electrons to form double bonds.

Double covalent bonds

Oxygen is two electrons short of a full shell – so, in a normal oxygen molecule, two atoms share *two* pairs of electrons in a covalent **double bond**.

For non-metals, the number of covalent bonds that can be made is the same as the number of 'arms' (see 3.2).

Non-metals get together

Covalent bonds can also form between different non-metals, forming **covalent compounds**. Nitrogen, with five electrons in its outer shell, needs to share three pairs of electrons. This can take the form of three single bonds – as with hydrogen in ammonia, NH_3.

Carbon, with only four electrons in its outer shell, needs to share four pairs. This can take the form of four single covalent bonds, as with hydrogen in methane CH_4, or two double bonds, as with oxygen in carbon dioxide (CO_2). Carbon can also make covalent bonds with itself. Ethane has just two carbon atoms, but much longer **carbon chains** are possible (see 7.4).

Compound	Structural formula	Outer-shell dot and cross diagrams
ammonia NH_3	H—N—H | H	
carbon dioxide CO_2	O=C=O	
methane CH_4	H—C—H (with H above and below)	
ethane C_2H_6	H—C—C—H (with H above and below each C)	

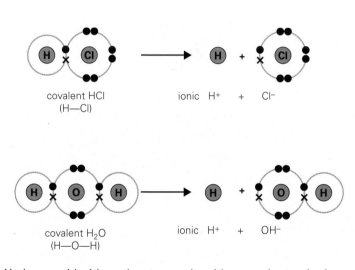

Hydrogen chloride and water can be either covalent or ionic.

covalent HCl (H—Cl) → ionic H^+ + Cl^-

covalent H_2O (H—O—H) → ionic H^+ + OH^-

Covalent or ionic?

Hydrogen is in a rather strange position as, with its one electron, it can either *lose* an electron to form an H^+ ion like a metal, or *gain* an electron to get a full shell like a non-metal. This can lead to strange effects. Hydrogen chloride gas, for example, is a covalent compound. As soon as it dissolves in water, however, it **dissociates**, forming H^+ and Cl^- ions, giving hydrochloric acid.

Water itself shows a similar effect: *pure* water is covalent and does not conduct electricity. But as soon as any ionic impurities are added, such as a trace of acid, the conductivity increases.

QUESTIONS

1 Draw full-shell diagrams showing the covalent bonding in F_2 and O_2 molecules.

2 Draw outer-shell, 'shared-pair' diagrams for:
 a tetrachloromethane, CCl_4
 b phosphorus trichloride, PCl_3 (phosphorus has 5 outer shell electrons, like nitrogen)
 c nitrogen, N_2 (this forms a triple bond)
 b carbon disulphide, CS_2.

3 Distilled water is made up of covalent water molecules. Explain what happens to some of these if a drop of acid is added to the distilled water.

4 Molecules have to break up when chemical reactions occur. Suggest a reason why nitrogen gas (N_2) seems so unreactive (see question **2c**).

4.5 Covalent materials

Molecular materials

Many covalent molecules such as hydrogen (H_2), nitrogen (N_2), oxygen (O_2) and carbon dioxide (CO_2) are gases at room temperature. Why is that?

Covalent molecules have no net electrostatic charge. So although there are strong covalent bonds *within* the molecules, there are only weak interparticle forces *between* them. This means that they melt and boil at very low temperatures, as only a little heat energy is needed to keep the molecules moving apart.

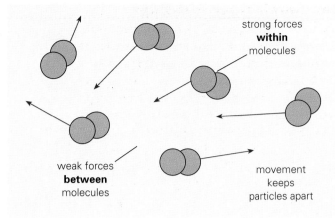

strong forces **within** molecules

weak forces **between** molecules

movement keeps particles apart

Boiling point and molecule size

In general, the smaller the molecule, the lower its melting and boiling points. Hydrogen has the smallest molecule of all and boils at minus 253°C – that's just 20° above absolute zero, which is as cold as you can get!

A few molecular materials, such as iodine (I_2), have large enough molecules to be solids at room temperature. But even here they are very easily vaporised.

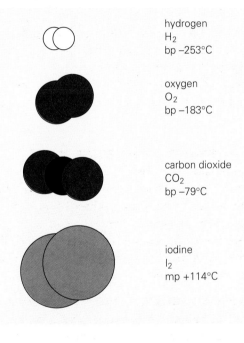

hydrogen
H_2
bp –253°C

oxygen
O_2
bp –183°C

carbon dioxide
CO_2
bp –79°C

iodine
I_2
mp +114°C

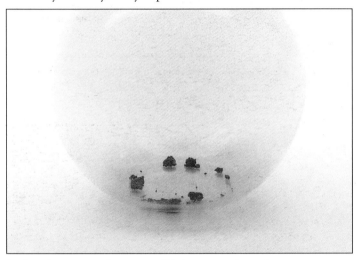

Iodine forms purple vapour if it is warmed gently.

Molecular solids

Covalent molecules stack up to form a weak **molecular lattice** when they solidify. The lack of strong forces between the molecules means that they are generally very soft and are easily melted or vaporised.

As the particles are not charged and have no 'loose' electrons, they do not conduct electricity or heat well. They do not dissolve in water. They may, however, dissolve in other solvents such as white spirit or petrol. These solutions do not conduct electricity.

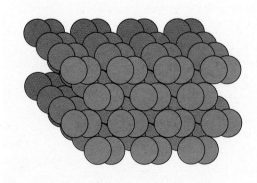

Iodine molecules stack up to form a simple, loosely held molecular lattice.

Macromolecular materials

Hydrogen, oxygen, nitrogen and iodine all form **diatomic** (two-atom) molecules where each atom uses a single, double or triple covalent bond to achieve a shared, full outer shell. But carbon is unable to bond with itself like this, as quadruple bonds are not possible. In **diamond**, however, carbon atoms are arranged so that each atom has a single bond with four neighbouring atoms arranged around it. This forms a complex, three-dimensional macromolecular (giant structure) structure in which billions of atoms are joined together in one gigantic molecule.

Because every bond in diamond is a strong covalent bond, it is very hard (it is the hardest material known) and has a very high melting point (3500°C). Diamond is also a typical macromolecular material in that it is a poor conductor of electricity, and does not dissolve in any solvents.

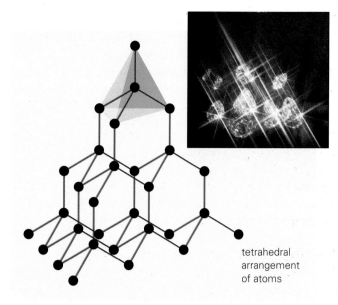

tetrahedral arrangement of atoms

A simple, repeating pattern forms the basis of the complex structure of a diamond.

A different arrangement

Carbon atoms can also stack up in a different pattern, with each carbon atom joined to three neighbours, forming a two-dimensional sheet with a honeycomb pattern. These sheets then stack up to form crystals of silvery-grey **graphite**. This looks very different to diamond, but has an equally high melting point.

Within each sheet the atoms are joined by strong, covalent bonds. But between the sheets there is just the weak force of interparticle attraction. The result is that graphite is very soft. If you rub it, the sheets slide easily over one another. This is what you are doing when you write with a pencil.

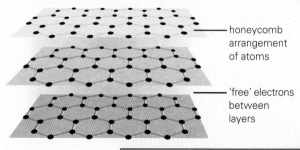

honeycomb arrangement of atoms

'free' electrons between layers

Graphite's unusual properties are a direct result of its macromolecular structure.

Another effect is that, for each carbon atom, only three of the four possible bonds are used. Only three of the four outer-shell electrons is paired up with a neighbour. The fourth is left 'loose'. As a result, 'free' electrons form a cloud between the honeycomb layers. This means that graphite, unlike diamond and other non-metals, can conduct electricity.

QUESTIONS

1 Why are hydrogen, oxygen and nitrogen gases at room temperature?

2 Why are iodine crystals so soft?

3a How does the structure of diamond account for its great hardness?
  b Compare the physical properties of diamond and graphite, and explain them in terms of their macromolecular structure.

4 Silicon dioxide (silica) forms crystals of quartz that have a similar 3D macromolecular structure to diamond. Predict the general properties of quartz from this (hardness, melting point, etc.)

4.6 *Models and equations*

More models!

In 4.5, covalent molecules such as oxygen are shown as **bubble models**, with their outer electron shells 'popped' together. In many ways, this is a quite an accurate view of what happens, but it is sometimes more useful to think in terms of the chemical bonds involved. **Ball and stick** models (like that used for diamond) show these bonds clearly, and so are often used to display the structure of compounds. Most laboratories will have some of these models around, built from coloured plastic balls and short springs.

You can represent these models on paper by writing the symbols of the elements linked by lines to show the chemical bonds. These are the **structural formulae** mentioned in 4.4.

Simple chemical formulae do not show the bonds. They give you a little less information, but they are quicker to write down.

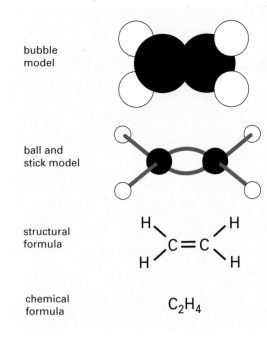

bubble model

ball and stick model

structural formula

chemical formula C_2H_4

Ethene is the same molecule, however it is represented.

	chlorine	oxygen	water	ammonia	carbon dioxide	methane	propane
bubble model							
ball and stick model							
structural formula	Cl–Cl	O=O	H H O	N H H H	O=C=O	H C H H H	H H H H–C–C–C–H H H H
formula	Cl_2	O_2	H_2O	NH_3	CO_2	CH_4	C_3H_8

Some common molecules represented in four different ways.

Representing reactions

In a chemical reaction, the chemicals you start with are the **reactants**, and the new chemicals that form are the **products**. You can write this as a word equation:

reactants $\longrightarrow$ products

So, for example, when an acid reacts with an alkali:

acids + alkali $\longrightarrow$ salt + water

The reaction between hydrochloric acid and sodium hydroxide:

$$\text{hydrochloric acid} + \text{sodium hydroxide} \longrightarrow \text{sodium chloride} + \text{water}$$

Keeping in balance

If you weigh the hydrochloric acid and sodium hydroxide before and after they have been mixed, you will find that there is no change in the mass. This follows one of the fundamental rules of chemistry: **matter is neither created nor destroyed** during a chemical reaction.

It makes sense, because you still have the same number of atoms – you have just rearranged them. If you keep this in mind, you will find chemical equations easier to follow.

Before and after mixing – no change!

Chemical equations

You can write the reaction down using the chemical formulae of the reactants and products instead of just the names. If you do this, you must make sure that there are the same number of each type of atom on each side of the equation. For the reaction shown above, it is easy to get the reaction to balance.

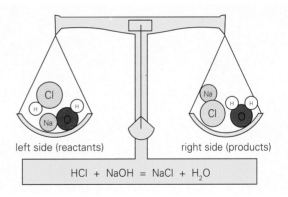

left side (reactants)   right side (products)

$$HCl + NaOH = NaCl + H_2O$$

A balanced chemical equation.

QUESTIONS

1 Here are the structural formulae of some compounds. Write the simple chemical formula for each of them.
   a chlorine monoxide Cl—O—Cl
   b carbon disulphide S=C=S
   c trichloromethane

$$\text{Cl}-\overset{\displaystyle H}{\underset{\displaystyle Cl}{\overset{|}{\underset{|}{C}}}}-\text{Cl}$$

2 For the following equations, how many of each type of atom are there on each side of the equation? Do they balance?
   a $CuSO_4 \longrightarrow CuO + SO_3$
   b $Mg + H_2SO_4 \longrightarrow MgSO_4 + H_2$
   c $CaCO_3 + H_2SO_4 \longrightarrow CaSO_4 + H_2O + CO_2$
   d $Pb(NO_3)_2 + CuSO_4 \longrightarrow Cu(NO_3)_2 + PbSO_4$

4.7 Balancing equations

Balanced equations

Word equations are useful, but chemical equations give you much more detail as they tell you what atoms are involved and how they become rearranged. In a balanced equation, the number and type of atom on each side of the equation must be the same.

For example, if black copper(II) oxide dissolves in sulphuric acid, you get blue copper(II) sulphate (the salt) and water.

Extra information

In the equation shown, some extra letters have been added in brackets after the formula of each chemical. These letters tell you the **state** of the chemical involved:

(s) means solid,
(l) means liquid,
(g) means gas and
(aq) means dissolved in water (**aqueous** solution).

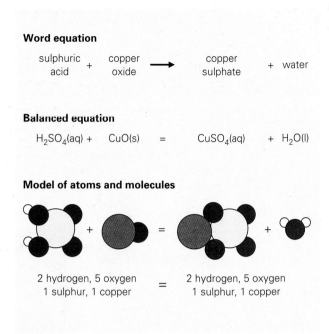

Word equation

sulphuric acid + copper oxide ⟶ copper sulphate + water

Balanced equation

$H_2SO_4(aq) + CuO(s) = CuSO_4(aq) + H_2O(l)$

Model of atoms and molecules

2 hydrogen, 5 oxygen 1 sulphur, 1 copper = 2 hydrogen, 5 oxygen 1 sulphur, 1 copper

Balancing chemical equations

To write a balanced chemical equation, you need to follow a series of steps. How many steps it takes depends on the reaction. Some can be quite simple. For example, calcium carbonate breaks down when it is heated to give calcium oxide and carbon dioxide:

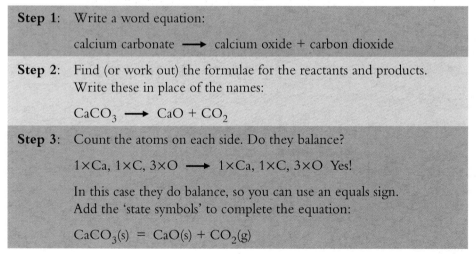

Step 1: Write a word equation:

calcium carbonate ⟶ calcium oxide + carbon dioxide

Step 2: Find (or work out) the formulae for the reactants and products. Write these in place of the names:

$CaCO_3 \longrightarrow CaO + CO_2$

Step 3: Count the atoms on each side. Do they balance?

$1 \times Ca, 1 \times C, 3 \times O \longrightarrow 1 \times Ca, 1 \times C, 3 \times O$ Yes!

In this case they do balance, so you can use an equals sign. Add the 'state symbols' to complete the equation:

$CaCO_3(s) = CaO(s) + CO_2(g)$

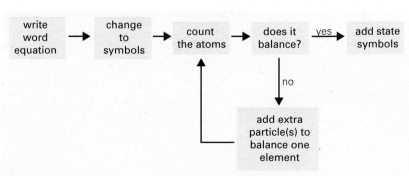

You can use this flow chart to help you balance your own equations. The equations for some reactions will work first time but others will need to go around the loop a few times before they balance.

A harder example

Sulphuric acid reacts with sodium hydroxide to give sodium sulphate and water. This is a harder example as it does not balance on the first attempt, so more steps are needed:

Step 1: Write a word equation:

sodium hydroxide + sulphuric acid $\longrightarrow$ sodium sulphate + water

Step 2: Find (or work out) the formulae for the reactants and products. Write these in place of the names:

$NaOH + H_2SO_4 \longrightarrow Na_2SO_4 + H_2O$

Step 3: Count the atoms on each side:

$1\times Na$, $1\times S$, $3\times H$, $5\times O \longrightarrow 2\times Na$, $1\times S$, $2\times H$, $5\times O$ not balanced

Step 4: If unbalanced, look for places where the products contain more atoms than the reactants. In this case, more sodium is needed, so add more NaOH. The number 2 in front of the formula shows you have two particles of that compound:

$2NaOH + H_2SO_4 \longrightarrow Na_2SO_4 + H_2O$

Step 5: Recount the atoms:

$2\times Na$, $1\times S$, $4\times H$, $6\times O \longrightarrow 2\times Na$, $1\times S$, $2\times H$, $5\times O$ not balanced

Step 6: The products are short of $2\times H$ and $1\times O$ – H_2O – so add it:

$2NaOH + H_2SO_4 \longrightarrow Na_2SO_4 + 2H_2O$

Step 7: Recount to check. You can change the arrow to an equals sign if it does balance.

$2\times Na$, $1\times S$, $4\times H$, $6\times O = 2\times Na$, $1\times S$, $4\times H$, $6\times O$ balanced

Step 8: Once the equation balances, you can add symbols to show what state the particles are in:

$2NaOH(aq) + H_2SO_4(aq) = Na_2SO_4(aq) + 2H_2O(l)$ completed

QUESTIONS

1 Balance the following incomplete equations (show the steps):

a $CuSO_4 + NaOH \longrightarrow Cu(OH)_2 + Na_2SO_4$
b $Ca(OH)_2 + HCl \longrightarrow CaCl_2 + H_2O$
c $Na_2CO_3 + HNO_3 \longrightarrow NaNO_3 + CO_2 + H_2O$
d $Al + O_2 \longrightarrow Al_2O_3$
e $Fe_2O_3 + C \longrightarrow Fe + CO_2$

2 Turn the following word equations into balanced chemical equations, showing each step you take:

a magnesium + oxygen $\longrightarrow$ magnesium oxide
b copper(II) sulphate + sodium carbonate $\longrightarrow$ copper(II) carbonate + sodium sulphate
c zinc + hydrochloric acid $\longrightarrow$ zinc chloride + hydrogen

SECTION A: QUESTIONS

1 Use particle theory to explain the following.

a Molten metal may be poured freely in and out of a mould, but once it has set it will retain the shape.

b A tight bottle top may be loosened by running it under hot water.

c The diagram shows how the hydraulic brakes of a car use a liquid to transmit pressure from the brake pedal to the wheels. Sometimes bubbles of air get trapped in the liquid, and this stops the brakes working properly.

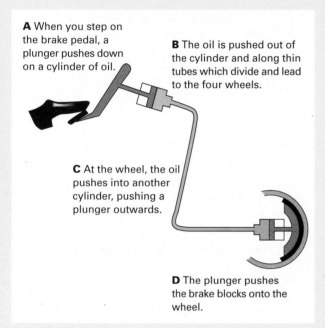

A When you step on the brake pedal, a plunger pushes down on a cylinder of oil.

B The oil is pushed out of the cylinder and along thin tubes which divide and lead to the four wheels.

C At the wheel, the oil pushes into another cylinder, pushing a plunger outwards.

D The plunger pushes the brake blocks onto the wheel.

2 Use particle theory to explain the following.

a Iodine dissolves in the greasy marks left by fingerprints, staining them brown. Fingerprints on paper are 'developed' (made visible) by standing the paper in a jar that has a few crystals of iodine at the bottom.

b Copper sulphate and potassium carbonate solutions react to give a green solid. If you drop a crystal of copper sulphate on one side of a beaker of water, and a crystal of potassium carbonate on the other, a green solid will slowly start to form between them.

c If trifles are kept for a few days, the lower parts of the custard turn the same colour as the jelly.

d Why does **a** happen faster than **b** which is in turn faster than **c**?

3a Sodium thiosulphate forms hexagonal crystals which melt at 40°C. If the liquid is cooled carefully, however, it will drop below this temperature *without* crystallising, forming a 'supercooled' liquid. If this is then 'seeded' with a small crystal, or is tapped with a needle, crystals grow rapidly and the temperature rises again. Why is this?

b Sodium acetate behaves in a similar way, but melts at 54°C. Mountaineers use packs of sodium acetate to warm their hands in cold weather. These are put into boiling water and then allowed to cool. When required, a button is pressed, and crystals can be seen growing in the pack, which warms up.

i What is the maximum temperature that the pack could reach?

ii Sketch the temperature curve that might be found if the pack was triggered on a freezing day (at 0°C).

iii What advantage would there be in having a pack containing twice the amount of sodium acetate?

4 Are the following substances metals or non-metals? Give reasons for your answers.

X is a liquid at room temperature. It is 13 times as dense as water and conducts electricity and heat.

Y is a shiny brown solid that melts at 1400°C. It is three times as dense as water but does not conduct heat or electricity well.

Z is a soft, silvery substance that floats on water and melts at 98°C. It conducts electricity.

5 Cheques can sometimes be forged so that they are worth more money than intended. Six pounds could be changed to six<u>ty</u> pounds, for example. The inks used may look the same, but how could you tell if they really were the same? Black ink is usually made from a mixture of dyes, and different inks have different mixtures. How could you:

a extract the dye from the ink,

b separate out the dyes it is made from, and

c compare the two?

6a Lead iodide forms as a yellow, insoluble solid (precipitate) when lead nitrate solution is mixed with sodium iodide solution. Describe how you would obtain a dry sample of lead iodide.

b If the sodium iodide solution was made up with tap water, some lead carbonate solid would also be formed. Lead carbonate is insoluble in hot or cold water, whilst lead iodide will dissolve in very hot water. How could you obtain a pure sample of lead iodide from these mixed solids?

7a Are each of the following substances elements, compounds or mixtures?

i sulphur   **vi** beer
ii calcium carbonate   **vii** ethanol (alcohol)
iii iron   **viii** oxygen
iv soil   **ix** water
v sodium chloride   **x** air

b Atoms of which elements are found in the following compounds?

i carbon dioxide   **iv** iron sulphate
ii copper sulphate   **v** potassium nitrate
iii copper carbonate

c How many of each type of atom is there in a molecule of:

i nitric acid HNO_3
ii calcium nitrate $Ca(NO_3)_2$?

8a Give the relative mass and charge on each of the three main sub-atomic particles.

b Elements are often shown by their symbols, with two numbers. For example:

$$_Z^{A_r}X$$

What do the numbers A_r and Z tell you?

c List the numbers of each type of particle in the following atoms:
sodium ($_{11}^{23}Na$), carbon ($_6^{12}C$), oxygen($_8^{16}O$), magnesium ($_{12}^{24}Mg$), neon ($_{10}^{20}Ne$), iron ($_{26}^{56}Fe$), barium ($_{56}^{137}Ba$), iodine ($_{53}^{127}I$), lead ($_{82}^{207}Pb$), uranium ($_{92}^{238}U$).

d Draw the electron configuration of sodium, carbon, oxygen, magnesium and neon atoms.

e List the numbers of each type of particle in the following ions:
sodium (Na^+), barium (Ba^{2+}), iodine (I^-), oxygen (O^{2-})

f Draw the electron configuration of sodium and oxygen ions.

9ai Draw the electron structure of calcium (Ca).

ii What is it about this arrangement that makes calcium a metal?

iii What happens when calcium forms its ion?

bi Draw the electron structure of fluorine (F).

ii What is it about this arrangement that makes fluorine a non-metal?

iii What happens when fluorine forms its ion?

c Explain, in terms of their electron structures, what happens when calcium and fluorine react together.

10a Why is it that solid metals conduct electricity, but crystals of ionic compounds do not?

b What particles move when a molten ionic compound conducts electricity?

c If you pass electricity through molten salt (sodium chloride) a gas is given off at the positive electrode (anode).

i What is this gas?

ii Why is it found at the positive terminal, rather than the negative one?

11a Describe, in terms of the electron structure, how the fluorine molecule F_2 is formed.

b Repeat this for the molecule O_2 (oxygen). What kind of bond is this? Draw it as a structural formula.

c Repeat this for the molecule N_2 (nitrogen). What kind of bond is this? Draw it as a structural formula.

12 Carbon atoms can join together in chains, linked by single covalent bonds. Draw the structural formula for the simple chain molecules

a propane (C_3H_8)
b pentane (C_5H_{12})
c octane (C_8H_{18}).

13a Sketch diagrams showing how the particles might be arranged in:

i solid carbon dioxide
ii sodium chloride
iii diamond.
Use these to help explain the following:

b Solid carbon dioxide is a soft material that turns to gas at $-78°C$.

c Salt crystals are hard but break if struck; they are not at all flexible.

d Rock boring drills are usually studded with industrial diamonds.

e Sodium chloride crystals do not conduct electricity; molten salt does.

f Diamonds do not conduct electricity at all.

5.1 *Acids and alkalis*

The litmus test

This test may have been one of your first chemistry experiments. Acids, such as vinegar or lemon juice, turn the dye in blue litmus red, whilst **alkalis**, such as soap or ammonia, turn red litmus blue.

Many dyes, such as those in red cabbage or raspberries, change colour in acids and alkalis. Dyes like this are called **indicators**. In the science laboratory you may come across others such as phenolphthalein or methyl orange.

More about acids

Weak acids such as citric acid and ethanoic (acetic) acid are sometimes used in cooking and taste sour – but that is not a test you should ever try with other acids, as many are poisonous or corrosive.

Some acids are used to remove limescale from kettles or toilet bowls. Limescale is calcium carbonate, and acids dissolve this. The limescale fizzes as carbon dioxide gas is given off.

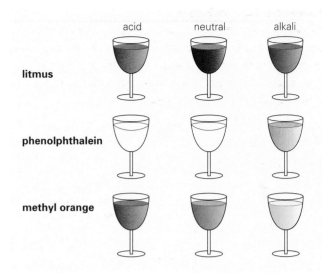

Some common indicators.

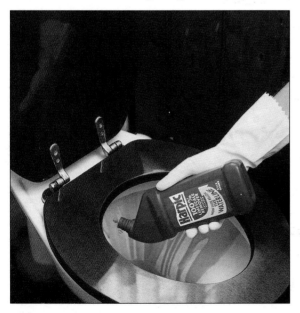

Your stomach contains hydrochloric acid, which helps to digest your food. If you have bad acid indigestion, this sometimes bubbles up into you throat and gives a nasty burning sensation.

Sulphuric acid is used in car batteries. It reacts with plates of the metal lead, producing electricity.

Citric acid in lemon juice and ethanoic acid in vinegar improve the flavour of some foods.

More about alkalis

Alkalis such as sodium carbonate (washing soda) and ammonia are used as household cleaners as they are good at dissolving grease. Sodium hydroxide (caustic soda) is a very strong alkali that is sometimes used to remove thick grease from cookers.

Soap is made by reacting sodium hydroxide with oils or fats. Because of this, most soaps and detergents are alkaline.

Some adverts for skin cleansers point out how alkaline most soap is.

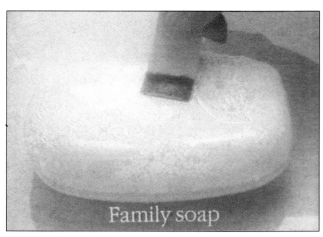

Family soap

From one extreme to the other

Acids and alkalis come in a wide range of strengths. The strongest acids and alkalis are very corrosive and need to be handled carefully. Weaker acids and alkalis are quite safe to handle. Between them comes water, which is neutral.

The strength of an acid or alkali is measured against the **pH scale**. This stretches from 0 (for the strongest acids) through 7 (for neutral water) to 14 (for the strongest alkalis). It is possible to measure pH directly using a special probe attached to a meter or computer. This can be very useful if you are monitoring the progress of a reaction in the environment, laboratory or in industry.

A simpler and cheaper method, however, uses **universal indicator**. This consists of a mixture of different indicator dyes which change colour at different pH values. The overall effect is to give a range of colour changes across the pH scale. This can be used in solution, or as test papers.

pH	
0	**(strongest acid)**
1	hydrochloric acid stomach acid
2	lemon juice
3	vinegar
4	acid rain
5	
6	rain water (contains dissolved carbon dioxide)
7	pure water **(neutral)**
8	sea water
9	
10	
11	ammonia
	washing soda
12	lime water
13	
14	sodium hydroxide **(strongest alkali)**

Universal indicator solution and the pH scale.

QUESTIONS

1 Make a list of some common acids and alkalis.

2 What reactions do acids give with
 a blue litmus **b** calcium carbonate?

3 What colour would:
 a methyl orange turn in distilled water
 b phenolphthalein turn in vinegar
 c phenolphthalein turn in ammonia?

4a Why is the pH scale so useful?
 b How does universal indicator help us to use it?

5 What colour would universal indicator turn in **a** ammonia, **b** pure water, **c** vinegar, **d** sodium hydroxide?

6 How could you tell pure distilled water from rain water?

5.2 Cancelling out

Making a salt ...

Acids and alkalis also react with each other. If they are mixed in the right proportions, **neutralisation** occurs – they cancel each other out. During this reaction a new substance called a **salt** forms. You can get crystals of this salt if you let the water evaporate. If you use hydrochloric acid and sodium hydroxide, you get common salt, sodium chloride.

Chemicals that neutralise acids like this are called **bases**. Copper oxide is base, but it does not dissolve in water. If you put it on damp litmus paper, nothing would happen, so it is not an alkali. Sodium hydroxide is a base that does dissolve in water. If you put some of that on damp litmus paper it would turn blue, so it is also an alkali. Alkalis are just bases that dissolve in water.

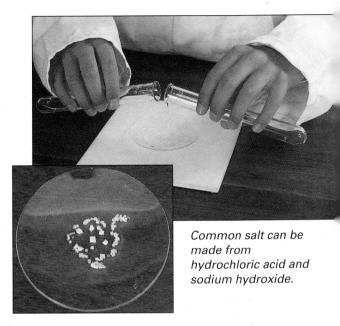

Common salt can be made from hydrochloric acid and sodium hydroxide.

... and water

All acids contain hydrogen, joined either to a single atom (such as chlorine in hydrochloric acid) or to a radical (such as the sulphate SO_4 in sulphuric acid).

Bases are the oxides (O) or hydroxides (OH radical) of metals. When they react, the hydrogen from the acid combines with the oxygen (or hydroxide radical) from the base to give water (H_2O), whilst the metal and radical combine to form a salt (see 3.3).

Neutralisation is a case of 'swapping partners'!

acid + base ⟶ salt + water

Useful neutralisation

If you suffer from acid indigestion, you may chew an 'antacid' tablet to settle your stomach. They are sometimes made of magnesium oxide. How do they help?

Your stomach contains hydrochloric acid, which helps dissolve your food. You get acid indigestion if your stomach makes too much. Magnesium oxide is a harmless base. When you swallow a magnesium oxide tablet, it neutralises some of the acid in your stomach.

Example 1

hydrochloric + sodium ⟶ sodium + water
acid   hydroxide   chloride
        (soluble alkali)   (salt)

$$HCl + NaOH \longrightarrow NaCl + H_2O$$

Example 2

sulphuric + copper ⟶ copper + water
acid   oxide   sulphate
     (insoluble base)   (salt)

$$H_2SO_4 + CuO \longrightarrow CuSO_4 + H_2O$$

Example 3

hydrochloric + magnesium ⟶ magnesium + water
acid   oxide   chloride

$$2HCl + MgO \longrightarrow MgCl_2 + H_2O$$

If you drop an antacid tablet into a glass of acid coloured with universal indicator, the colour changes, showing that the acid is becoming weaker until there is none left.

Soil troubles

Most plants grow best if the soil is neutral or slightly acidic (pH 6–7), but some soils become much more acidic than this. The peat soils on the moors of Yorkshire and Scotland may have a pH as low as 3 or 4. This is fine for pine forests, but is no good for crops.

These soils can be neutralised by sprinkling them with calcium hydroxide (slaked lime), a base made from limestone (see 5.5).

Farmers world-wide use lime to neutralise acidic soil and so increase their crop production.

Useful salts

You are most familiar with the uses of common salt, sodium chloride. But many other salts have important uses. Here are some examples.

- Potassium nitrate is used in gunpowder.
- Potassium chloride is used in medicine for diarrhoea.
- Calcium sulphate is used in plaster of Paris.
- Iron sulphate is used in iron tablets, which some people take to help their blood carry oxygen.
- Magnesium sulphate is used in medicine for constipation,
- Copper sulphate is sprayed onto grape vines to prevent disease.

Copper sulphate in use at a vineyard.

QUESTIONS

1 Write out the general word equation for neutralisation.

2 *Alkalis* are a sub-set of *bases*. Explain what is meant by this. What is the difference between an alkali and a base?

3 Explain how antacid tablets work.

4 Some antacid tablets contain aluminium oxide (Al_2O_3).

  a What salt will form in your stomach if you take one of these tablets?

  b Write a word equation for the reaction.

5 For each of the 'useful salts' listed:

  a What acid and base could be used to make it?

  b Write a word equation for the reaction.

6 Write balanced chemical equations for the reactions you have described in questions **4** and **5**.

7 Rusty iron can be prepared for painting by coating it with phosphoric acid. This forms a hard layer of iron(III) phosphate. Assume rust is iron(III) oxide.

  a Write down this reaction as a word equation.

  b The phosphate radical PO_4 has a valency of 3 (see 3.3). Write down this reaction as a balanced symbolic equation.

5.3 *Acids, salts and ions*

Charge it!

There is another important part to the story of acids. The acid molecules split apart into charged particles called ions when they are in water (see 4.2). The hydrogen atoms form positively charged ions called cations. The radicals form negatively charged ions called anions. Some of the water molecules **ionise** as well, as shown.

a sulphuric $\longrightarrow$ hydrogen + sulphate
    acid   cations   anions

$$H_2SO_4 \longrightarrow 2H^+ + SO_4^{2-}$$

b   water $\longrightarrow$ hydrogen + hydroxide
                 cations   anions

$$H_2O \longrightarrow H^+ + OH^-$$

Alkalis also ionise in a similar way – the important part here being the hydroxide anion, as shown.

c   sodium $\longrightarrow$ sodium + hydroxide
    hydroxide   cations   anions

$$NaOH \longrightarrow Na^+ + OH^-$$

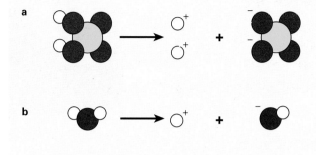

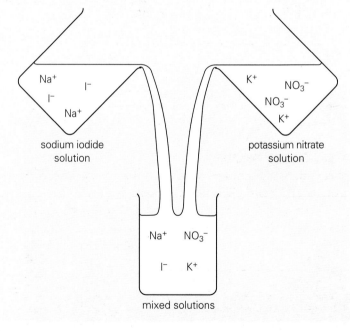

When acids and alkalis dissolve they encourage water molecules to ionise as well.

Making water

When neutralisation occurs, the hydrogen and hydroxide ions get back together – to make water again!

$$H^+ + OH^- \longrightarrow H_2O$$

This happens in *all* acid–alkali reactions.

sodium iodide solution

potassium nitrate solution

mixed solutions

All mixed up

Soluble salts also ionise in aqueous (water) solution. This time it is the metal that forms the cation, whilst the radical or other non-metallic part becomes the anion. A mixture of two soluble salts is just a mixture of the four ions, as the ionic partners will have separated and will move and mingle freely. So, for example, in solution:

sodium + potassium $\longrightarrow$ sodium + potassium + iodide + nitrate
iodide   nitrate   cations   cations   anions   anions

$$NaI + KNO_3 \longrightarrow Na^+ + K^+ + I^- + NO^{3-}$$

The result is the same as if you had mixed sodium nitrate and potassium iodide, both of which give clear solutions.

Changing partners

If you mix sodium iodide with water-soluble lead nitrate, however, you get a different effect, because lead iodide is insoluble in cold water. When the lead cations collide with iodide anions, they stick together to form a solid mass and 'fall out' of solution – you see a **precipitate** of yellow lead iodide. When salts 'change partners' like this it is called **double decomposition**.

sodium + lead ⟶ sodium + lead
iodide   nitrate   nitrate   iodide
(clear solutions)   (clear)   (precipitate)

$$2NaI + Pb(NO_3)_2 \longrightarrow 2NaNO_3 + PbI_2$$

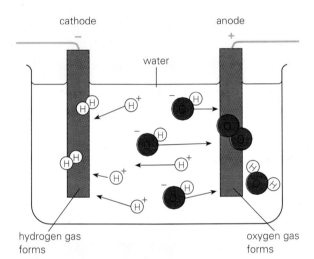

cathode   anode
water
hydrogen gas forms   oxygen gas forms

Hydrogen and oxygen gases form during the electrolysis of water.

Watch them move

Copper cations give copper sulphate its blue colour. Permanganate anions give potassium permanganate its purple colour. Put crystals onto moist filter paper as shown and you can watch the ions move.

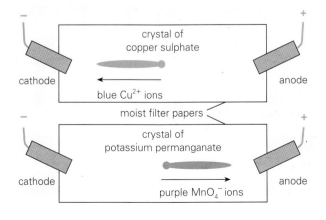

cathode — crystal of copper sulphate + anode
blue Cu²⁺ ions

moist filter papers

cathode — crystal of potassium permanganate + anode
purple MnO₄⁻ ions

Pull them apart

If you pass an electric current through slightly acidified water, using platinum electrodes, gases start to form.

At the anode (the positive electrode), the gas relights a glowing splint. This shows that it is oxygen. At the cathode (the negative terminal) twice as much gas collects. This goes 'pop' if you hold a lighted splint to it. It is hydrogen.

Acidified water ionises. Negative hydroxide <u>an</u>ions are attracted to the positive <u>an</u>ode (unlike charges attract). At the anode, the charges cancel out, and the hydroxide ions break down to oxygen and water.

The positive hydrogen <u>cat</u>ions are attracted to the negative <u>cat</u>hode. Again, the charges cancel out and this time hydrogen gas is formed.

This process is called electrolysis (see 4.3).

QUESTIONS

1 Describe what happens to acids and alkalis when ionisation occurs.

2 What are the ionisation products of
   a hydrochloric acid (HCl)
   b potassium hydroxide (KOH)?
   Which are the anions, and which the cations?

3 Copper carbonate is insoluble in water. Describe what would happen if solutions of copper sulphate and sodium carbonate were mixed. Write a word equation for this.

4 Ionic compounds conduct electricity when molten. What would collect at the anode and the cathode if molten common salt was electrolysed?

5.4 *More acid reactions*

Metals and acids

If you put a metal such as magnesium in an acid, it will start to **effervesce** (fizz). You can fill a test tube with this gas by **collecting it over water**.

If you hold your thumb over the tube as you take it out of the water, then hold a lighted splint over the tube and release your thumb, the gas will 'pop' with a mini explosion. This shows that it is hydrogen. The other product is the metal/acid salt.

$$\text{acid} \quad + \quad \text{metal} \quad \longrightarrow \quad \text{salt} \quad + \quad \text{hydrogen}$$

For example:

$$\text{magnesium} + \begin{array}{c}\text{sulphuric} \\ \text{acid}\end{array} \longrightarrow \begin{array}{c}\text{magnesium} \\ \text{sulphate}\end{array} + \text{hydrogen}$$

$$Mg \quad + \quad H_2SO_4 \quad \longrightarrow \quad MgSO_4 \quad + \quad H_2$$

Many (but not all) metals react like this. Different acids produce different salts, but the gas is always hydrogen.

Chemical bullies

All acids contain hydrogen. You might think of them loosely as 'salts' of hydrogen: sulphuric acid is hydrogen sulphate, nitric acid is hydrogen nitrate, and so on.

When a metal reacts with an acid this way, it is pushing the hydrogen out of its compound, like a kind of chemical bully. This is called a **displacement reaction**.

Magnesium – the big bully

Some metals are better at 'bullying' out the hydrogen than others. Magnesium is so good at it that it can even displace hydrogen from hot water or steam.

If you pass steam over heated magnesium ribbon it will glow brilliant white as it 'steals' the oxygen from the water. Hydrogen gas can be burnt off at the end of the tube:

$$\text{magnesium} + \text{steam} \longrightarrow \text{magnesium oxide} + \text{hydrogen}$$

$$Mg \quad + \quad H_2O \quad \longrightarrow \quad MgO \quad + \quad H_2$$

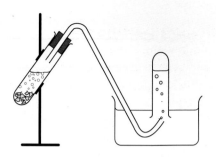

You can collect a tube full of this gas 'over water' by bubbling it up into an inverted tube full of water, as shown.

Magnesium can bully hydrogen out of acid . . .

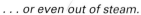

. . . or even out of steam.

Damp rocksil wool gives off steam when heated

Acids and carbonates

Limestone or marble chips (calcium carbonate) also fizz in acid. But this time the gas produced makes a flame go out, rather than explodes with one. It is carbon dioxide – the same gas that you breathe out.

acid + metal carbonate ⟶ salt + carbon dioxide + water

For example:

sulphuric acid + calcium carbonate ⟶ calcium sulphate + carbon dioxide + water

$$H_2SO_4 + CaCO_3 \longrightarrow CaSO_4 + CO_2 + H_2O$$

You cannot collect carbon dioxide over cold water, as it is soluble and will dissolve! One way to collect carbon dioxide is by **downward delivery**, as it is denser than air and so will sink to the bottom of a tube.

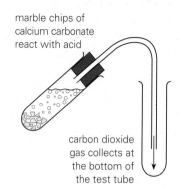
marble chips of calcium carbonate react with acid

carbon dioxide gas collects at the bottom of the test tube

This is the same reaction that happens when you dissolve limescale with an acid cleaner.

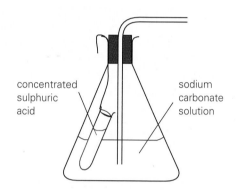
concentrated sulphuric acid

sodium carbonate solution

Put out the fire

The simple acid/carbonate reaction is used in red fire extinguishers. They contain a strong solution of sodium carbonate and a glass bottle of concentrated acid. When the extinguisher is used, the acid bottle is broken, and a violent reaction starts. The gas produced froths up the solution and squirts it out of the nozzle onto the fire – like opening a can of cola that has been badly shaken.

This simple model fire extinguisher will start as soon as the acid tube is tilted over.

Testing for carbon dioxide

Carbon dioxide is not the only gas that puts out a burning splint. If you want to be sure that the gas is carbon dioxide, you should use lime water. Carbon dioxide turns lime water milky.

Lime water is a solution of calcium hydroxide. When you react it with carbon dioxide, you get insoluble calcium carbonate which forms a white 'milky' precipitate.

calcium hydroxide + carbon dioxide ⟶ calcium carbonate + water

$$Ca(OH)_2(aq) + CO_2(g) \longrightarrow CaCO_3(s) + H_2O$$

You can easily try out the carbon dioxide test by breathing out through lime water.

QUESTIONS

1 Describe how you could fill a test tube with hydrogen gas safely in the science laboratory.

2 Calcium metal reacts with cold water to give hydrogen.
 a Do you think it will react with hydrochloric acid?
 b What would be formed?

3 Some people take baking soda (sodium hydrogencarbonate, $NaHCO_3$) for acid indigestion.
 a Gas is given off. What is it?
 b Complete the equation:
  $NaHCO_3 + HCl \longrightarrow$

4a Write a word equation for the 'simple model fire extinguisher' reaction.
 b Sodium has a valency of 1. Write a balanced symbolic equation for this reaction.

5.5 *Useful rocks*

Using limestone

Limestone (calcium carbonate) is a common rock that has been quarried and used for building for thousands of years. Many buildings throughout the world – from the pyramids of Egypt to Canterbury Cathedral – were built from limestone.

Limestone is still important today, with 130 million tonnes a year being quarried in Britain alone. Some of this is used directly for building or as road 'chippings'. But much of it is changed by chemical processes into other useful products.

Slaked lime has been used for centuries as a simple fertiliser, reducing soil acidity and improving its texture. Remains of simple lime kilns – where the limestone was roasted over charcoal fires – may be found all over the world.

Heat it up – break it down

If limestone is heated strongly, the compound is broken in two. Carbon dioxide is driven off and calcium oxide – **quicklime** – is left.

$$\text{calcium carbonate} \xrightarrow{\text{heat}} \text{calcium oxide} + \text{carbon dioxide}$$

$$CaCO_3 \longrightarrow CaO + CO_2$$

Quicklime is a dangerously corrosive alkali. It reacts with water, forming calcium hydroxide (**slaked lime**). This reaction gives out a lot of heat energy.

$$\text{calcium oxide} + \text{water} \longrightarrow \text{calcium hydroxide} + \text{heat energy}$$

$$CaO + H_2O \longrightarrow Ca(OH)_2$$

Bricks and mortar

Slaked lime was also used in **mortar**. It was mixed into a paste with water and used to hold bricks together. Over time, this mortar reacted with carbon dioxide in the air and hardened as it turned back to 'limestone'.

$$\text{calcium hydroxide} + \text{carbon dioxide} \longrightarrow \text{calcium carbonate} + \text{water}$$

$$Ca(OH)_2 + CO_2 \longrightarrow CaCO_3 + H_2O$$

Bricks are made from clay that has been heated in a kiln. The heat causes chemical reactions which permanently harden the clay.

Mortar is made from roasted limestone, bricks from baked clay.

Cement and concrete

Today, most limestone is used to make **cement**. The limestone is heated with clay in a special kiln to form a complex compound of calcium, **silica** (silicon dioxide) and aluminium. This powder recrystallises when water is added, in a similar way to plaster of Paris, but the resultant solid is much stronger.

Most cement is mixed with sand and gravel to make **concrete**. This versatile material forms a slurry when first mixed with water, and can be poured into any shape mould. But slow chemical reactions make it set after a few hours and eventually it becomes rock-hard. It is used to make pavements, bridge supports, building frameworks and foundations. It is often covered with brick or decorative stone, though some architects think it looks great on its own.

The Royal Festival Hall in London was built in the 1950s to show off the beauty of concrete. Not everyone thinks this was such a good idea.

Sand and sandstone

Sand and sandstone are also common rocks. They are mostly made from silica. Every year, 160 million tonnes of **sand** (or the coarser gravel) are used as **aggregates** – the fillers mixed in with the cement in concrete. They may be quarried from ancient sand beds, or dredged from rivers.

Very pure sand is needed to give colourless, transparent glass.

Making glass

Some sands are very pure, consisting of nothing but worn grains of crystalline silica – **quartz**. These pure sands are heated with limestone and a little sodium carbonate to make **glass**. The chemicals react and melt, driving off carbon dioxide. In the main reaction with calcium carbonate:

$$\text{calcium carbonate} + \text{silicon dioxide} \longrightarrow \text{calcium silicate} + \text{carbon dioxide}$$

$$CaCO_3 + SiO_2 \longrightarrow CaSiO_3 + CO_2$$

When calcium silicate cools it forms a hard but brittle, transparent material – glass. Glass is a strange material as the molecules do not stack up neatly as they would in a crystal, but keep the haphazard arrangement of a liquid.

QUESTIONS

1 Some soils can become quite acidic. How did farmers overcome this using the local rock?

2 Describe the chemical reactions that lead from calcium carbonate in limestone through to calcium carbonate in hardened mortar.

3 What is odd about the way glass solidifies?

4 Iron ore contains silicon dioxide impurities. Explain how limestone could help to remove these impurities when the mixture is heated.

5 Copper(II) carbonate is a green powder which turns black when heated. Lime water turns milky when held above the powder as it changes colour.
a What is happening?
b Write a word equation and a balanced symbolic equation for this.

6.1 *Metals in the rocks*

Our technology relies on metals, from the iron and steel in cars and bridges to the copper in electrical wires. The surface layers of the Earth's **crust** contains 70 metals. Of these, iron and aluminium are quite common, but most of the other metals are much rarer.

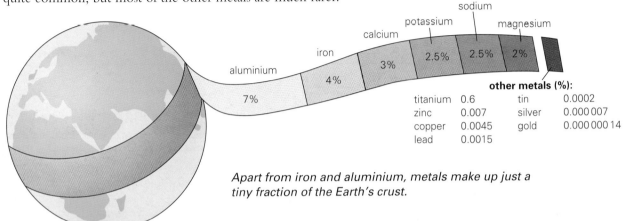

other metals (%):			
titanium	0.6	tin	0.0002
zinc	0.007	silver	0.000 007
copper	0.0045	gold	0.000 000 14
lead	0.0015		

Apart from iron and aluminium, metals make up just a tiny fraction of the Earth's crust.

Finding the ores

Most of the elements contained in the Earth are found as natural compounds (**minerals**) which are mixed together in rock. Most metals are found either combined with oxygen (as oxides) or sulphur (as sulphides). If these compounds are found in large enough amounts they are called **ores**, and may be worth mining.

Iron is the commonest metal, so suitable ores are easy to find. Aluminium is also common, but it is usually locked up in complex compounds with silica. Its oxide ore (**bauxite**) is far less common than you might expect.

Other metals are much rarer. Fortunately, natural processes sometimes concentrate these compounds so that they can be mined and processed economically. How can this happen?

Iron ore like this is fairly common, but most metal ores are rare.

Concentration by water

Rocks containing metal ores get broken down and eroded away by the wind and rain (see 9.2). Some ore minerals are hard and resistant, and remain as gravel or pebble-sized pieces at the bottom of rivers. But a pebble of ore may weigh two or three times as much as an ordinary pebble of the same size. Because of this, water currents may wash away the lighter material, leaving the ore in concentrated patches.

Tin ore pebbles are often found at the bottom of Cornish rivers, and gold could be found in the sea-washed river sands of Sierra Leone.

Prospectors often helped this process along by 'panning' the gravels to wash out the lighter material and leave the gold behind.

Finding the vein

In many areas of the world, new mountain chains are forming and there are many active volcanoes (see 9.1). Where this is happening, huge volumes of rock (tens of thousands of cubic kilometres or more) melt deep within the crust. Some of this molten rock escapes to the surface as lava, but most remains to cool and set slowly, deep underground.

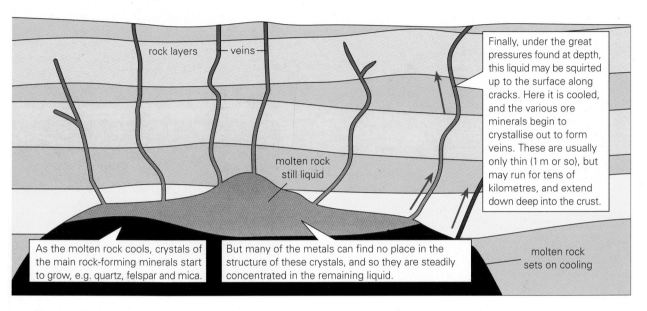

rock layers — veins —

Finally, under the great pressures found at depth, this liquid may be squirted up to the surface along cracks. Here it is cooled, and the various ore minerals begin to crystallise out to form veins. These are usually only thin (1 m or so), but may run for tens of kilometres, and extend down deep into the crust.

molten rock still liquid

As the molten rock cools, crystals of the main rock-forming minerals start to grow, e.g. quartz, felspar and mica.

But many of the metals can find no place in the structure of these crystals, and so they are steadily concentrated in the remaining liquid.

molten rock sets on cooling

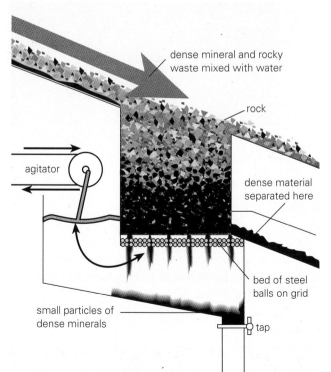

dense mineral and rocky waste mixed with water

rock

agitator

dense material separated here

bed of steel balls on grid

small particles of dense minerals

tap

When the mixture is jigged, the denser particles sink to the bottom. Try shaking a tin of ball-bearings and peas to see what happens.

Now it's our turn

Even metal ores from veins need to be concentrated further before you can extract them economically.

This usually involves crushing the rock, to break the ore particles free. The denser metal ores can then be separated from the waste rock. 'Jigging' works like panning, trapping the denser ore while the lighter waste particles are washed away.

QUESTIONS

1 Why are iron ores more common than tin ores?

2 How do rivers help to concentrate ore minerals?

3 Why are many metals 'left over' when molten rock solidifies?

4 How do mineral veins form?

5 How can metal ore fragments be separated from the waste rock?

6.2 *Reactivity and discovery*

Discovering metals

From the composition of the Earth's crust alone, which metal would you have expected to have been discovered first? If you said iron or aluminium it would make sense as they are the commonest metals. Yet if you study the table, you will see it was gold – the rarest metal! Why was that? The puzzle may be solved by looking at the way metals react with air, water and acids.

Metal	Percentage of crust	First discovered
gold	0.000 000 4	10 000 years ago
copper	0.0045	7000 years ago
lead	0.0015	6500 years ago
tin	0.0002	6000 years ago
iron	4	3000 years ago
zinc	0.007	2000 years ago
aluminium	7	170 years ago
magnesium	2	130 years ago

Metals react with oxygen

Most metals will react with oxygen in the air, to form a metal oxide.

$$\text{metal} + \text{oxygen} \longrightarrow \text{metal oxide}$$

For example:

$$\text{magnesium} + \text{oxygen} \longrightarrow \text{magnesium oxide}$$

$$2Mg + O_2 \longrightarrow 2MgO$$

But the way in which they react varies considerably.

Some metals, such as sodium and potassium, will catch fire spontaneously in oxygen. Others, such as magnesium, may be lit easily in thin strips and burn vigorously in air. Iron, zinc and aluminium are not usually thought of as materials which burn – but if finely powdered they too will flare up, as in sparklers and other fireworks. Copper dust will not burn, but it still does react with oxygen in the air, turning black. Finally, gold and the other precious metals do not react at all.

Magnesium burns with a brilliant white flame.

Metals react with acids

Many metals are able to displace hydrogen from acids (see 5.4).

$$\text{acid} + \text{metal} \longrightarrow \text{salt} + \text{hydrogen}$$

For example:

$$\text{hydrochloric acid} + \text{magnesium} \longrightarrow \text{magnesium chloride} + \text{hydrogen}$$

$$2HCl + Mg \longrightarrow MgCl_2 + H_2$$

Potassium and sodium react so violently that they would be far too dangerous to try in the school laboratory. Calcium and magnesium react very vigorously, iron and zinc more slowly. Lead and tin will only react with warm, strong acid. But copper and gold will not react in this way at all.

How some different metals behave in hydrochloric acid.

Metals react with water

Some metals can even displace hydrogen from water. Potassium and sodium react furiously with water, whizzing round on the surface and getting so hot that they melt to a silvery ball.

sodium + water ⟶ sodium hydroxide + hydrogen

$$2Na + 2H_2O \longrightarrow 2NaOH + H_2$$

The other metals are less spectacular. Calcium fizzes in cold water. Magnesium will bubble with hydrogen in hot water. But the others react much more slowly or not at all. In the long term, however, many will react – like iron rusting.

Sodium reacts spectacularly with water. The flame is from burning hydrogen coloured by the sodium ions.

very reactive – strong compounds

potassium
sodium
calcium
magnesium
aluminium
zinc
iron
tin
lead
copper
gold

unreactive – weak compounds

The reactivity series ...

So different metals react at different rates. You can list them in **order of reactivity**, from most to least reactive. The interesting thing is that this order of reactivity is the same, no matter what the reaction. This list is called the **reactivity series** of metals.

... and the discovery of metals

The more reactive a metal is, the stronger its compounds will be. The stronger the compound, the harder it is to get the metal out. Aluminium and iron may be common, but they are so reactive that they are normally tightly locked up in compounds. Copper and lead are also found in compounds, but these are easier to break down. Lead was discovered early, because the heat from an ordinary cooking fire would have been enough to free it from its ore. Gold is so unreactive that it may be found **native**, as pure metal. It may be rare but, if you were very lucky, you might find a pure, glistening lump of it.

So discovery was in reverse order of reactivity. And don't forget that far back in history nobody was actually trying to find the metals because nobody knew they existed! The first discovery had to be accidental.

QUESTIONS

1 List the metals in order of discovery. How does this compare to **a** their abundance and **b** their reactivity?

2 Write word and symbolic equations for the reactions of three different metals with oxygen.

3 Calcium (valency 2) displaces the hydrogen from water, leaving calcium hydroxide solution. Write word and symbolic equations for this reaction.

4 Write word and symbolic equations for the reaction of three different metals with hydrochloric acid.

5 Where should these 'unknown metals' fit on the reactivity series?

a Metal X reacts vigorously with acid and just starts to bubble in very hot water.

b Metal Y does not fizz with acid at all.

c Metal Z bubbles slowly in very strong acid.

6.3 *Extracting metals*

Getting the metals out

Given that most metals are only found locked up in their ores, how do you go about getting them out? For a few metals, such as mercury, heat alone will do the trick (see 4.1). But for most ores the temperatures needed are far too high to make this a practical possibility. Another approach is needed.

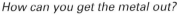

copper ore

How can you get the metal out?

Iron forces the copper out of copper sulphate solution.

Displacement again

If you dip a clean penknife blade or iron nail into blue copper sulphate solution, you will find that it comes out an orangey-brown colour – it has been copper-plated. Some of the the metallic iron atoms, coming into contact with the copper ions in solution, have swapped places with them. Indeed, if enough iron was added, the solution would lose its blue colour as all of the copper ions turned back into metallic copper, whilst iron ions took their place.

$$Fe \quad + \quad Cu^{2+} \quad \longrightarrow \quad Fe^{2+} \quad + \quad Cu$$
(metal)   (cation)   (cation)   (metal)

This is called a displacement reaction (see 5.4). It happens because iron is more reactive than copper and so displaces it from solution.

Displacement and reactivity

A less scientific view is that iron is a 'chemical bully', and pushes weaker copper from its compound. Whichever way you choose to think of it, the rule is that a more reactive metal will be able to displace a less reactive one from its compounds.

$$\text{iron} \quad + \quad \text{copper} \quad \longrightarrow \quad \text{copper} \quad + \quad \text{iron}$$
(metal)   sulphate   (metal)   sulphate

$$Fe \quad + \quad CuSO_4(aq) \quad \longrightarrow \quad Cu \quad + \quad FeSO_4(aq)$$

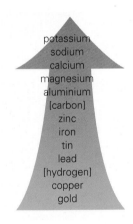

The reactivity series again. Those above can bully those below.

potassium
sodium
calcium
magnesium
aluminium
[carbon]
zinc
iron
tin
lead
[hydrogen]
copper
gold

A spectacular displacement

Displacement reactions can take place between solids, too. Aluminium is more reactive than iron. If you mix aluminium with iron oxide and give it a kick-start of energy, the aluminium pushes the iron from its oxide ore in a strongly **exothermic** reaction – it gives out heat and light energy. This is called a **thermit** reaction, and it can be very spectacular, with sparks flying and molten iron left behind.

$$\text{aluminium} \quad + \quad \text{iron} \quad \longrightarrow \text{aluminium} \quad + \quad \text{iron}$$
oxide   oxide

$$2Al \quad + \quad Fe_2O_3 \quad \longrightarrow \quad Al_2O_3 \quad + \quad 2Fe$$

This is a great way to get iron from its ore in the laboratory, so why not use it in industry? Unfortunately, as aluminium is more expensive than iron, this is a very costly way to get iron from its ore. What is needed is some other reactive element that can be found in an uncombined form and so is cheap to use.

Thermit reactions like that between aluminium and iron oxide are spectacular but do not make economic sense.

Carbon to the rescue!

Fortunately non-metals fit into our reactivity list as well. Hydrogen, for example, fits in between lead and copper. That is why copper can never push hydrogen from an acid.

Carbon fits above iron and zinc and so is quite capable of pushing lead, copper, zinc or iron from their compounds in a displacement reaction. Unlike aluminium, however, it is in plentiful supply in a fairly pure form as coal.

Redox reactions

When an element combines with oxygen, it is called **oxidation**. If the oxygen is taken away, however, it is called **reduction**. Both of these reactions occur when carbon is used to push lead from its oxide ore. Carbon reacts with lead oxide by combining with the oxygen – it is oxidised. But at the same time, the lead has oxygen taken away from it – it is reduced.

Oxidation and reduction always go hand in hand like this, so reactions like this are referred to as **redox** (or RedOx) reactions.

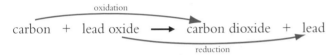

$$\text{carbon} + \text{lead oxide} \longrightarrow \text{carbon dioxide} + \text{lead}$$

Carbon can be used to push less reactive metals such as lead from their ores in a redox reaction.

QUESTIONS

1 Which of these metals can push lead from a solution of lead nitrate – iron, copper, zinc?

2 Metal X is pushed out of its salts by iron and zinc. But a piece of metal X dipped into copper sulphate solution gets copper-plated. What could it be?

3 Thermit reactions make good chemical but poor economic sense. Explain this statement.

4 Lead ore is first converted to lead oxide (PbO_2) before it is reacted with carbon to extract the lead.
a Write a word equation for the lead oxide/carbon reaction.
b Write a balanced symbolic equation for this reaction.

5 Copper can be pushed from heated copper oxide by hydrogen.
a Describe this as a redox reaction.
b What is the oxidation product?

6.4 *Making iron*

The iron age

Although iron can be displaced from its ores by carbon, very high temperatures are needed to kick-start the reaction, so it cannot be demonstrated easily in the laboratory. For the same reason, iron was not discovered until long after copper and lead. Lead melts at 327°C, copper at 1083°C, but iron needs a temperature of 1535°C. But, as the table of annual production figures shows, iron is very definitely 'top of the league' of useful metals.

Annual production figures for metals in Britain, 1990	
Metal	**Million tonnes/year**
iron	400
aluminium	12.5
copper	8
zinc	6
chromium	6
lead	3
nickel	0.7
tin	0.2
silver	0.01

The raw materials

Iron is produced by carbon reduction in a **blast furnace**. For this, the following raw materials are needed:

- **Iron ore** – The commonest iron ores are the oxides, **haematite** (Fe_2O_3) and **limonite**, which are found in sediments in Britain. The biggest and purest deposits are found in ancient sediments in Canada, South America, Africa and Australia.
- **Coke** – Carbon is needed to fire the furnace and reduce the ore. At first charcoal was used, but modern furnaces use coke. This is coal which has been heated to drive off oils and gases, leaving fairly pure carbon.
- **Limestone** – This natural source of calcium carbonate ($CaCO_3$) is added to the mixture to remove the impurities (mostly silicon dioxide).

The Ashdown Forest in Kent was a source of trees to make charcoal for early blast furnaces – and it shows!

The earliest blast furnaces were sited where these raw materials were close at hand. At first trees were needed to make charcoal, but later iron production moved to areas rich in coal, iron ore and limestone.

How it works

In simple terms, carbon is more reactive than iron so it reduces the iron oxide – pulling the oxygen away from the iron. In reality, this happens in three stages, as shown opposite.

Unfortunately iron ore is never pure iron oxide – it normally contains about 40% of silicon dioxide (SiO_2 – sand). The limestone in the furnace reacts with this impurity to form molten **slag**, which floats on top of the iron and can be tapped off separately and removed. When it sets, it looks just like volcanic lava. This is not surprising really as, being mostly calcium silicate, it is chemically very similar.

Most iron ore today is shipped in bulk from Australia.

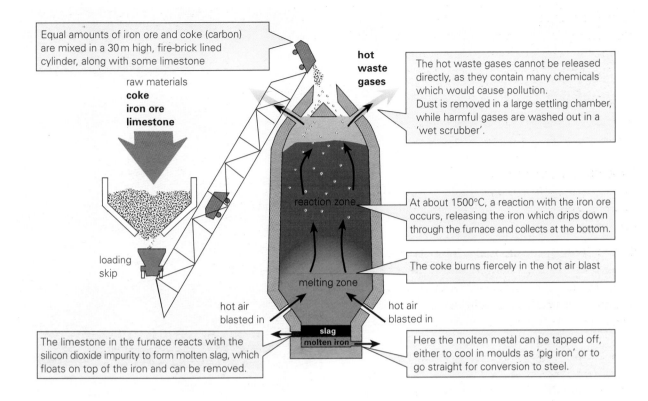

Equal amounts of iron ore and coke (carbon) are mixed in a 30 m high, fire-brick lined cylinder, along with some limestone

raw materials
coke
iron ore
limestone

loading skip

hot waste gases

The hot waste gases cannot be released directly, as they contain many chemicals which would cause pollution.
Dust is removed in a large settling chamber, while harmful gases are washed out in a 'wet scrubber'.

reaction zone

At about 1500°C, a reaction with the iron ore occurs, releasing the iron which drips down through the furnace and collects at the bottom.

The coke burns fiercely in the hot air blast

melting zone

hot air blasted in

hot air blasted in

The limestone in the furnace reacts with the silicon dioxide impurity to form molten slag, which floats on top of the iron and can be removed.

slag
molten iron

Here the molten metal can be tapped off, either to cool in moulds as 'pig iron' or to go straight for conversion to steel.

Stage 1: The coke burns, giving off lots of heat.

carbon + oxygen $\longrightarrow$ carbon dioxide + heat energy

$$C + O_2 \longrightarrow CO_2$$

Stage 2: The carbon dioxide reacts with more carbon.

carbon dioxide + carbon $\longrightarrow$ carbon monoxide

$$CO_2 + C \longrightarrow 2CO$$

Stage 3: The carbon monoxide reduces the iron oxide.

carbon monoxide + iron oxide $\longrightarrow$ carbon dioxide + iron

$$3CO + Fe_2O_3 \longrightarrow 3CO_2 + 2Fe$$

The limestone reaction

calcium carbonate + silicon dioxide $\longrightarrow$ calcium silicate + carbon dioxide

$$CaCO_3 + SiO_2 \longrightarrow CaSiO_3 + CO_2$$

Waste not ...

The hot air blast is produced by heating air in a gas stove. But once the furnace is running, great energy savings can be made by preheating the fresh air in a heat exchange unit using the hot waste gases, and thus recycling a lot of the heat energy.

QUESTIONS

1a What are the two main raw materials needed for iron production?

b Why is limestone added?

2a Why are there so few trees left in the Ashdown Forest?

b Why did iron production move to Wales?

c Why are large harbours needed in areas where iron is produced?

3 Describe in words and symbols the key chemical reactions that take place in a blast furnace.

4a Draw an annotated diagram of a blast furnace or draw a flow diagram showing the main systems, processes and reactions involved.

b Why can't iron be produced in the laboratory like this?

6.5 *Using electricity*

Carbon reduction is a relatively cheap way to get metals from their ores, but cannot work for metals above zinc in the reactivity series. For very reactive metals such as aluminium, the only choice left is to tear the metal from its molten ore using electrical energy, that is by electrolysis. This method is also used with *less* reactive materials in *solution*.

Electrolysis from solution

One of the simplest examples of electrolysis, often seen in school laboratories, is that of copper sulphate solution. If electrodes connected to a battery are dipped into this blue solution, the cathode gets coated with fresh, metallic copper. This is because the positive copper cations in solution are pulled towards the negative cathode (unlike charges attract). Here the charges cancel out (the cations gain electrons, see 4.3), and metallic copper is deposited.

$$Cu^{2+}(aq) + 2e^- \longrightarrow Cu(s)$$

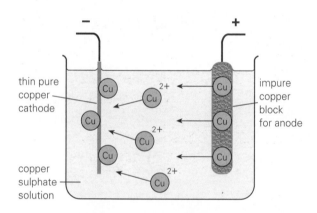

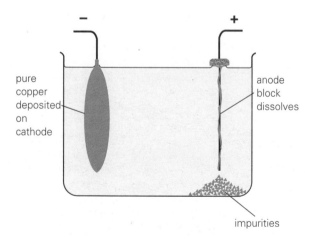

Copper can be purified like this because copper is less reactive than hydrogen and so does not react with the water in the solution.

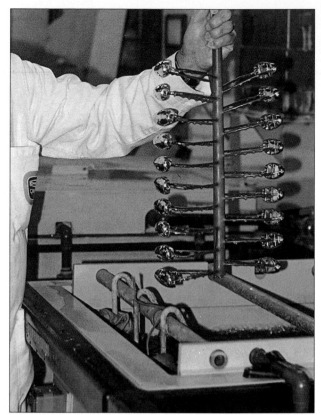

Electrolysis can be used to plate one metal onto another. If a solution of a silver salt is used, spoons connected up as the cathode in an electrolytic cell will be silver-plated.

Purifying copper

This process is used industrially to purify copper. A block of impure copper from a blast furnace is connected up as the anode, and a strip of pure copper as the cathode. These electrodes are placed in a conducting solution (**electrolyte**) such as copper sulphate.

When the current is switched on, electrons are pumped out of the anode to the cathode. The copper atoms in the anode block have their 'loose' electrons stripped away, and so become copper cations, which go into solution.

These copper cations are then attracted to the cathode. When they reach it, their positive charge is cancelled out as they pick up electrons. They turn back into copper atoms again, which are deposited onto the pure copper cathode.

As the reaction continues, the copper steadily migrates from the impure anode block (which gets smaller) and onto the pure copper cathode (which gets bigger). Eventually, no copper is left on the anode, and the cathode is a full-sized block of purified metal.

Extracting aluminium

Aluminium cannot be made by electrolysis in solution as it would react with the water – giving hydrogen gas instead. It must therefore be extracted by the electrolysis of its molten ore. Unfortunately aluminium's common oxide ore bauxite has a very high melting point – over 2000°C – so vast amounts of energy would be needed to melt and split the ore. Fortunately, by adding a little **cryolite** (a less common aluminium ore) the melting point can be lowered to 950°C. Even so, aluminium costs five or six times as much as iron, despite being more common in the Earth's crust. When you recycle your aluminium cans, what you are saving is not so much the material itself, but the vast amount of energy that was used to produce it in the first place.

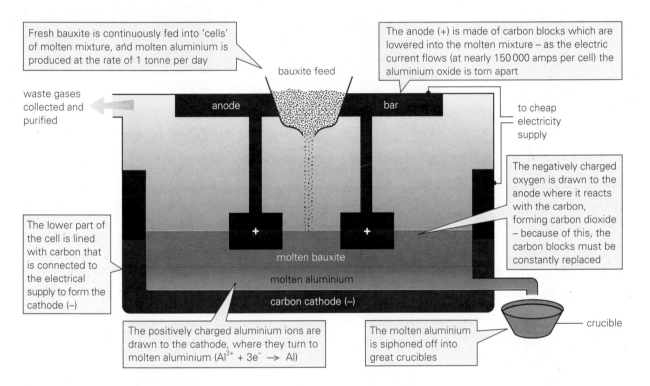

Fresh bauxite is continuously fed into 'cells' of molten mixture, and molten aluminium is produced at the rate of 1 tonne per day

The anode (+) is made of carbon blocks which are lowered into the molten mixture – as the electric current flows (at nearly 150 000 amps per cell) the aluminium oxide is torn apart

bauxite feed

waste gases collected and purified

anode

bar

to cheap electricity supply

The negatively charged oxygen is drawn to the anode where it reacts with the carbon, forming carbon dioxide – because of this, the carbon blocks must be constantly replaced

The lower part of the cell is lined with carbon that is connected to the electrical supply to form the cathode (–)

molten bauxite

molten aluminium

carbon cathode (–)

The positively charged aluminium ions are drawn to the cathode, where they turn to molten aluminium ($Al^{3+} + 3e^- \rightarrow Al$)

The molten aluminium is siphoned off into great crucibles

crucible

Aluminium is a very useful metal. It is light and strong and doesn't corrode, so it's great for cans and saucepans … and aircraft!. Unfortunately it is very expensive to produce.

The price we pay

Because of the high production costs involved, aluminium plants tend to be very large. It is cheaper (per tonne) to make a lot rather than a little. A typical plant may have 300 cells like the one shown, using a total of 200 megawatts of power. Indeed, most plants have a power station of their very own – preferably hydroelectric, as that gives the cheapest electricity.

QUESTIONS

1 Why is electrolysis used only when all other ways to extract the metal do not work?

2 How could you silver-plate a metal spoon?

3 Describe how electrolysis is used to purify copper.

4 Why is cryolite added to bauxite before electrolysis?

5a Why are aluminium plants usually built near power stations?
 b Which method of power generation is preferred and why?

6a Draw an annotated diagram of an aluminium electrolysis cell, showing the main processes and reactions.
 b Why do the carbon anode blocks from this process have to be replaced regularly?

6.6 Useful metals

The big one...

Many of the common uses of metals, in construction or for machinery, rely on the fact that metals can be shaped easily but are very strong. Iron, usually used in the form of steel, is so important because of this. Just think of how much iron and steel there is in use around the world in cars, trains, ships, bridges, railway lines... the list is endless. Because of this, more iron is used than all of the other metals put together.

Iron is also used to reinforce concrete in most modern buildings.

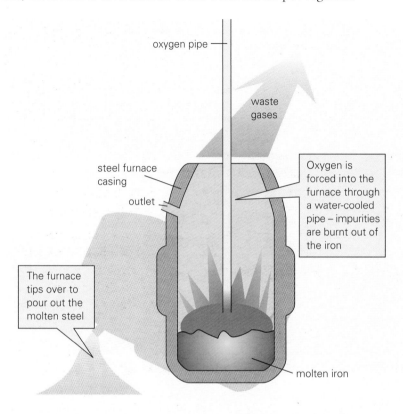

oxygen pipe

waste gases

steel furnace casing

outlet

Oxygen is forced into the furnace through a water-cooled pipe – impurities are burnt out of the iron

The furnace tips over to pour out the molten steel

molten iron

Once enough carbon has been removed from the iron, the whole furnace is tipped and the molten steel is poured out.

What is steel?

Iron straight from the blast furnace can be poured into moulds to make cast iron. This is hard, but is too brittle for most uses. Most iron today is used in the form of **steel**, which is a carefully blended mixture called an **alloy**. Usually, alloys are mixtures of different metals, but in steel iron is alloyed with a small amount of carbon.

Iron from the blast furnace already contains more carbon than is needed for steel. Some of this is removed by burning it out with a blast of oxygen.

How much carbon?

The amount of carbon to be left in the steel depends on what it is to be used for. With between 0 and 1% of carbon, the strength trebles as hardness also increases. **Mild steel** is bendable in thin sheets and is used for car bodies, 'tin' cans and ships' hulls. **Medium steel** is harder, and is now strong enough for use in hammer or axe heads. With above 1% carbon, however, the strength drops a little, while the hardness still increases. Scissors, knives, chisels, files and drill bits benefit from this **high carbon steel**, as they 'keep their edge' – but they may snap if badly used.

How the strength and hardness of steel change with carbon content.

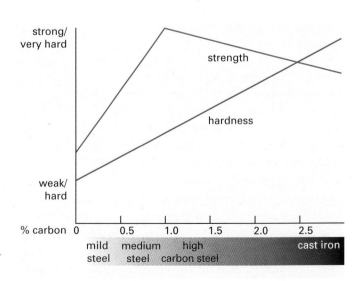

strong/ very hard

strength

hardness

weak/ hard

% carbon   0   0.5   1.0   1.5   2.0   2.5

mild steel   medium steel   high carbon steel   cast iron

The alloy age

Very few metals are used in the pure, elemental form. Aluminium is used for food wraps and copper is used for wiring, for example, but both are too soft when pure to be used for much else. Most of the metals you see in use around you are alloys.

Copper and tin were discovered 7000 years ago, but were of little use until they were put together to make the hard and strong alloy **bronze** about 4500 years ago.

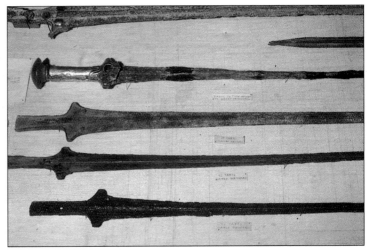

Bronze age swords and knives.

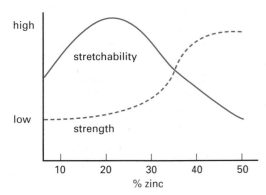

How the properties of brass vary.

More than just a mixture

The properties of alloys are not simply an 'average' of the individual metals involved. They may be quite different.

Brass is a very useful, corrosion-resistant alloy made from copper and zinc, but its hardness and 'stretchability' vary with the proportion of zinc involved. Ship fitments need to be very strong, so a higher proportion of zinc is needed than, for example, in shell-cases, which have to be stretched into shape.

Some more alloys

Copper and tin make bronze, copper and zinc make brass. All three make gun metal – a tough, hard-wearing metal that resists corrosion and is used for ship fittings, as well as guns! Copper is also used to make alloys that resist corrosion. With nickel it forms cupronickel – a resistant alloy that does not corrode, even when passed through many sweaty hands, and so is ideal for coinage.

Aluminium has a very low density for a metal, but is too weak to be of much use in construction when pure. Magnesium is even weaker, yet a combination of the two produces a strong alloy. The addition of a small amount of copper improves things even further, making duralumin. This is used in aircraft construction, where its combination of great strength yet low density makes it almost ideal.

Lead melts at 327°C, tin at 232°C. Yet mixed together they make solder, which can melt as low as 183°C, and so is useful for joining together wires in electrical circuits.

QUESTIONS

1a What is unusual about the main alloy partner for iron in steel?

b How is steel produced from iron?

2a Which percentage of carbon in steel gives the best combination of strength and hardness?

b Which would be best for razor blades?

3 Why was the discovery of bronze 4500 years ago such an important technological advance?

4 A firm making 'ship' brass with 40% zinc wants to increase to 45% zinc to save money. Will the brass be strong enough? Could they use this for shell cases? (Explain your answers.)

5 Why is aluminium used rather than iron in the aircraft industry?

6 Which of the alloys mentioned above would be used for each of the following? Give reasons for your answer.

a helicopter body frame   **c** low value coins

b a car body frame   **d** a shotgun barrel.

6.7 *Corrosion problems*

Useful aluminium

At first glance, you might well think that aluminium is an unreactive metal, as kitchen foil stays shiny and untarnished, and doesn't catch fire in the oven. Yet, as you have also seen from the thermit reaction, it is much more reactive than iron.

The trick is that aluminium is so reactive that it forms a microscopically thin oxide layer over its surface the instant it is exposed to air. This forms a protective barrier, preventing further reaction and making the metal seem inert.

aluminium + oxygen $\longrightarrow$ aluminium oxide

$$4Al + 3O_2 \longrightarrow 2Al_2O_3$$

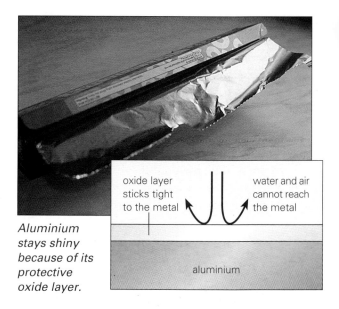

Aluminium stays shiny because of its protective oxide layer.

The trouble with iron

Unfortunately, iron does not form a protective oxide layer like aluminium. As all car owners will tell you, iron – whether 'pure' or in the form of steel – **rusts**. So what is different?

A simple experiment in the laboratory is enough to show that both air and water are needed for rusting. The process is quite complex, but iron(II) hydroxide forms first.

$$2Fe + O_2 + 2H_2O \longrightarrow 2Fe(OH)_2$$

This then reacts with more oxygen and water, forming **hydrated** iron(III) oxide. This can absorb more and more water, so the rust swells and blisters, flaking away and exposing fresh iron… which then starts to rust, and so on. Eventually, the whole structure collapses into dust. The formula of hydrated iron(III) oxide is $Fe_2O_3.nH_2O$

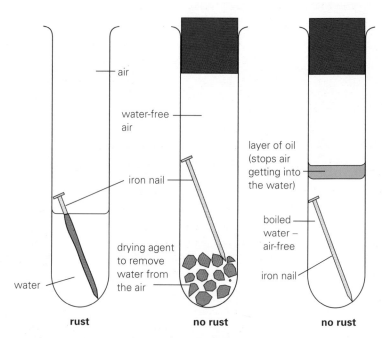

Both air and water are needed for iron to rust.

It's no good just painting over rust. It soon blisters out through the paint, letting the water and air in again.

How do we stop rusting?

The simplest way to stop rusting is to stop the water and air getting to the iron. Paint seals off the metal surface and so stops rust forming. But if this protective coating is chipped or scratched, rust will soon start to work underneath it. Rusting will continue unless all of the rust is removed and the metal is cleaned and repainted.

New cars have several layers of special paint beneath their top coat to stop rusting. The underside is very open to corrosion, so this is **undersealed** with a layer of bitumen. Coatings of oil or grease also keep out air and water and so prevent rusting.

Car bodies coated with paint ensure complete protection from rust.

Tin cans and barbed wire

Steel is useful for making many things, but rusts very easily. It is often protected by coating with a thin layer of another metal, such as tin for food cans or zinc for things like barbed wire. If the tin coating of a food can is broken, the iron rusts very fast indeed – yet if a zinc coated sheet is scratched, it is the zinc that corrodes. This is because when two metals are joined by water a small electric current flows, which causes the more reactive metal to corrode while leaving the less reactive one intact. Zinc is more reactive than iron, tin is less reactive.

It's the iron that rusts in a rusty 'tin' can.

What a sacrifice!

Zinc can also be used to protect ships from corrosion. Sea water is very corrosive, so steel-hulled ships need to be well protected. They sometimes have blocks of zinc or magnesium bolted to their hulls, which then corrode in place of the iron of the hull. These sacrificial blocks are much easier to replace than the hull itself!

When this zinc block has corroded it will need replacing – but the hull will be undamaged by rust.

QUESTIONS

1 Aluminium is very reactive, so why doesn't it corrode away?

2 Why doesn't rust protect iron in the same way that aluminium oxide protects aluminium?

3 How are cars protected against rust? Can you think of any reasons why manufacturers do not make their cars of totally rust-proof stainless steel?

4 How could you tell if some steel was tin-plated or zinc-plated if it was scratched and corroded?

5 Why is it not good enough just to 'paint over the rust' on an old car?

6 Some cars have aluminium engines. What would happen if these were bolted directly onto the steel body of the car?

6.8 *The trouble with metals*

In Britain we live in a 'high consumption' society. What effect does this have on our environment?

Mine it ... refine it!

If an ore deposit has been discovered near the surface, the simplest way to get at it is to dig a big hole. Mining companies like this 'open-cast' method of mining because it is relatively cheap, and miners like it because it is relatively safe.

The freshly mined ore then has to be concentrated further, and this generates vast amounts of 'useless' rock debris which has to be disposed of, often in ugly heaps. Yet even this might seem better than the sprawl of refineries and industrial plants that produce and shape the metals we use.

This copper mine at Bingham Canyon, Utah, USA covers an area of 7 km², and goes down 800 m – and they're still digging!

Use or abuse it

Some people say that our use of metals – in railway lines, in cars, and reinforcing the concrete buildings in our cities – has done nothing but harm to our environment. Others say that all these things are great improvements – providing better communications, better housing for the growing population, and a better quality of life.

Are cities like New York a use or abuse of technology?

Throw it away...

Between 10 and 20% of the metal produced every year is simply thrown away. This can spoil the appearance of the environment, but it is more serious than that. Rusting metal can cut or injure children or wild animals, and chemicals spreading into the soil may stunt or kill vegetation. Zinc or lead-based batteries discarded in or near water will eventually corrode and start to release their metals, causing environmental poisoning. If we use the bins provided for our waste, and the services made available for disposal of wrecked cars and other 'technological debris', we can limit this damage to chosen dump sites, rather than spreading its menace across the countryside. But there are other solutions.

Left to rust – but at what cost?

70

Separating out cans from household rubbish helps recycle valuable metals.

All mined out?

Earth is sometimes compared to a spaceship. It is where we all live, and from it we must get all that we need. It may seem enormous to you and me, but there are nearly 4 billion people on the planet and we are consuming the Earth's resources at an ever increasing rate. You will have heard about the energy crisis and how our fossil fuels will soon run out. But that is also true of the metal ores, on which so much of our modern technology depends. At present rates, and using today's mining techniques, many important metals will have been 'mined out' within the next 100 years or so.

Some optimists think that this is not really a problem. As our technology improves it becomes possible to extract metals from poorer quality ores – so long as we have plentiful supplies of cheap energy!

. . .or use and use again!

If we could recycle all of the metals we use, our problem would be solved. This is happening to some extent. You may have seen scrap metal yards near you – often full of rusting cars, waiting to be recycled. Aluminium cans can be deposited in collection bins for recycling.

We already recycle a significant proportion of some metals in the UK, but there are still many problems to overcome.

Metal recycling in Britain	
Metal	**% recycled**
aluminium	28
copper	18
iron	50
lead	60
tin	30
zinc	30

QUESTIONS

1   Our technology relies on metals – to build the machines, factories, homes and transport systems we take for granted, as well as the wires to carry the electricity that powers it all.

a In a small group, talk about the benefits and problems of modern technology.

b Decide on the five most important benefits, and the five biggest problems.

c Try to think of possible solutions for the problems.

d Report your findings to the whole class.

7.1 *Fossil fuels*

Trees are energy stores

Trees contain vast amounts of stored energy, which they got from the sun when they grew (see 8.1). They use the green pigment **chlorophyll** in their leaves to trap the energy in sunlight and use it to build complex chemicals from carbon dioxide and water. This process is called **photosynthesis**.

Most of this energy is released again when trees die and rot away. The complex chemicals react with oxygen to make carbon dioxide and water again. But if the plant material is buried in the mud, so that no oxygen can get to it, it breaks down in a different way.

Trees are solar-powered energy stores.

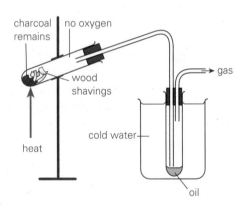

Distillation of wood – millions of years modelled in a few minutes!

Breaking down the wood

You can model what might happen by heating wood in a closed container, away from the oxygen that would make it burn. As the wood is heated, the complex chemicals break down and **oil** and **gas** are produced. These boil away, but can be collected elsewhere. What is left behind is almost pure carbon – **charcoal**.

Trees that have been buried in the mud break down like this too – but it may take millions of years. As the mud is buried deeper and deeper, the pressure increases enormously from the weight of the overlying sediment, and the temperature also rises. The mud hardens to rock and the wood is slowly reduced to carbon which is left in the beds of rock as **coal**. The oil and gas that form escape up towards the surface.

Fossil fuels

Coal, oil and gas can all be burnt as fuels. They are called **fossil fuels**, and they contain the energy store that was built up by the plants, using sunlight, millions of years ago.

If you burn wood, you are using energy that has been trapped and stored in a similar way, but you can grow new trees to take their place. Wood is a **renewable** source of energy. If you burn fossil fuels, you are using up an energy store that took millions of years to form, so fossils fuels are a **non- renewable** source of energy. Once they have been used up, they cannot be replaced.

Fossil fuels could all be used up within 300 years – what can be used instead?

Trapping oil and gas

Oil and gas can also be formed when any animal or plant remains are buried. Sediments that are deposited in the sea contain large amounts of **organic material** like this. If this material is buried quickly, the tiny droplets of oil and bubbles of gas which form may be trapped for millions of years under hundreds or thousands of metres of sediments, which slowly turns to rock.

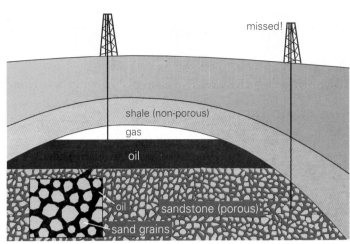

Sandstone soaks up water like a sponge. Oil and gas can float up through this water and collect under domes of shale.

The search for oil and gas

The search for oil involves looking for places where oil might be trapped. Scientists need a way to look into the rocks of the Earth's crust. This is now done by setting off explosions and monitoring the complex shock-wave reflections that bounce back to the surface from the rock layers below. Computer analysis then produces a picture of any hidden structures. These techniques are now so powerful that **oil traps** have been discovered buried deep in the sediments under the North Sea. But, despite this advanced technology, the only way to see if there is actually any oil or gas there is to drill a 'wildcat' well! It is still a very expensive, high risk business.

These controlled explosions could help to find a new oil trap.

Oil slick!

Oil is very big business, as it is used as a fuel and a source of chemicals for industry. Huge supertankers carry billions of tonnes of oil around the world. If they have accidents, oil slicks spread across the sea and shorelines, killing the wildlife. This is one industrial by-product that won't be missed when the oil runs out!

This seabird was killed when it was covered by oil from an oil slick

QUESTIONS

1 Where did the stored energy in fossil fuels originally come from? Why was it not lost?

2 Compare the formation of fossil fuels to the products of the distillation of wood.

3 How is it possible to find an oil trap in rocks beneath the sea?

4 The world's store of fossil fuels formed over the last 300 *million* years. It is likely to have been exhausted within just 300 years. What problems can you foresee this causing?

7.2 *Uses of crude oil*

The oil you get from an oil well – called **crude oil** – is a complex mixture of chemicals. As crude oil, it is not much use. But if the different chemicals are separated out, it is a different story. Crude oil is one of the most important raw materials available to industry. It is used for everything from fuels to the manufacture of medicines. What is in it, and how can these things be separated?

The chain gang

Crude oil is mostly a mixture of **hydrocarbons** – chemicals made from hydrogen and carbon only. Carbon has the ability to form long chain molecules, so a range of hydrocarbon compounds are possible, depending on the length of the carbon chain. Molecules like this are often called **organic** compounds, as similar carbon-chain chemicals, with added oxygen and nitrogen, form the basis of all life (**organisms**) on our planet.

Methane (natural gas) is the simplest hydrocarbon, with one carbon to four hydrogen atoms. But by linking carbon atoms together by single bonds, a whole family of compounds with similar chemical properties may be produced.

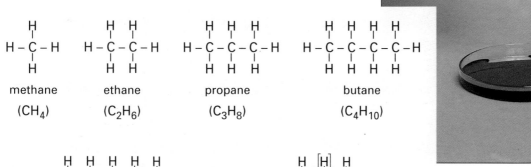

Crude oil is a mixture of hydrocarbons with chain lengths from 1 to over 100.

A range of properties

All hydrocarbons will burn in air to give carbon dioxide, water and energy. How easily they do this depends on the chain length. The physical properties also vary with chain length as shown.

As the different molecules have different boiling points, they can be separated by **fractional distillation** (see 2.5). You could do this in the laboratory by steadily heating the oil and collecting the separate fractions by changing the tubes. In industry, the process is reversed. The oil is completely vaporised in a furnace and then passed up a tower, which gets cooler and cooler. The different fractions condense out at different levels in the tower and can be tapped off. This means that the whole process can run continuously, which is more efficient and so saves money, which keeps the price of oil products down.

Properties of hydrocarbons and molecule size		
Property	**Short chains** ⟶	**long chains**
boiling point*	low ⟶	high
easily vaporised?	yes ⟶	no
easily lit?	yes ⟶	no
viscosity	runny ⟶	thick
example	**petrol**	**engine oil**

* very short chain hydrocarbons are gases at room temperature, very long chain hydrocarbons are solids at room temperature

The fractional distillation of crude oil

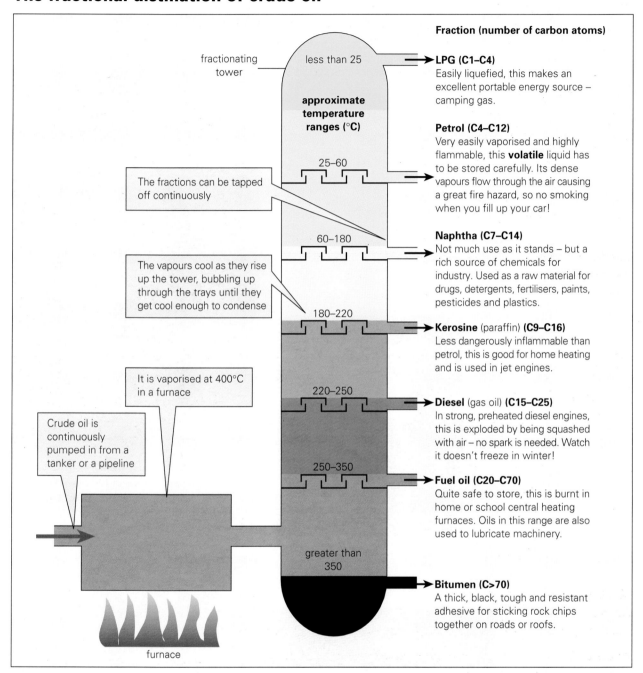

Fraction (number of carbon atoms)

fractionating tower

less than 25

approximate temperature ranges (°C)

LPG (C1–C4)
Easily liquefied, this makes an excellent portable energy source – camping gas.

Petrol (C4–C12)
Very easily vaporised and highly flammable, this **volatile** liquid has to be stored carefully. Its dense vapours flow through the air causing a great fire hazard, so no smoking when you fill up your car!

25–60

The fractions can be tapped off continuously

Naphtha (C7–C14)
Not much use as it stands – but a rich source of chemicals for industry. Used as a raw material for drugs, detergents, fertilisers, paints, pesticides and plastics.

60–180

The vapours cool as they rise up the tower, bubbling up through the trays until they get cool enough to condense

180–220

Kerosine (paraffin) **(C9–C16)**
Less dangerously inflammable than petrol, this is good for home heating and is used in jet engines.

It is vaporised at 400°C in a furnace

220–250

Diesel (gas oil) **(C15–C25)**
In strong, preheated diesel engines, this is exploded by being squashed with air – no spark is needed. Watch it doesn't freeze in winter!

Crude oil is continuously pumped in from a tanker or a pipeline

250–350

Fuel oil (C20–C70)
Quite safe to store, this is burnt in home or school central heating furnaces. Oils in this range are also used to lubricate machinery.

greater than 350

Bitumen (C>70)
A thick, black, tough and resistant adhesive for sticking rock chips together on roads or roofs.

furnace

QUESTIONS

1 What do you think is the main difference in physical property between methane (CH_4) and octane (C_8H_{18})?

2 How does the industrial method of oil distillation differ from the method used in the school laboratory? Why is it different?

3 Why is the 'no smoking' rule so important when filling a car with petrol?

4 Fuel oil is safe to store and has to be sprayed as tiny droplets before it will burn. Why is it so different to petrol?

5 Lubricating oil can be thick or runny, depending on the job it is needed for. Which type is likely to have the longer carbon chain?

7.3 Burning up

Combustion

When a fuel burns, it reacts with the oxygen in the air to give waste gases in a **combustion** reaction. During this reaction the fuel is oxidised. More importantly, the reaction gives out heat (and light) energy, which means that combustion reactions are strongly exothermic.

What fuels do we use?

The fuels we use contain hydrogen, carbon or the two combined, sometimes with oxygen.

● **Hydrogen** is only rarely used on its own, as it is found combined in nature and so has to be manufactured.
It is a pollution-free fuel, however, as the only waste product it produces is water.

$$hydrogen + oxygen \longrightarrow water + energy$$
$$2H_2 + O_2 \longrightarrow 2H_2O$$

● **Carbon** occurs in an almost pure form in the rocks as coal. This is not so easy to set alight but, once it is burning, it gives off a lot of energy, forming carbon dioxide gas. On a large scale, this can cause problems with the 'greenhouse effect' (see 8.3), but it is not a poisonous gas – it is the gas you breathe out!

$$carbon + oxygen \longrightarrow carbon\ dioxide + energy$$
$$C + O_2 \longrightarrow CO_2$$

● **Hydrocarbons** from crude oil contain hydrogen and carbon. So when they burn, they produce both carbon dioxide and water. So for natural gas (methane):

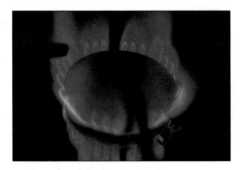

$$hydrocarbon + oxygen \longrightarrow carbon\ dioxide + water + energy$$
$$(e.g.\ methane)$$
$$CH_4 + 2O_2 \longrightarrow CO_2 + 2H_2O$$

The main rocket motors of the Space Shuttle use liquid hydrogen as a fuel, which they carry with them into space, along with liquid oxygen.

Flash point

With liquid hydrocarbons, it is their vapour that burns and, the lower their boiling point, the more vapour will be produced at room temperature. Each fuel has its own **flash point** temperature, above which this vapour will ignite from the smallest spark or flame. You can smell petrol when you fill up a car because it has a low boiling point and so is very **volatile**, and its dense vapour spreads through the air.

The flash point of petrol is well below room temperature, so there is always a risk of fire. Because of this, petrol must be stored in sealed containers. The flash points for paraffin or fuel oil are much higher, so it is easier to store them safely.

Heat is most easily taken from a fire by water, which uses the heat energy to boil it away. But water conducts electricity so can't be used on electrical fires. Also it vaporises oil in a burning chip pan, spreading the fire further.

Flammable materials left lying around are a fire hazard. Supermarkets should take away cardboard boxes for safe disposal.

heat

fuel

oxygen

Throwing a damp cloth over a chip-pan fire takes away the oxygen from the burning oil. Some fire extinguishers use non-flammable materials to engulf a fire in the same way.

Fire!

To make a fire you need three things: fuel, a supply of oxygen (usually air), and a high enough temperature to keep the reaction going. This is often shown as the **fire triangle** – remove one thing and the fire will go out.

Gas heaters need good ventilation.

Incomplete combustion

All these equations have assumed that there is enough oxygen available to complete the reaction. If there is not enough oxygen to go around, however, the carbon is not fully oxidised to give carbon dioxide. Instead, colourless, odourless but deadly poisonous carbon monoxide (CO) gas is produced.

Some carbon monoxide is found in car exhaust gases, so car engines should never be run inside garages. Carbon monoxide can also be produced if the ventilation of gas heaters is faulty. The flame should be like a miniature roaring Bunsen flame. If it is yellowish and sooty – get it checked at once!

QUESTIONS

1 What are the advantages and disadvantages of hydrogen as a fuel?

2 Write balanced symbolic equations for the complete combustion of **a** methane, **b** propane (C_3H_8).

3 Which side of the fire triangle is being removed to extinguish the following:
 a a fire break cut around a forest fire
 b carbon dioxide blown over an electrical fire
 c water poured onto glowing barbecue charcoal?

4 What would you do if the following caught fire:
 a a frying pan of sausages
 b your friend's clothes
 c paper in a waste paper basket?

5 A Bunsen burner with the air hole closed burns with a sooty flame.
 a Where is this carbon coming from and why?
 b What poisonous gas might also be formed?
 c Why does this stop happening when the airhole is opened?

7.4 *More about hydrocarbons*

Naming the chains

In the simple hydrocarbons found in crude oil, every carbon atom has four single bonds, either attached to a neighbouring carbon atom or a hydrogen atom. Simple hydrocarbons like this are called **alkanes**. As all of the bonds are single, they are said to be **saturated**.

The whole collection, from short chain gases, through medium chain liquids, to long chain solids, make a family of compounds with graded chemical properties. To make sense of this, they have similar names. The first part (prefix) tells you the chain length, whilst the *–ane* ending tells you that they are part of the simple alkane family.

Alkane reactions

As you have seen, the alkanes are all fuels which burn in oxygen to produce carbon dioxide and water. For example:

propane + oxygen $\longrightarrow$ carbon dioxide + water

$$C_3H_8 + 5O_2 \longrightarrow 3CO_2 + 4H_2O$$

Despite this, these simple chain hydrocarbons are relatively unreactive. As all the bonds are single bonds, the main reactions apart from combustion are **substitution** reactions, where one or more of the hydrogen atoms is replaced. If methane reacts with chlorine, for example, the hydrogen atoms may be 'picked off' in turn:

$$CH_4 + Cl_2 \longrightarrow CH_3Cl + HCl$$
$$CH_3Cl + Cl_2 \longrightarrow CH_2Cl_2 + HCl$$
$$CH_2Cl_2 + Cl_2 \longrightarrow CHCl_3 + HCl$$
$$CHCl_3 + Cl_2 \longrightarrow CCl_4 + HCl$$

$$CH_4 + Cl_2 \longrightarrow CH_3Cl + HCl$$

Chlorinated hydrocarbons can form by substitution.

This reaction does not proceed in the dark, but may be explosive in sunlight. One of the final products is tetrachloromethane (carbon tetrachloride, CCl_4). Longer chain molecules will burn steadily in chlorine, and a wide range of chlorinated hydrocarbons are possible. They are unreactive and are commonly used as solvents. If fluorine is substituted as well, chlorofluorocarbon products (**CFCs**) are formed, which were once widely used as aerosol propellants and refrigerator gases.

The first ten members of the alkane family			
No. of carbon atoms	Standard prefix	Alkane name	Boiling point °C
1	meth-	methane	–162
2	eth-	ethane	–87
3	prop-	propane	–42
4	but-	butane	–1
5	pent-	pentane	36
6	hex-	hexane	69
7	hept-	heptane	99
8	oct-	octane	126
9	non-	nonane	151
10	dec-	decane	174

CFCs seemed the ideal chemicals for refrigerator coolants and aerosol propellants – until it was discovered that they damaged the Earth's ozone layer (see 8.2).

Variations on the theme

This basic theme of carbon chains has many variations. An important parallel family (the **alkenes**) has a double bond in place of one of the simple carbon-carbon single bond links in the chain.

As before, the first part of the name tells you the number of carbon atoms in the chain. The ending *-ene* tell you that there is a double bond.

The presence of these double bonds makes members of this family more reactive. With chlorine, for example, the double bond springs open – each 'free arm' grabs a chlorine atom to form a chlorinated hydrocarbon. This is an **addition** reaction.

Organic compounds with double bonds are said to be **unsaturated**.

H–C=C–H
| |
H H
ethene
(C_2H_4)

H
|
H–C–C=C–H
| | |
H H H
propene
(C_3H_6)

H H
| |
H–C–C–C=C–H
| | | |
H H H H
butene
(C_4H_8)

Telling them apart

This reactivity can be used as a test. Unlike alkanes, alkenes react rapidly with bromine water in this way, decolourising it.

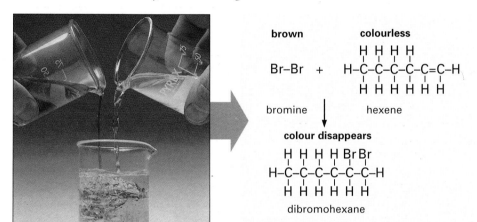

Alkenes decolourise bromine water.

In structural formulae, molecules are usually written with the bonds at right angles. This does not show their shape but is easier to read.

Saturated or unsaturated?

Fats have a more complex version of the carbon chain molecule. Those in butter are saturated, like the alkanes. Those in olive oil are unsaturated, like the alkenes. Those in sunflower oil and margarine are **polyunsaturated**. That means they have lots of double bonds in their molecules. Some research suggests that unsaturated and polyunsaturated fats may be better for your heart than saturated fats. So margarines which contain unsaturated fats are sometimes considered a healthier option than butter.

QUESTIONS

1a Plot a graph of number of carbon atoms against boiling point for the first 10 alkanes, leaving yourself enough room to extend the graph to number 15.
b Predict the boiling point of alkane number 15.

2a Describe the differences in chemical properties between alkanes and alkenes.
b Explain the cause of these differences.

3 Draw one possible structural formula for
a butene **b** pentene **c** octene.

4 What colour will bromine water be if mixed with an alkane?

5a Write a word equation for the complete combustion of ethene in air.
b Write this as a balanced symbolic equation.

7.5 *Cracking it*

Supply and demand

Crude oil is a rich source of hydrocarbons and, as you have seen, may be separated out into useful components by fractional distillation. One problem, however, is the fact that the demand for the lighter fractions such as petrol is proportionally much greater than their percentage in the crude oil, because the lighter fractions make better fuels.

Getting what you need

The answer is to crack it! In this process, long carbon chains are split into shorter sections by the action of heat. This works efficiently at relatively low temperatures (about 400°C) by using finely powdered aluminium oxide as a catalyst (see 13.2). The new products are then separated by further fractional distillation. For example, decane from unwanted naphtha may be cracked to give octane which is used in petrol:

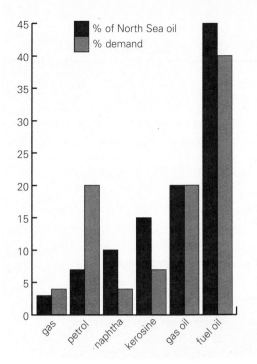

The demand for different oil products does not match their natural occurrence in crude oil.

$$C_{10}H_{22} \xrightarrow{\text{cracking}} C_8H_{18} + C_2H_4$$

$$\text{decane} \longrightarrow \text{octane} + \text{ethene}$$

$$\underset{\substack{|\\H}}{\overset{\substack{H\\|}}{H-C}}-\overset{H}{\underset{H}{C}}-\overset{H}{\underset{H}{C}}-\overset{H}{\underset{H}{C}}-\overset{H}{\underset{H}{C}}-\overset{H}{\underset{H}{C}}-\overset{H}{\underset{H}{C}}-\overset{H}{\underset{H}{C}}-\overset{H}{\underset{H}{C}}-\overset{H}{\underset{H}{C}}-H \longrightarrow H-C-C-C-C-C-C-C-C-H + H-C=C-H$$

Methylated spirit (meths) is used as a solvent for some paints, amongst other things.

Using ethene

As you can see, a second product of this is the alkene ethene. It can be made to undergo an addition reaction with water (by passing ethene and steam over a phosphoric acid catalyst at 300°C) to make ethanol (ethyl alcohol).

$$\text{ethene} + \text{steam} \xrightarrow{\substack{\text{phosphoric acid}\\\text{catalyst at 300°C}}} \text{ethanol}$$

$$C_2H_4 + H_2O \longrightarrow C_2H_5OH$$

Vast quantities of ethanol are produced for industry in this way, where it is widely used as a solvent. Methylated spirit is made from this. Ethanol is also the active ingredient in wines, beers and spirits, but this is made by the more traditional, organic method of fermentation (see 13.5).

Petrol's 'octane rating'

The hydrocarbons used in petrol must be volatile enough to vaporise easily – they must have low boiling points. Within a petrol engine, the vapour/air mixture is exploded by a spark from the spark plug, and this forces the piston down to turn the engine. The problem is that simple alkanes explode too fast, causing a jerky and inefficient engine action known as 'knocking'. But hydrocarbons can exist in different forms, with branching rather than straight carbon chains. The 'best' molecule for petrol is a form of octane that has three branches. All petrol blends are compared to this 100% 'octane rating'.

Straight-chain octane causes an engine to 'knock'.

Branched chain octane is just right.

Unleaded fuel is taxed less to encourage motorists to change from leaded to unleaded petrol.

Unfortunately, petrol has to be re-refined to reach this high standard, and that is expensive. One answer was to add a lead compound to poorer quality fuel to help it burn more smoothly, but this means that poisonous lead comes out in the exhaust. Fortunately, branched-chain hydrocarbons are produced in the cracking process. These are added to modern **unleaded** fuel, to improve its octane rating.

Hydrogenation

Some branched chains produced by cracking are alkenes. They need to be turned back to alkanes – **reformed** – before they can be added to petrol. This is done by reacting them with hydrogen.

$$\text{alkene} + \text{hydrogen} \xrightarrow{\text{hydrogenation}} \text{alkane}$$

So, for the hydrogenation of ethene to ethane:

When this happens, the double bond snaps open, 'grabbing' the two extra hydrogen atoms. This process is called hydrogenation.

QUESTIONS

1 Explain why some of the naphtha fraction from crude oil is sent to be cracked.

2 What are the two types of product from cracking naphtha?

3 Alcoholic drinks are highly taxed, industrial ethanol is not. Why do you think industrial alcohol is commonly mixed with an unpleasant tasting poison, before being sold as 'methylated spirit'?

4a What is the significance of the octane rating of petrol?

 b How does lead help to improve this?

 c What are the problems associated with this use of lead?

 d How does cracking help?

5a Explain the term hydrogenation.

 b Write a balanced symbolic equation for the hydrogenation of propene (C_3H_6).

7.6 *Addition polymers*

Very long carbon chain molecules occur widely in nature. But starting with alkenes, new types can be made to order.

Addition polymers

You have seen how addition reactions occur with alkenes, when the double bond breaks open. This gives each carbon atom a spare 'bond arm', which can then grab an additional atom, such as chlorine or hydrogen. If this happens when only alkene molecules are available, they can be made to join together, each linking to its neighbour in a growing chain. As each addition still leaves one spare bond, this process could go on indefinitely. In practice many thousands of molecules may link together to form a long, thin molecule called an **addition polymer**. The process is called **polymerisation**.

Polythene has many uses, but this is still the most visible of them.

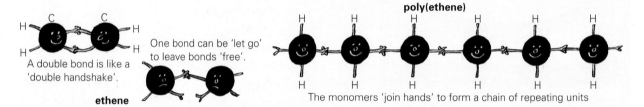

A double bond is like a 'double handshake'.

ethene

One bond can be 'let go' to leave bonds 'free'.

poly(ethene)

The monomers 'join hands' to form a chain of repeating units

Poly(ethene)

Ethene may be polymerised to poly(ethene) (better known as **polythene**) in this way, by the action of heat and pressure (though catalysts are now used to speed up the reaction). Polythene is a waxy solid that is resistant to corrosion and is an excellent electrical insulator. It is very easy to shape or mould (hence the general term plastic) and may be formed into thin, tough, flexible and waterproof sheets – ideal as food wrap or the familiar plastic bag. It is also used to make some plastic bottles.

Brightly coloured, hardwearing polypropylene has many uses.

In theory, any alkene may be polymerised in this way. The starting alkene is called the monomer, and the resultant polymer is named by simply putting *poly-* in front of its name.

Poly(propene)

Propene is used to make the tougher plastic poly(propene) (better known as **polypropylene**). This may be coloured easily, and is used to make hardwearing items such as bowls, crates or moulded school chairs. It can also be made into fibres for ropes or carpets.

Poly(chloroethene)

The old name for chloroethene was vinyl chloride, and its polymer is better known as **polyvinyl chloride (PVC)**. This is widely used for everything from electrical insulation to 'artificial leather'. It was, for many years, vital to the music industry for records, though these are now being replaced by CDs. It is, however, steadily replacing metals for gas and water piping.

PVC is used for a range of objects from records to shoes.

Expanded polystyrene is widely used in packaging.

Polystyrene

Polystyrene is made from styrene, an alkene with a 'side-arm' of a carbon-ring molecule found in crude oil. It is a harder, more brittle plastic, used for electronic equipment and toy casings, as well as 'Airfix' models. It is acid resistant, so it is also used for car batteries. It is even more common in its expanded form – frothed up with air to form a fairly rigid, insulating and protecting foam.

QUESTIONS

1   Describe with the aid of diagrams how polythene is formed from ethene.

2   Draw structural diagrams for the addition polymers formed from the following:
 a ethene ($CH_2=CH_2$)
 b 'vinyl chloride' ($ClCH=CH_2$)
 c styrene ($\bigcirc$–$CH=CH_2$)

3   In the 1970s, oil prices rose dramatically. Explain why the price of LP records also rose.

4   List the uses shown for each of the addition polymers in question 2.
    In each case, describe the key properties that make the material suitable.

7.7 *The plastic age*

Isn't it great?

Plastics are wonderful, aren't they? No-deposit, shatter-proof bottles for our soft drinks, hygienic cartons for our hamburgers, insulated cups for our coffee… even our fresh meat from the supermarket comes wrapped in cling film on a nice plastic tray. At home, our plastic-cased electronic equipment comes packed in plastic foam to keep it safe, and we put our rubbish into the plastic bags we got for our shopping before we throw it all out.

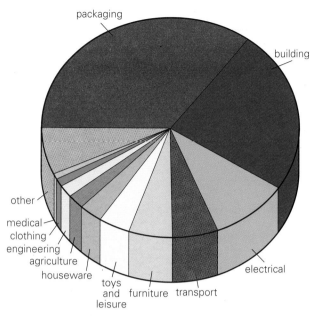

Plastics have many uses…

…but they are difficult to get rid of.

The downside

That last part is, of course, the problem. The plastic age is also the over-packaged, throw-away age (over a million tonnes of plastic packaging are produced per year in the UK). In the worst case, this plastic ends up as litter – an ugly reminder of our waste on our streets, in the countryside, and on the beach.

Paper is thrown away too, but this natural material rots down rapidly in the soil – it is **biodegradable**. Plastics, however, are not biodegradable, and may take tens or even hundreds of years to break down.

Most plastic rubbish does end up in the dustbin, where it forms about 7% of the 'municipal solid waste' by weight. It then ends up on the local tip, which is usually a landfill site – perhaps an old quarry. The problem here is that the available landfill sites are filling up fast. Because of their low density, plastics make up as much as 20% of the volume of this waste. How long will it be before we drown in the sea of our own refuse?

What happens when the old quarries are full?

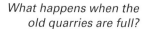

Some ways out

Chemical firms such as ICI are working on the development of new plastics which are biodegradable. Some of these are 'altered versions' of current plastics so, even if they do decay, their products may harm the soil. Others are based on natural polymers such as starch, and it is hoped that these could fit more easily into the natural decay cycles.

Some environmental groups argue that all plastics should be banned. Although a total ban seems unlikely at present, one county in New York State, USA did ban polystyrene and PVC, forcing supermarkets to return to traditional ways of selling their meat and vegetables: the paper bag made a comeback!

The return of the brown paper bag?

Different types of plastics have to be sorted by hand before recycling.

Recycle

Plastics are produced from a scarce resource (oil) by processes that use large amounts of energy. What a waste to just throw it all away. The solution is to recycle wherever possible. The problem is that there are many different types of plastic, and these are not easy to separate.

Where individual plastics can be separated out, however, the uses are more varied. Clear soft drink bottles are made from **PET (polyethene terephthalate)**, which may be recycled as fibre-fill for pillows or in carpets, for example. This can save up to 90% on energy costs, but the low density/large volume factor does cause problems. Around 20 000 drinks bottles must be collected to give 1 tonne of recycled PET!

QUESTIONS

1 Draw up a list of the advantages and disadvantages of the way we use plastics.

2 Most household waste is now disposed of in landfill sites. What does this mean, and why is this becoming a problem? Why are plastics a particular problem in landfill sites?

3 Explain the term 'biodegradable'.

4 Explain how the law is being used to control plastic waste in some areas.

5 Why is it thought to be a good idea to recycle plastics wherever possible?

6 What are the problems surrounding the recycling of plastics? How may these be overcome?

8.1 *The atmosphere*

The blue and white planet

Space exploration has produced many wonderful images of distant planets – but nothing to match the stunning appearance of our own Earth from space. You can see the continents and the oceans, but it is the swirls of blue and white weather patterns that capture the imagination. The blanket of air that covers the Earth is called the **atmosphere**. Without it, we could not exist. What is it made of, and how did it form?

What's in the air?

Approximately one fifth of dry air is oxygen, the gas you need to breathe. Most of the rest is the unreactive gas nitrogen, plus a little carbon dioxide and other gases. Normal air also contains varying amounts of water vapour.

The Earth viewed from space

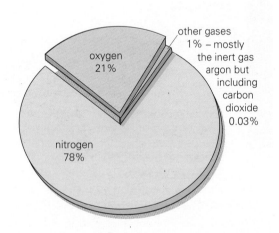

The composition of dry air.

How can you tell?

You can find the exact amount of oxygen in the air by passing a set volume of dry air backwards and forwards over heated copper, using two gas syringes. Only the oxygen reacts with the copper, forming copper oxide.

As the oxygen is removed from the air by this reaction, the total volume of air in the syringes is reduced. When the reaction is complete and the apparatus has cooled down, you can find the volume of oxygen-free air that is left. For every $100\,cm^3$ of air used, only $79\,cm^3$ is left, so $21\,cm^3$ of oxygen is removed by the reaction with the copper. That means that 21% of the original air was oxygen.

$$copper + oxygen \longrightarrow black\ copper\ oxide$$
$$2Cu + O_2 \longrightarrow 2CuO$$

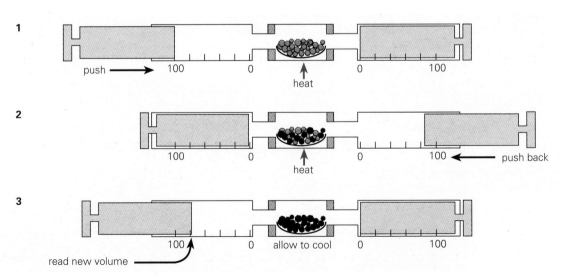

You can use gas syringes to push hot air backwards and forwards over heated copper.

Why oxygen?

As oxygen is so reactive, you might wonder why it exists as an element in the air at all. In fact, it is only there because of the action of plants, for oxygen is produced as a waste gas during photosynthesis. If plants suddenly disappeared from Earth, the oxygen level in the atmosphere would steadily fall back to zero.

Keeping it in balance

Why doesn't the oxygen content of the air go on increasing all the time? The answer is life! Living things – including humans – change the atmosphere by **respiration**. They take in food and oxygen and combine them in a reaction that is chemically the same as combustion. From this, they produce the waste gases carbon dioxide and water, and get the energy they need for life. But plants give out much more oxygen than they do carbon dioxide. So animals and plants between them keep the composition of the air in balance.

Green plants make oxygen as a waste gas during photosynthesis.

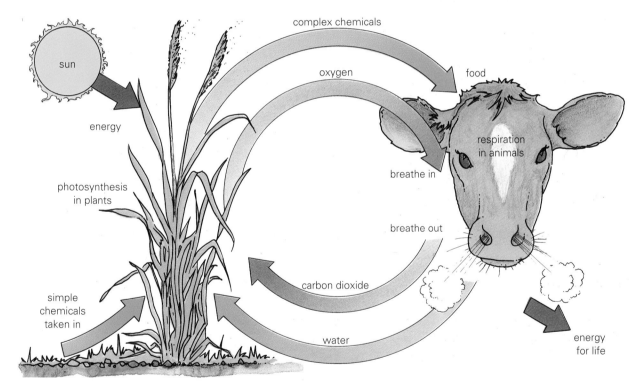

Between them, plants and animals keep the composition of air in balance – all driven by energy from the sun.

QUESTIONS

1a Describe an experiment that can be used to find the proportion of oxygen in the air.

b What percentage of oxygen would you expect this to show?

2 Why are all animals reliant on plants, apart from eating them as food?

3 Explain how the current balance of gases in the air is maintained.

4 What would happen to the oxygen in the air if plants disappeared from the Earth?

8.2 *The evolving atmosphere*

4.5 billion years ago

Chaos as the Earth is born.

3 billion years ago

Primitive life evolved in a calmer but still oxygen-free environment.

Our evolving atmosphere

When the Earth first formed, 4½ billion years ago, things were very different. The Earth was molten at first, and any original atmosphere of hydrogen and helium boiled away into space. Eventually the surface rocks cooled and hardened, forming a thin crust. But volcanic activity continued to blast out gases such as steam, carbon dioxide, carbon monoxide, ammonia and methane.

In time, the Earth cooled enough for the steam to condense back to water, forming the oceans. But the atmosphere was very different from that of today, with no free oxygen. The main gas in the atmosphere was probably carbon dioxide.

Simple forms of life evolved on Earth in this oxygen-free environment, like primitive bacteria. Most 'fed' by breaking down complex chemicals they found in the sea. About 3 billion years ago, one group evolved a way to build up their own complex food chemicals by trapping the energy in sunlight. These were simple algae, the ancestors of all modern plants, and they literally changed the world.

The process that the algae evolved was photosynthesis, which produces oxygen as a waste product. But oxygen is a very reactive chemical. To all the other life forms at the time, it was as poisonous as chlorine would be to you! So the growth and spread of simple plants led to massive pollution of the world's oceans – with oxygen. By 2 billion years ago, other life-forms were wiped out, or restricted to oxygen-free environments such as deep ocean muds or stagnant pools.

The ozone layer

As plants evolved and spread, the oxygen started to build up in the atmosphere. By about 1 billion years ago, there was enough oxygen in the air to develop an **ozone layer**. The Earth is bombarded by dangerous cosmic rays, but these react with oxygen, changing the usual molecule (O_2) to ozone (O_3). Ozone then collects in the upper atmosphere, where it absorbs the cosmic rays (including high energy ultraviolet rays) and so protects the surface of the Earth.

2 billion years ago

Killer algae produced the deadly toxin oxygen!

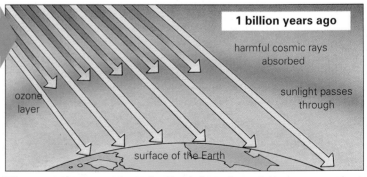

1 billion years ago

harmful cosmic rays absorbed

sunlight passes through

ozone layer

surface of the Earth

The ozone layer protects the Earth from harmful rays.

In this new protected environment, higher forms of life – plants and animals – could evolve. There was a sudden explosion of life in the seas. By 400 million years ago, plants spread over the land, and animals followed. By 200 million years ago, the atmosphere was virtually identical to today's. The plant/animal balance was established.

The greenhouse effect

The atmosphere has another function – keeping the Earth warm at night. The Earth is warmed by the sun on the 'daylight' side, but loses heat energy to space at night. The atmosphere helps to reduce the amount of heat energy lost, and keeps the temperature of the Earth fairly constant.

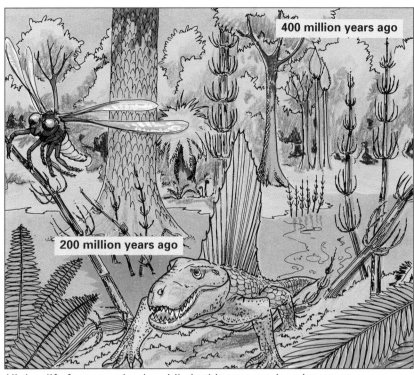

Higher life forms evolved rapidly in this protected environment.

Of all the gases in the air, it is carbon dioxide that has the biggest effect. Carbon dioxide in the atmosphere allows sunlight energy through but stops some of the heat being radiated from the Earth before it can escape into space. This keeps the Earth warm, just like a glass greenhouse. This is called the **greenhouse effect**. How much heat energy escapes depends on how much carbon dioxide there is. The current proportion of 0.03% in dry air is just right.

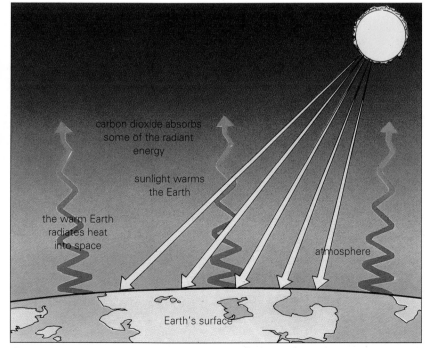

Carbon dioxide acts like a greenhouse to keep the Earth warm at night.

QUESTIONS

1a Plants have caused the worst pollution that this planet has ever seen. Explain this statement.
b Where can you find oxygen-hating bacteria today?

2a What is the ozone layer?
b How does it form?
c Why is it important?

3 What has happened to the atmosphere over the last 200 million years?

4 How does the level of carbon dioxide in the atmosphere control the temperature of the Earth?

8.3 *The Earth in balance*

Carbon dioxide in the atmosphere controls the Earth's temperature balance by way of the greenhouse effect (see 8.2). The more carbon dioxide there is in the atmosphere, the greater the warming effect. The current levels of carbon dioxide suit us fine – but it is a question of balance. If there was not enough carbon dioxide, the Earth would get colder and the ice caps would grow. The Earth would move into another ice age. If there was too much, however, the Earth would warm up and the ice caps would melt. This would raise the sea level and flood low-lying areas. To see what would happen if conditions got more extreme, you can look at some other planets.

The red (and dead) planet

If you want to see what the Earth would be like without any greenhouse effect, look at Mars! This dead planet is unable to retain enough of the Sun's heat to keep water liquid at the surface. The little carbon dioxide that is there freezes at the poles in winter.

Mars

Hothouse Venus

If you want to see what a runaway greenhouse effect can do to a planet, look at Venus. The temperature has risen so much there, that the oceans have boiled and the atmospheric pressure is hundreds of times as high as on Earth – far too hot for life as we know it.

Checks and balances

The plant/animal link plays a major part in maintaining carbon dioxide as well as the oxygen levels. Plants store massive amounts of carbon in their tissues. When animals eat plants, they release carbon dioxide, but new plants grow to take their place, which take it back in.

Venus

Usually all the carbon is released when a plant dies, but sometimes some is preserved, fossilised in the rocks as coal. The oceans also act as a great carbon reservoir as carbon dioxide dissolves in water, and shellfish extract it to build their shells, which may later form limestone rock. These processes may take carbon out of the system for millions of years. But rocks are eventually 'recycled' (see 9.5) and the carbon gets back into the atmosphere from volcanic eruptions.

Shellfish help to reduce the greenhouse effect by locking up carbon dioxide.

The carbon cycle

The way that carbon is naturally recycled can affect the levels of carbon dioxide in the atmosphere.

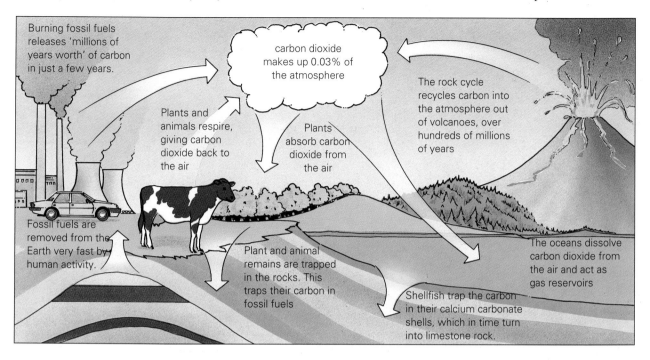

Burning fossil fuels releases 'millions of years worth' of carbon in just a few years.

carbon dioxide makes up 0.03% of the atmosphere

The rock cycle recycles carbon into the atmosphere out of volcanoes, over hundreds of millions of years

Plants and animals respire, giving carbon dioxide back to the air

Plants absorb carbon dioxide from the air

Fossil fuels are removed from the Earth very fast by human activity.

Plant and animal remains are trapped in the rocks. This traps their carbon in fossil fuels

Shellfish trap the carbon in their calcium carbonate shells, which in time turn into limestone rock.

The oceans dissolve carbon dioxide from the air and act as gas reservoirs

Tipping the balance?

Our modern, energy-consuming industrial and social lifestyle is upsetting this delicate balance. Fossil fuels are being converted back to carbon dioxide a million times faster than they form. Making cement from limestone also sends extra carbon dioxide into the atmosphere. Over the last 100 years or so, this has raised the percentage of carbon dioxide in the air from 0.02% to 0.03% and, if some predictions are correct, this could double in another 50 years. The effect of this may seem small – the overall, average temperature of the planet might rise by a degree or two. Yet even this is enough to upset the weather systems, perhaps even beginning to melt the polar ice caps. Again, the effect may seem small – a one metre rise in 50 years – but not if you happen to live on 'sea level' Pacific Islands – or parts of East Anglia, for that matter.

QUESTIONS

1 Why is it very unlikely that there is any life on the planet Venus?

2 What would happen on Earth if the carbon dioxide level in the atmosphere became **a** too high or **b** too low?

3 A tree may have a mass of many tonnes, 40% of which is carbon.
  a Where did all this carbon come from?
  b Where does it go when the tree dies and rots?

4 How do shellfish keep down the levels of carbon dioxide in the atmosphere?

5 Why has burning fossil fuels 'upset the balance'? What effects might this have?

8.4 *The water cycle*

You may be familiar with the simple idea of the solar-powered **water cycle**. When the sun shines onto the sea it makes some of the water evaporate and warm, moist air forms. This begins to rise but, as it rises, it cools down. As it cools, some of this water vapour turns back to tiny droplets – clouds form. If the clouds rise further and cool even more, these droplets get bigger and start to fall – it rains. This can happen anywhere where moist air rises, but it is very common over mountains where air currents are forced upwards. The rain falling on the land collects in streams and rivers, and so runs back to the sea, completing the cycle.

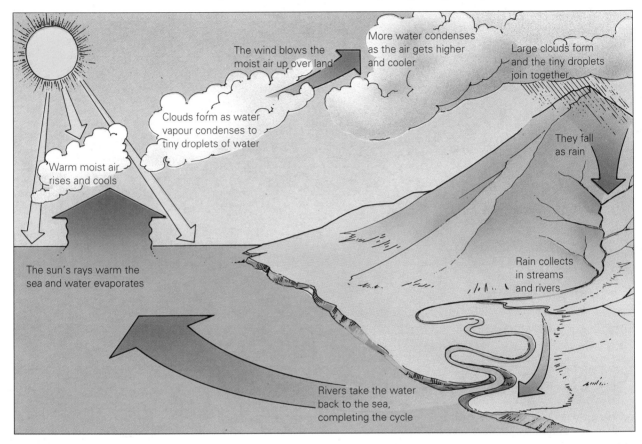

The wind blows the moist air up over land

More water condenses as the air gets higher and cooler

Large clouds form and the tiny droplets join together

Clouds form as water vapour condenses to tiny droplets of water

They fall as rain

Warm moist air rises and cools

The sun's rays warm the sea and water evaporates

Rain collects in streams and rivers

Rivers take the water back to the sea, completing the cycle

Humidity and saturation

Why does cooling the air make clouds form? There is a limit to how much water vapour air can contain and, when it reaches this, it is said to be **saturated** – the **humidity** is 100%. When it reaches this level, no more water can evaporate. If you exercise when the air is humid, you will feel uncomfortable as your sweat cannot evaporate and cool you down.

But the amount of water that the air can hold depends upon the temperature. So air that is saturated at 20°C, would have a humidity of only 60% at 30°C. On the other hand, if saturated air at 30°C was cooled to 20°C, it would become 'supersaturated' and the excess would come out as tiny droplets of liquid water. So clouds form as warm, humid air rises and cools – the warmer and more humid the air is in the first place, the greater the possible effect.

Sport can be uncomfortable on hot, humid days!

Why does it rain?

Tiny droplets of water are kept up in the cloud by the updraught of rising air. If the drops merge together, however, they will fall faster and so drop out of the cloud as rain. If the temperature is below zero, ice crystal – not water droplets – will form and it will snow. Indeed, as it is below freezing high up in the clouds, most British rain is actually snow that melted on the way down!

It's snowing over London – if you look high enough!

The water you use

You need to drink about 2 litres of water a day, to replace the water you lose in urine, sweat and by breathing. This water must be 'fresh' – not necessarily totally pure, but with only small amounts of dissolved salts. However, each person in Britain uses on average 145 litres of water per day – 9 litres go down the sewer each time you flush the toilet. Industry uses about half as much again so, over the whole country, that's about 15 billion litres of fresh water a day.

All of that water must be taken from the environment. Unfortunately, the largest source of water, the sea, is far too salty for most purposes, and purification by distillation is far too expensive. Only 3% of the world's water is fresh water, and most of this is locked up in glaciers and icebergs. So we are limited to rivers, lakes and groundwater supplies for the water we need. If managed carefully, however, most countries in the world have sufficient supplies.

Where all the water goes!

Water used at home (litres/day)		Industrial production (litres water used to make ...)	
drinking	2	1 kg aluminium	1500
cooking	3	1 kg steel	200
washing up	15	large newspaper	200
laundry	15	bag of cement	180
washing/bathing	50	1 litre of beer	8
flushing the toilet	50	1 litre of milk	6
other	10	1 litre of petrol	1000
Total	**145**		

QUESTIONS

1 Draw an annotated diagram of the water cycle from memory.

2a Why is it that clouds form when air rises, but evaporate if air falls?

 b Do you think the air is usually rising or falling over desert regions? Explain your answer.

3a What are the main sources of drinking water?

 b Why is sea water not normally used?

4 Water purification for drinking is an expensive process. Is it an efficient use of our resources to purify *all* of the water we use at home in this way? (Use the table of water usage to help you.)

8.5 *Nitrogen and its uses*

The importance of nitrogen

Plants need nitrogen in order to make proteins and grow – this may not seem a problem since they are surrounded by it in the air. However, they are unable to use the nitrogen in the air directly and, up until recent times, they have had to rely on recycled nitrogen-containing chemicals in animal waste (manure) or dead plants and animals (compost).

The nutrients from organic material are released as bacteria and fungi feed on them. These **decomposers** break down complex organic chemicals such as proteins for 'food', recycling carbon dioxide and water. The problem is that some bacteria break proteins down completely, releasing their nitrogen into the air. These **denitrifying bacteria** reduce the amounts of useful nitrogen available to plants in the soil.

Fortunately there is another group of bacteria which can reverse this process. These **nitrifying bacteria** trap the nitrogen from the air and 'fix' it. That is, they turn it into chemicals such as nitrates, which the plants can use. Plants such as peas and beans (the legumes) 'grow' these special bacteria in nodules on their roots, to make their own supply of fertiliser. Scientists hope to use genetic engineering to transfer this ability to other plant groups.

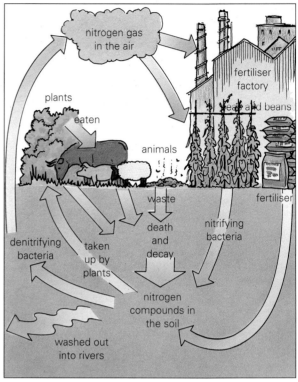

The nitrogen cycle: nitrogen is recycled by the action of nitrifying and denitrifying bacteria.

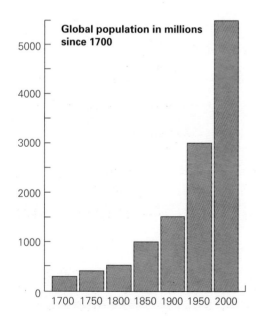

Fertilisers

Farmers have used manure and compost for thousands of years, but the population explosion over the last 200 years has increased the need for food crops dramatically. The increased **yield** required has been achieved by using artificial **fertilisers** – nitrogen-rich chemicals produced industrially.

Fertilisers must contain nitrogen in a form that the plants can take in and use to make proteins. Compounds of ammonia (NH_3) and nitric acid (HNO_3) are suitable. The one most commonly used is ammonium nitrate (NH_4NO_3) made by combining the two. This has a 'double dose' of accessible nitrogen.

The rapid increase in the world's population shows why fertilisers such as ammonium nitrate are so important for food production.

Some of these fish are dying because of a lack of oxygen in the water caused by algal bloom.

Fertiliser problems

Manufactured fertilisers have worked wonders on crop production, raising yields and keeping food prices down. But there are problems. If fertilisers wash into rivers, they can upset the natural balance and make the algae grow out of control (**eutrophication**). These 'algal blooms' end up by poisoning the fish in the river.

Nitrogen in the air

Nitrogen in its elemental form (that is, not combined with any other elements) makes up four-fifths of the air. This is not so surprising, as nitrogen gas is unreactive under normal conditions. But the original atmosphere of the Earth probably contained nitrogen combined with hydrogen in ammonia, so how did this change?

In part, this is linked to the rise of oxygen in the atmosphere. Oxygen is more reactive than nitrogen, so it can 'steal' the hydrogen from ammonia in a displacement reaction.

ammonia + oxygen $\longrightarrow$ water + nitrogen

$$4NH_3 + 3O_2 \longrightarrow 6H_2O + 2N_2$$

But bacteria also had a role. Nitrifying bacteria removed ammonia and converted it to nitrates, which were then used by plants. Denitrifying bacteria then decomposed the plant remains, releasing nitrogen into the air.

Manufacturing fertilisers

Ammonia is the starting chemical for fertilisers. It is made by combining nitrogen from the air directly with hydrogen in the **Haber process** (see 15.3), which uses high pressures and temperatures as well as a catalyst.

Step 1

nitrogen + hydrogen $\xrightarrow{\text{Haber process}}$ ammonia

$$N_2 + 3H_2 \longrightarrow 2NH_3$$

Ammonia dissolves in water to form the alkaline solution of ammonium hydroxide (NH_4OH). This is often simply called 'ammonia solution'.

Step 2

ammonia + water $\longrightarrow$ ammonium hydroxide

$$NH_3 + H_2O \longrightarrow NH_4OH$$

Nitric acid is made by oxidising ammonia using a platinum catalyst and then dissolving the nitrogen oxides produced in water. It is a complex, three-stage oxidation reaction.

Step 3 (simplified)

ammonia + oxygen $\xrightarrow{\text{catalyst}}$ nitric acid + water

$$NH_3 + 2O_2 \longrightarrow HNO_3 + H_2O$$

Nitric acid and ammonium hydroxide are then combined in a neutralisation reaction, and the solution is evaporated to give the salt, ammonium nitrate.

Step 4

ammonium hydroxide + nitric acid $\longrightarrow$ ammonium nitrate + water

$$NH_4OH + HNO_3 \longrightarrow NH_4NO_3 + H_2O$$

QUESTIONS

1a Why do plants need nitrogen?

b What are the 'natural' ways in which plants can get the nitrogen they need?

2 Why are scientists studying the genes of peas with such interest?

3 Why have fertilisers become so important over the last century?

4 In East Anglia recently, there was concern about the levels of nitrate found in tap water, which was thought to damage young babies. How might this nitrate have got into the water?

5 How did elemental nitrogen get into the air?

6a Why is ammonium nitrate such a good fertiliser?

b Draw a flow chart for the manufacture of ammonium nitrate.

8.6 *The atmosphere at risk*

Where plants left off

Plants may have been the original polluters of the atmosphere, but humans seem to be doing their best to catch up. The enhanced greenhouse effect caused by burning fossils fuels has already been described (see 8.3). But there are other dangers to our atmosphere.

Transport and traffic

Petrol and diesel engines work by exploding a fuel vapour/air mixture inside the engine. The basic reaction is the simple oxidation of hydrocarbons in the fuel to produce carbon dioxide and water.

$$\text{petrol/diesel} + \text{oxygen} \longrightarrow \text{carbon dioxide} + \text{water}$$

If this was all that was produced, there would not be a problem, as this is the same mixture that you breathe out. Unfortunately, exhaust gases from both petrol and diesel engines also contain dangerous chemical pollutants such as carbon monoxide, nitrogen oxide and finely divided carbon particles (soot). How do these form?

Unfortunately, exhaust gases contain more than just carbon dioxide and water. The danger is greatest at pushchair level!

Internal combustion

The problem is that the amount of oxygen the fuel can react with is limited, as the reaction takes place inside the engine. If the oxygen supply is not quite sufficient for total combustion, some is only partially oxidised to give carbon monoxide (see 7.3), while some is left as tiny particles of elemental carbon. In addition, the air in the engine is four-fifths nitrogen. During the petrol/air explosion, some of this reacts with oxygen to give nitrogen oxides.

Carbon monoxide and nitrogen oxides are poisons in their own right. But in sunlight they combine with the air to make small quantities of ozone which, at ground level, is also a deadly poison. Together they are also responsible for **photochemical smog**, the brown haze that can often be seen over cities. This looks bad and stings your eyes, but it also has severe effects on asthma suffers, amongst others. Athens has the same problem and is now banning most cars from the city centre during the day. Could London be next?

London in the 1950s suffered life-threatening 'pea souper' smogs causes by soot and smoke from burning coal.

Today's 'photochemical' smog from exhaust pollution may not be as thick, but is just as dangerous to our capital.

Acid rain

The use of fossil fuels threatens the atmosphere with pollution in another way. Fossil fuels often contain sulphur and so, when they are burnt, sulphur dioxide is released into the atmosphere. This then dissolves in the rain and reacts with oxygen to make a weak solution of sulphuric acid. Similarly, nitrogen dioxide from car exhausts reacts with water and oxygen to make nitric acid. Between the two, the pH of polluted rain may be as low as 3.5, almost as acidic as vinegar.

This **acid rain** corrodes metalwork and limestone on buildings and statues, but also damages trees and the fish in lakes. Polluted clouds may be blown long distances by prevailing winds – the lakes and forests of Norway have been damaged by pollution from British power stations on the other side of the North Sea.

Acid rain is one export that Britain should not be proud of.

Cure...and prevention

One attempt to solve the problem of acid rain involves dropping great quantities of quicklime (calcium oxide) or ground limestone (calcium carbonate) into the affected lakes to neutralise the acid. Once the pH has stabilised, the lake must be re-stocked with fish. Prevention is the best approach, however. Power stations today must have chemical plants to remove the sulphur dioxide from their waste gases. This is done using a spray of quicklime to neutralise the acid.

The police are now stopping vehicles and checking their exhaust fumes. Heavy fines are on the way for offending vehicles.

Cars, too

New cars must be fitted with **catalytic converters** to reduce the toxicity of their exhausts. These use a catalyst to react the nitrogen and carbon monoxides in the exhaust together to form harmless nitrogen and carbon dioxide (see 13.4).

$$2CO + 2NO \xrightarrow{\text{catalyst}} 2CO_2 + N_2$$

harmful   harmless

So we have the chemical technology to eliminate the problem – but at a financial cost. You, the consumer, must always be prepared to pay for a cleaner environment.

QUESTIONS

1a What causes the brown smog in London?
b How do these chemicals form?
c How easy will this be to cure?

2 Sulphur burns in air to give sulphur dioxide. Write this out as word and symbolic equations.

3 Acid rain contains sulphuric and nitric acids.
a What salts will form when these are neutralised by quicklime (calcium oxide)?
b Write separate word equations for the reaction of these acids with quicklime.

4 How does the use of a catalyst help to reduce the pollution from car exhausts?

9.1 *The igneous rocks*

The first rocks

The Earth formed 4½ billion years ago, as a ball of hot and molten rock (**magma**). As this cooled, crystals started to grow and the molten mixture set to form a crust of rock. Rocks that form when magma cools and sets are called **igneous rocks**. They were the first rocks on Earth, but you can still find them forming today.

Looking at granite

Granite is a hard, speckled grey or pinky-grey igneous rock. It forms the knobbly tors of Dartmoor and much of the Highlands of Scotland. If you look closely, you can see that it is made of a mixture of tightly interlocking crystals that grew as the molten rock set. They include glassy quartz and grey or pink felspar, arranged in a random pattern. The individual crystals are easy to see. They are several millimetres across.

The very first rocks were igneous – but this Dartmoor granite is much younger – just a few hundred million years old!

... and basalt

Basalt is a hard black rock. It often forms thick layers that can cover large areas. Parts of Northern Ireland and the West Coast of Scotland are covered by basalt.

With the unaided eye, you cannot see the internal structure of basalt. But if you cut a thin slice of the rock and look at it through a microscope, you can see that it is made of a mass of interlocking crystals, in a similar way to granite. Basalt also formed from magma.

The Giant's Causeway in Northern Ireland was formed when molten rock set to form basalt.

Why are they different?

You can model the way crystals grow from magma using a chemical called **salol**. You can make salol crystals grow by carefully melting it in a test tube and then pouring a few drops onto a microscope slide. If the slide is cold, the salol cools and sets rapidly, and you get a lot of small crystals. But if the slide is warm, the salol cools more slowly. This time, you get fewer but larger crystals.

The size and number of crystals depends on how quickly the molten salol cools.

cold slide – fast cool

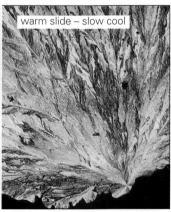

warm slide – slow cool

Volcanoes

The crust may have set and cooled, but it is still very hot inside the Earth. The deeper you go underground, the hotter the rocks become. In places it is hot enough to melt the rocks – 1000°C or more! If this magma reaches the surface, it pours out as **lava**. A **volcano** forms as the lava cools and turns to rock. Often the lava contains dissolved gas under pressure, which bubbles out as it reaches the surface. This can sometimes make volcanic eruptions explosively dangerous – but very spectacular.

As the surface of the Earth is very cold (compared to molten rock) the lava cools very rapidly, so it has lots of tiny crystals. Basalt formed in this way, too, which is why it has such small crystals. Rocks that form on the surface like this are called **extrusive** igneous rocks.

Gas bubbling out of a liquid when pressure is released can blast molten rock out of a volcano.

What's underneath?

In places where there are active volcanoes and newly forming mountains, vast amounts of rock melt deep within the crust. Only a fraction of this reaches the surface of the Earth to form lava. The rest of the magma stays trapped deep within the crust.

Eventually this will start to cool and set. But it will take a very long time to cool down, as it is very well insulated – surrounded by hot rock. Because of this, the crystals have time to grow large. Granite forms when magma is trapped deep within the crust like this. That is why granite has large crystals.

Rocks that form within the crust like this are called **intrusive** igneous rocks.

Granite formed in gigantic magma chambers, deep in the Earth's crust.

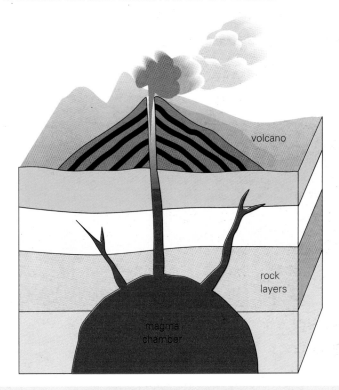

QUESTIONS

1 Why were igneous rocks the first rocks on Earth?

2a Describe granite and basalt.
 b In what ways are they the same?
 c In what ways are they different?
 d Why does granite have larger crystals than basalt?

3 You can see basalt forming today in some volcanoes. Why can't you see granite form?

4 When you open a can of coke that has been heated or shaken, the contents squirt out everywhere. How does this compare to an erupting volcano?

9.2 *Breaking down the rocks*

Rocks such as granite appear hard and everlasting. Yet granite forms deep underground and so is seen only once vast amounts of rock have been removed. How does this happen? The rocks must be broken up and carried away.

Breaking up

Rocks can get broken in many ways. In the desert, the extreme temperature changes from day to night may be enough to shatter the rocks over many years, as they continually expand by day and contract at night.

High in the mountains, water seeps into cracks by day and freezes at night. Water, unlike most substances, expands on freezing. This is why water pipes burst if they get frozen in winter. This expansion can also push open the cracks in the rock, wedging off great slabs from cliffs. These fragments collect at the foot of the cliffs. When rocks are physically broken up like this it is called **physical weathering**.

The piles of rock at the bottom of this cliff have been broken off by ice action.

Chemical attack

Igneous rocks also come under attack from the air and rain, which is slightly acidic, even when 'pure'. The felspar in granite, for example, breaks down to form clay. This releases the quartz crystals, which form sand. The chemical breakdown of rocks like this is called **chemical weathering**. If this debris is left in place it forms **soil** – which is vital for plant growth as it traps water and also provides the nutrients they need to grow. The plants then help the process by forcing their roots into cracks in the rock, breaking it up further – a form of **biological weathering**.

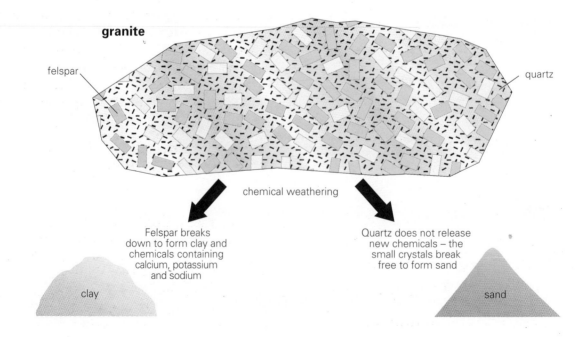

granite

felspar

quartz

chemical weathering

Felspar breaks down to form clay and chemicals containing calcium, potassium and sodium

clay

Quartz does not release new chemicals – the small crystals break free to form sand

sand

Carry it all away

When rain falls on the land, some soaks into the ground, but much 'runs off', collecting to form streams, which join to form rivers, and so on down to the sea. This washes away any loose soil, carrying the debris along with the flow. When material is removed like this it is called **erosion**.

Angular rock fragments also get washed into rivers, where they will be rolled and tumbled by the current. As they knock against each other and the river bed, they are steadily worn away. The corners get chipped off first, so the further they travel, the rounder they become, as well as getting smaller. This process is continued by wave action in the sea, and beach pebbles are often very well rounded. In the same way, angular quartz crystals from weathered granite are gradually turned into rounded grains of sand.

Rock fragments get smaller and rounder as they are carried down to the sea.

Cutting gorges and valleys

The debris carried by a fast-flowing river also has an abrasive effect on the underlying rocks. In this way, the rocks beneath a river are eroded further, and the river cuts down through them. This then adds to the load of **sediment** being transported by the river.

The river's load

How much sediment a river can carry depends on how big it is and how fast it is flowing. Often more material will be carried in one short period of 'flood' after heavy rains than in the rest of the year put together. But the process is complex in detail, as the size of the particles carried depends on the water speed. Small particles such as clay are carried along in **suspension** by even the gentlest flow. Sand grains are only carried in suspension if the flow is very fast. Usually they are rolled or bounced along the bed of the river. Pebbles or larger boulders are rolled along only by the fastest flowing rivers.

This river is coloured brown by all the sand and mud it is carrying.

QUESTIONS

1a Describe the processes of physical weathering
 b Which type is common in Northern Britain?

2a How are sand and clay formed from granite?
 b Describe how soil forms.
 c Why is soil so important for plant growth?

3 A small, rounded beach pebble may have started off as a large, angular rock fragment in the mountains. Explain how this could happen.

4 What makes up the sediment carried by a river?

5 Which is more likely to move a large pebble, a large but slow-moving lowland river or a small mountain stream? Explain your answer.

9.3 *Sedimentary rocks*

Down to the sea

Most of the sediment carried by a river will eventually reach the sea. Here the river's power is lost and the river dumps its load of sediment. If a vast amount of sediment is being brought in, this may build a wedge of new land out into the sea – a **delta**. The Nile delta is so big that it can easily be seen from space. It is an important farming area in Egypt, where the rest of the land is mostly desert and no good for growing crops.

But usually wave action gets to work, washing fine clay out into deeper water and spreading the sand and pebbles out along a beach.

The Nile delta – seen from the Space Shuttle.

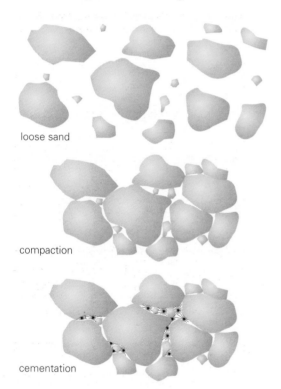

loose sand

compaction

cementation

From loose sand to hard sandstone.

Making sedimentary rock

Eventually, the sediments are deposited in more or less horizontal layers called **beds**. New sediments are very soft and may contain a lot of water. If sedimentation continues, however, they are steadily buried, and the weight of overlaying sediment starts to compact them down (**compression**). Clay, in particular, may be reduced to as little as a tenth of its original volume, as excess water is squeezed out.

In addition, the water contains dissolved chemicals such as calcite and silicon dioxide in low concentrations. These often crystallise between the grains, **cementing** the grains together. So, over tens, hundreds, thousands or even millions of years, by the processes of compaction and cementation, sediments turn into **sedimentary rocks**.

Evidence in the rocks

As the layers of rocks formed one on top of the other, the general rule is that the oldest rocks are found at the bottom and the youngest at the top of a sequence of sedimentary rocks. Sometimes the layers have been uplifted and older sedimentary rocks are exposed (see 10.1 and 9.2).

The oldest sedimentary rocks are at the bottom of the Grand Canyon.

The common sedimentary rocks

Pebbles become cemented together to form **conglomerate**, which is like natural concrete. Conglomerate from a river shows pebbles of different sizes, often mixed up with clay. Beach conglomerates, however, are often made of uniform, well-rounded pebbles where they have been washed backwards and forwards by waves.

Sand forms **sandstone**. Sands that have been deposited rapidly in a delta may be mixed up with clay. Sands that have been reworked by the sea, however, may be 'clean' and clay-free. The sandstone in the photograph shows angular lines running between the beds. This is called cross-bedding and, on this scale, suggests formation in a sand dune which was wind-blown.

Clay minerals are flat, like small tiles. If clay is deposited slowly, these minerals lay flat on top of one another, making a soft rock that breaks easily into flakes. This is called **shale**, and it often contains fossils. If the clay is deposited rapidly, however, the minerals become trapped at different angles, forming unlayered **mudstone**.

Limestone is made from calcium carbonate. Many sea animals extract this from sea water to build their shells. When they die, these shells may be smashed up by wave action to make sand or mud-sized fragments. As this sediment is buried, some of the calcium carbonate recrystallises between the fragments and cements them together to make hard limestone.

In short …

There are many different variations on these basic types of sedimentary rock. What they all have in common is that they are made from fragments of earlier rocks which have become cemented together. The fragments are sometimes arranged in bands or thicker layers called beds.

This conglomerate probably formed on a beach as the pebbles are so well-rounded.

This cross-bedded sandstone formed in a desert sand dune.

This limestone is full of shell fragments. It formed in the sea.

QUESTIONS

1a Why is the Nile delta so important in Egypt?
b How did it form?

2 Describe the ways in which a soft sediment can turn into a hard sedimentary rock.

3 Where do you find the oldest rocks in the Grand Canyon? Why?

4 What would you call a rock:
a made from pebbles cemented together
b made from sea shells and corals
c made from layers of clay?

5 In what major environment are the following rocks most likely to have formed:
a a conglomerate with round pebbles
b a limestone with cockle and whelk shells?

9.4 *Fossils*

Sedimentary rocks are rarely exposed so clearly as in the Grand Canyon. Trying to work out what is going on from a few isolated outcrops or quarries is like trying to do a jigsaw puzzle where most of the pieces are missing. Fortunately, fossils can help to complete the picture.

What is a fossil?

A **fossil** is simply evidence of past life preserved in sedimentary rock. At one extreme, insects may be perfectly preserved in resin that later turned to **amber**. At the other extreme, there may just be a footprint! When most animals die, however, the soft parts soon rot away and only the hard parts are left. Shellfish leave their shells, sharks their teeth and other vertebrates (including the dinosaurs) their bones. These can become trapped in sediments which later turn into sedimentary rock. Not all rocks contain fossils – it takes both skill and luck to find them.

A perfectly preserved insect in amber.

Dinosaur bones from Utah, USA.

How do they help?

Some fossils are similar enough to living plants or animals to tell you about the environment in which the rock formed. The fossil tree trunks found in the rocks close to coal seams suggest a river flood-plain or delta-top swamp environment, for example. Other fossils are unlike anything found today, and it is this variation that helps to give a sense of time.

Splitting the country

In the south and east of England the rocks are often quite soft, barely changed from their original sediments. Many of these rocks contain the coiled shells of fossil **ammonites** (a distant relative of the squid), as well as **bivalve** shells, **snails**, **sea urchins** and **corals**, similar to those found in the sea today. In north and west Britain, however, the rocks appear harder and more changed. Here, strange fossil **trilobites** are found, alongside more unusual shellfish such as **brachiopods**, and strange, primitive corals.

Rocks containing ammonites are sometimes found *above* rocks with trilobites, but they are never found *below* them. This means that the rocks with ammonites must be younger than those with trilobites.

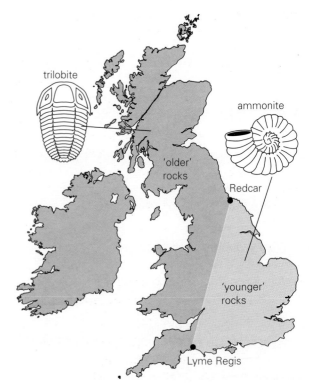
The rocks of Britain can be split into two main age groups by the fossils they contain.

The stratigraphic column

This simple idea has been greatly extended over the last 200 years to produce a standard sequence known as the **stratigraphic column**. Life on Earth has changed steadily – **evolved** – over millions of years, so the fossils found in each level act as a 'time fingerprint'. Any rock containing fossils can be matched against this to give its *relative* age. The three main **eras** are shown here, but these can be further subdivided into hundreds of different levels.

How old is this fossil?

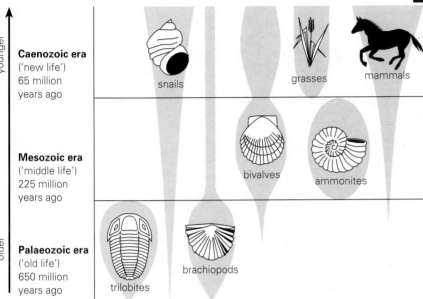

The stratigraphic column and some fossil ranges.

Absolute ages

Fossils may be used for dating sedimentary rocks but they cannot give an absolute age in millions of years. Recently, however, the study of radioactive decay has led to the development of **radioactive dating** techniques. These are most commonly used on igneous rocks but, by careful comparison, they can be used to add dates to the stratigraphic column. Radioactive dating also shows that fossils tell about only part of Earth's history. The oldest rocks dated go back 4 billion years – compare this to the paltry 650 million years for the oldest rocks with trilobites! Radioactive dating is therefore very useful, but it is difficult and expensive to do. By comparison, a fossil expert could match a fossil to the stratigraphic column in seconds – for nothing.

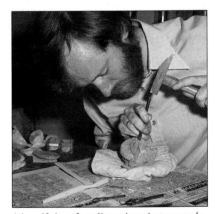

Identifying fossils – the cheap and easy way to date rocks!

QUESTIONS

1 If a rock was found containing sea-urchins, bivalves and ammonites, is it more likely to have come from Wales or Kent?

2 Why is it that the fossils in each level of the stratigraphic column are different?

3 In rocks of which era might you find the following collections of fossils:

a ammonites, snails and bivalves

b trilobites, brachiopods and corals

c snails, horse bones and grass seeds?

4 What are the advantages and disadvantages of radioactive and fossil dating?

9.5 *Completing the rock cycle*

Igneous rocks are weathered and eroded to make sedimentary rocks. Sedimentary rocks themselves may be uplifted and eroded to make new sediments. But they may also be changed by heat and/or pressure, and this process is called **metamorphism**.

Simple metamorphism

If rocks are deeply buried, the pressure and temperature increase enormously. Under these conditions, the minerals in the still-solid rocks may start to recrystallise. For rocks that are made of one simple mineral only, this simply makes them harder and more coarsely grained. In this way, the calcite in limestone recrystallises to form **marble**.

Fossil-rich limestone is metamorphosed to 'sugary' marble.

Changing grade

Deep in the roots of newly-forming mountains the temperature and pressure become intense. This increase comes in part from the mass of rock above, but added to this are enormous side-pressures generated by the processes of mountain building (see chapter 10). You can therefore get a range of metamorphic changes, becoming more and more intense as you go deeper in the crust. Shale or mudstone can form three different types of metamorphic rock, depending on the temperature and pressure to which it is exposed.

At low temperature and pressure, the rock is simply squashed and hardened, turning it to **slate**, which may be split into thin layers.

With increasing heat and pressure, wavy, sparkling layers form in a rock called **schist**.

At high temperature and pressure, the banding becomes coarser and **gneiss** is formed. These higher grade rocks often contain new minerals such as **garnet**.

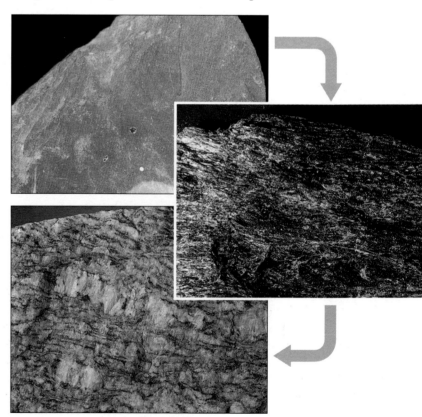

Shale changes to slate, schist or gneiss, depending on the temperature and pressure.

Completing the cycle

All of these metamorphic changes occur without the rock actually melting. It stays solid, so the new crystals that grow line up against the pressure. That is why metamorphic rocks are crystalline but usually have bands or layers, unlike the igneous rocks.

Finally, if the temperature becomes *too* great, the rock will start to melt. When this happens, the metamorphic rock turns into magma, making fresh igneous rock and so completing the **rock cycle**.

Gneiss and granite can be made of the same minerals – but in gneiss they are in bands.

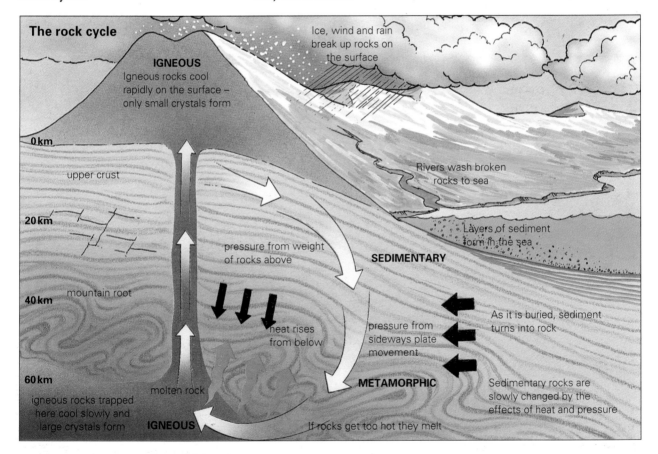

The rock cycle

IGNEOUS
Igneous rocks cool rapidly on the surface – only small crystals form

Ice, wind and rain break up rocks on the surface

0 km

upper crust

Rivers wash broken rocks to sea

20 km

pressure from weight of rocks above

Layers of sediment form in the sea

SEDIMENTARY

40 km   mountain root

heat rises from below

pressure from sideways plate movement

As it is buried, sediment turns into rock

60 km
igneous rocks trapped here cool slowly and large crystals form

molten rock

METAMORPHIC

If rocks get too hot they melt

IGNEOUS

Sedimentary rocks are slowly changed by the effects of heat and pressure

QUESTIONS

1 What happens to limestone when it is metamorphosed?

2 Describe the changes that clay goes through at different grades of metamorphism.

3 Granite and gneiss can contain the same minerals. How could you tell them apart?

4a What processes turn **i** igneous rock to sedimentary rock **ii** sedimentary rock to metamorphic rock **iii** metamorphic rock to igneous rock?

b Where do each of these changes happen?

c Draw a simple diagram to show the rock cycle.

10.1 *Faulting and folding*

Rocks under stress

Well-cemented sedimentary rocks can be very hard, but they are also brittle. If you hit a block of sedimentary rock with a sledgehammer, it will break. In parts of the Earth's crust, these rocks are put under great pressure. If they are hard rocks they may resist this pressure for some time but, if the pressure continues to build up, they will eventually break. This sudden fracture sends out a great shock wave – an **earthquake**. You get a similar effect if you bend a dry stick until it snaps! The **fault lines** that break up rock outcrops show where this has happened in the past.

The block to the right of this fault has moved down by 2 metres.

Evidence from faults

The movement on either side of the fault can give further information. In places, the Earth's crust is being stretched. The crust is cracked by sloping faults, and sometimes a central block sinks down to form a **rift valley**. With each earthquake the blocks might move just a few centimetres, but over millions of years these small movements can add up to hundreds of metres of vertical difference across a fault. The Midland Valley of Scotland formed in this way.

How a rift valley forms.

central block drops

sides are wedged apart

In other places the crust is being squeezed, and blocks are forced up over one another. Sometimes blocks are moved many kilometres in this way. The Moine thrust of Scotland formed like this, as did much of the Alps.

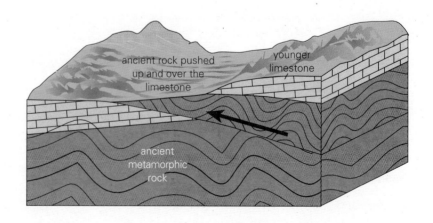

ancient rock pushed up and over the limestone

younger limestone

ancient metamorphic rock

The Moine thrust formed when ancient metamorphic rock thrust up over the top of younger limestone.

Sometimes the blocks of rock slip side-by-side. This has happened along the Great Glen in Scotland, splitting an outcrop of granite on either side by tens of kilometres.

Going down

As you go deeper in the crust, the temperatures and pressures get steadily higher and higher. Under these conditions the rocks behave differently, becoming increasingly plastic. Instead of breaking, they slowly change shape and are squeezed into **folds**.

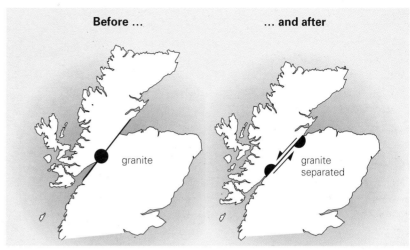

Before ...   **... and after**

granite   granite separated

The map of Scotland might have been very different without a fault!

How were these hard and brittle rocks folded?

Part-way down into the crust they may bend into open folds, but will still fracture if the pressure is too great. As you go deeper, these folds become more and more intense. In the deepest and hottest zones the rocks behave like plasticine, being squeezed into tight folds and changing their shape without breaking. Metamorphic rocks are often intensely folded like this.

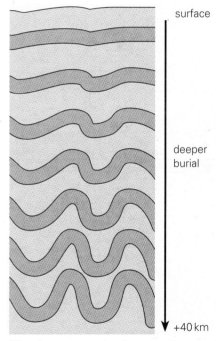

surface

deeper burial

+40 km

The deeper you go, the more intense the folding can be.

QUESTIONS

1 If an earthquake occurred every 10 years on average, and the rock moved just 10 cm each time, how far would the rock have moved in a million years?

2 Describe the difference between faults formed when the crust is being stretched and those formed when it is squashed.

3 In some places you can find beds of limestone that have been faulted. In other places you can find limestone that has been folded. How can the same rock behave in different ways like this?

4 Oil and gas are often found trapped under domes of rock (see 7.1). Explain how these domes may be formed.

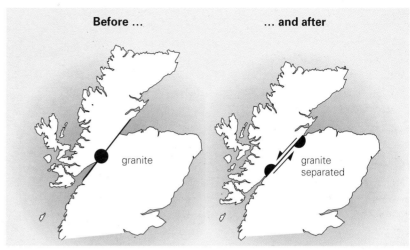

10.2 *Inside the Earth*

The processes of the rock cycle (see 9.5) take place on the surface of the Earth, or within the top 50 km or so of the crust. To understand why they occur, you need to know what is happening below the crust. The Earth has a diameter of 13 000 km – how is it possible to know what is happening inside it? The answer is found, in part, in the study of earthquakes.

What is an earthquake?

Earthquakes occur when rocks which have been under great stress finally snap, sending out shock waves from the spot where the faulting has occurred (see 10.1). Thousands of earthquakes are detected every year, though only a handful are very severe.

Clearing up after the Kobe freeway collapsed in an earthquake in Japan, 1995.

Useful earthquakes

The shock waves from an earthquake can be analysed by computer, to build up an internal 'picture' of the Earth. Some of the waves are bounced back by layers in the Earth. The base of the crust shows up clearly. This shows a surprising variation in depth, the crust being at it thickest beneath mountains and much thinner under the oceans. But the crust is still very thin compared to the diameter of the Earth – like a postage stamp on a football!

Detailed analysis also shows that the thick continental crust has the same density as granite, while the thinner oceanic crust is denser, like basalt. The rocks beneath the crust are similar to basalt, so the less dense continental crust is 'floating' on them. This is why the continents rise up above sea level.

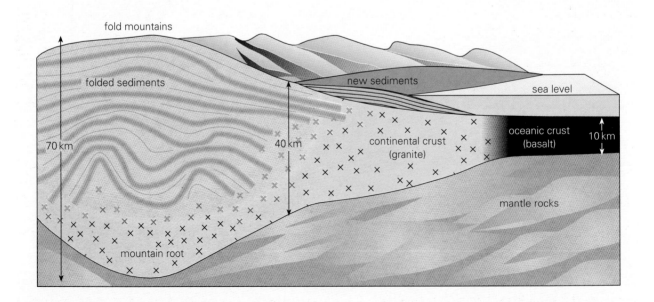

A section through the Earth's crust.

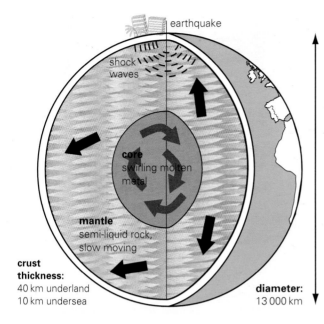

Diagram labels: earthquake; shock waves; core — swirling molten metal; mantle — semi-liquid rock, slow moving; crust thickness: 40 km underland, 10 km undersea; diameter: 13 000 km

Looking deeper

Shock waves that have passed right through the Earth show that it has a deeper layered structure – rather like a giant soft-boiled egg!

Beneath the thin crust is a layer of rock about 3000 km thick called the **mantle**. This hot rock acts like a very viscous liquid and can change shape over long periods of time.

In the centre is a dense, liquid **core.** Its diameter is about 7000 km. (More detailed analysis suggests that there may also be a solid **inner core**.)

The Earth is like a soft-boiled egg with a thin, cracked shell.

What are the layers made of?

Astronomical measurements suggest that the average density of the Earth is $5.5\,\text{g/cm}^3$, twice that of granite or the continental crust. Computer analysis of earthquake shock–wave evidence suggests that the average density of the mantle is $4.5\,\text{g/cm}^3$, while the inner core may be as high as $10\,\text{g/cm}^3$. What are these layers made of?

Some evidence comes from **meteorites**, which are thought to be the remains of a broken, Earth-like planet that once orbited the Sun between Mars and Jupiter. These come in two types. Some are made of a crystalline rock similar to basalt, but a little more dense. Scientists think that these are like the rocks of the mantle. Rocks like this have been found on Earth, where great faults have uplifted and exposed the very base of the crust.

Others are much denser ($7\,\text{g/cm}^3$), and are made of nickel and iron. These are thought to be of the same composition as the Earth's core.

The Troodos mountains in Cyprus contain uplifted rocks from the top of the mantle.

QUESTIONS

1a What useful information can scientists get from earthquakes?

b What does this tell us about the Earth's crust? (Draw a diagram of a section of the crust.)

c How does the thickness of the crust compare to the diameter of the Earth?

2 What is different about oceanic and continental crust apart from their thickness?

3a Draw a diagram of a section through the Earth.

b Label it to describe the layers.

4 What other evidence is there that helps to explain what might be inside the Earth?

111

10.3 *Introducing plate tectonics*

Active edges

If all the volcanic eruptions and earthquakes that occur are plotted on a map, they form a very definite pattern, ringing the Pacific Ocean and running from the Alps to the Himalayas. Less powerful earthquakes also occur along the middle of the oceans. This is because the crust of the Earth (and a thick slab of mantle beneath) is cracked into a gigantic jigsaw puzzle of pieces called **plates**.

All the activity is around the edges of these plates. It is caused by the fact that the plates are moving.

Britain today is 1000 km or so from the nearest plate margin, which is why we escape the most destructive effects of this activity.

THE DAILY

15th June 1993

QUAKE IN THE LAKES

THE Lake District felt its biggest earth tremor for ten years yesterday.

England's finest beauty spot was rocked by a tremor centred near Grangemouth at the southern end of the Lakes.

The tremor measured 4.2 on the Richter scale, the strongest since this country's biggest ever quake in 1984.

Then the entire country experienced a 5.7 quake that had its epi-centre at Portmadoc in North Wales. That one caused chimney pots in Liverpool and windows in North Wales to crack.

Yesterday's tremor caused a loud bang and made walls vibrate, but there was no serious damage.

The worst you can expect in Britain today.

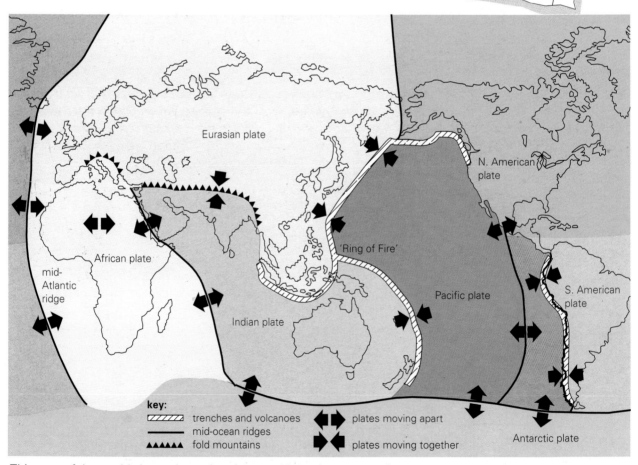

key:

////// trenches and volcanoes

—— mid-ocean ridges

▲▲▲▲▲ fold mountains

◀▶ plates moving apart

▶◀ plates moving together

This map of the world shows the major plates and how they are moving.

Slipping sideways

In a few places, the plates are simply slipping sideways against each other. Perhaps the most famous example of this is the **San Andreas Fault** in California. A narrow coastal strip is sliding northwards at a rate of 7cm a year, as is clearly shown in the photo of orange groves that were planted just a few decades ago.

Unfortunately, San Francisco has been built on top of this great fault. In places, the plates glide evenly against one another, but near San Francisco they are locked tight. There, pressure builds up until the rocks snap, generating powerful earthquakes. San Francisco was destroyed by fire after an earthquake in 1906 and it has been shaken regularly since then.

These Californian orange trees were planted in straight lines.

Cracking up

The rocks of the mantle are very hot, and slow-moving but immense **convection currents** are swirling around, driven by the heat from natural radioactivity. It is these currents that drag the plates around. When a rising convection current reaches the surface, it splits and moves apart, splitting the plate above and carrying it with it.

Africa is at present lying over an upcurrent, and this has cracked the continent, forming the Great Rift Valley. Volcanic activity along this rift has formed large volcanoes such as Mount Kilimanjaro. At the northern end, the process has gone further, however. Basalt magma has risen to fill the crack: this has set and then been cracked apart itself, and so on, moving Arabia away from Africa and creating the Red Sea.

The rate of separation is measurable at just a few centimetres a year. But, given the *millions* of years available in geological time, this process will split Arabia right away from Africa, forming a new ocean. The Atlantic ocean formed in a similar way over a period of 200 million years or so.

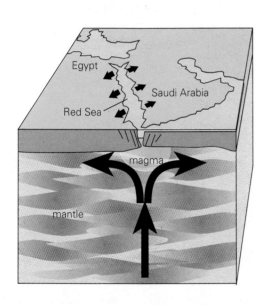

The Red Sea may become the Red Ocean in the far future!

QUESTIONS

1 British earthquakes are very rare and of low intensity. Japanese earthquakes are common and are often very destructive. Why is this?

2 New buildings in San Francisco have steel girder frames which survive being shaken. Why do they need this?

3 In places on the San Andreas fault where the plates move easily, you regularly get small earthquakes. Explain why the longer the time gap between earthquakes here, the more powerful they are likely to be.

4a What has caused the Rift Valley system to form in Africa?

b What will form between Arabia and Africa if the process continues for millions of years?

10.4 *Building continents*

Going down

If plates are moving apart in some places, they must be colliding in others. When this happens, the edge of the thin but denser oceanic crust slides beneath its neighbouring continent, dragged down by the sinking current in the mantle. Along the margin, the bed of the ocean is buckled down into a deep **trench**, up to 11 km below sea level.

As the oceanic crust slides into the **subduction zone** beneath the continent, some of its sediments melt to form vast volumes of granitic magma. This magma rises up into the crust above, where it causes explosive volcanic activity. The edge of the continent is buckled up as the oceanic crust pushes beneath it, forming new mountains. At the same time, powerful, deep-focus earthquakes are set off along the sinking plate, as it is slowly absorbed back into the mantle.

The Pacific plate is sliding beneath South America, forcing up the Andes mountains and causing volcanic eruptions.

Closing an ocean

The Atlantic Ocean is opening at an average rate of 2 cm per year. On the other side of the world, the Pacific Ocean is getting smaller at a similar rate. Although the Pacific also has a mid-oceanic ridge, there are subduction zones on either side, consuming the old ocean crust faster than the new ocean crust can form. Eventually, the Pacific Ocean will disappear completely!

The sinking oceanic plate triggers earthquakes and melts rocks in a subduction zone. The magma rises forming explosive volcanoes.

Making mountains

India and Asia were once separated by an ocean which disappeared like this. As the ocean between them got smaller and smaller, it began to fill up with sediment eroded from the continents. Eventually, this sediment formed a block of soft material between the continents – but they still continued to move towards each other. The soft sediment was too 'light' to sink back into the mantle. Instead, it was squeezed and folded upwards, forming new mountains – the Himalayas.

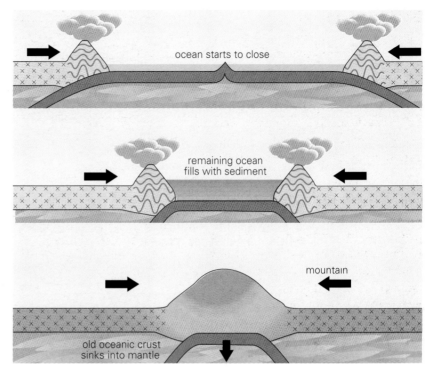

ocean starts to close

remaining ocean fills with sediment

mountain

old oceanic crust sinks into mantle

New mountains form when continents collide.

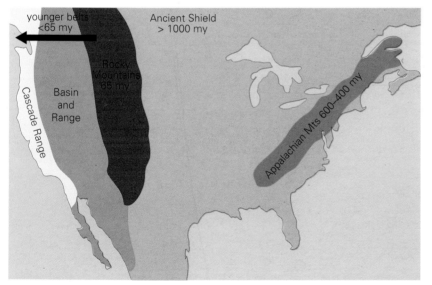

younger belts
<65 my

Ancient Shield
> 1000 my

Rocky
Mountains
65 my

Basin
and
Range

Cascade Range

Appalachian Mts 600–400 my

The North American continent has grown over the last 600 million years, as fold mountains have been added to the central 'shield' area.

Growing continents

So, while weathering and erosion are constantly wearing the mountains and continents away, plate activity is building them back up again. Because of this, the process is called **plate tectonics** ('tecton' means 'builder' in Greek). Indeed, the continental material is not simply recycled, because new material from the mantle is added in the process. In this way, the continents have steadily grown during the Earth's history.

QUESTIONS

1 Why are deep ocean trenches found directly in front of active continental margins such as the Pacific coast of South America?

2a Why do the Andes mountains suffer from explosive volcanic activity and powerful, deep-focus earthquakes?

 b What igneous features are forming deep within their roots?

3 Describe how the Himalaya mountains formed.

4 How has plate tectonics increased the size of the continents over hundreds of millions of years?

115

10.5 *Understanding the Earth machine*

Today, the processes that drive volcanoes and earthquakes, form new mountains and shape the surface of the Earth are well understood. But how did this understanding come about?

Early ideas

Mountain ranges such as the Alps and Himalayas are built from folded sedimentary rocks. A hundred years ago, some scientists thought that the Earth must have shrunk as it cooled down, and that this caused its crust to wrinkle up into mountains.

Other scientists looked at the way the continents on either side of the Atlantic Ocean seemed to fit together. Perhaps the Earth was getting bigger, and this had torn them apart? In 1912, Alfred Wegener looked in detail at the fit between South America and Africa and concluded that they must have split apart. He called this **continental drift**, but he couldn't explain how it could work, so nobody believed him.

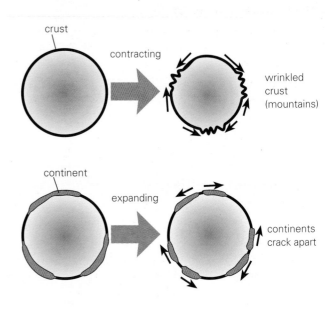

Conflicting evidence – was the Earth shrinking or getting bigger?

Fossil magnetism

In the 1950s, scientists studying the Earth's magnetic field found that it left a record in the rocks. From it, you could tell where the north pole must have been. To their surprise, they found that the position of the pole seemed to be different in older rocks. One explanation was that the pole was staying still, but the continents were drifting as Wegener had suggested. Over the last 600 million years, the rocks that now form Britain seem to have moved from south of the equator to their current position. The relative position of the pole found from rocks of different ages can be plotted on a map as a **polar wandering curve**.

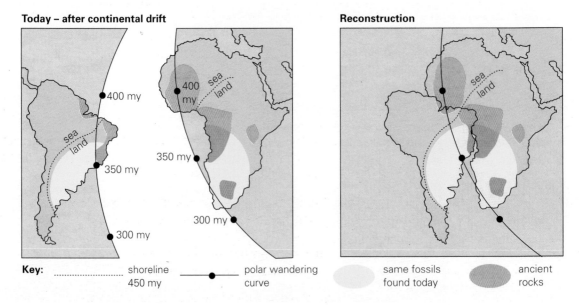

Polar wandering curves and fossil evidence show how South America and Africa could have fitted together like a jigsaw, supporting Wegener's ideas.

Unexpected mountains

Also in the 1950s, the floor of the Atlantic Ocean was surveyed in detail for the first time. The first, startling discovery was a chain of undersea volcanic mountains running along its centre. There was also a symmetrical pattern to the crust beneath the ocean, with thin ocean crust on either side of the volcanic ridge and its central rift system.

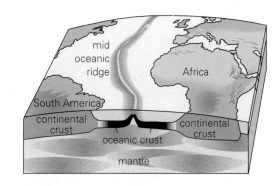

The Atlantic ocean is symmetrical.

Magnetic anomalies

By the 1960s, magnetic surveys yielded further remarkable discoveries. The Earth's magnetic field seemed to rise and fall in a symmetrical pattern on either side of the ridge. This was because the fossil magnetism trapped in the basalt rock of the oceanic crust sometimes added to the field, but sometimes opposed it. The Earth's magnetic field must have reversed every half million years or so, and this left a fingerprint-like pattern in the rocks. Also, this pattern was repeated symmetrically on either side of the ridge. The oceanic crust was splitting apart and new crust was forming in the gap (picking up the magnetic polarity of the time). This was then split apart in turn, and so on, slowly pushing the continents apart.

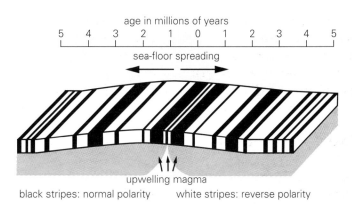

black stripes: normal polarity   white stripes: reverse polarity

The magnetic patterns either side of the Mid-Atlantic Ridge are like a mirror image.

Driving the machine

So, at last, direct evidence for continental drift was discovered. But what was driving the process? Heat measurements across the volcanic ridge showed that it was a zone of high heat loss – upwelling magma was carrying the heat energy up from deep within the mantle in convection currents (like those that form over the heater in an electric kettle, only on a gigantic scale).

QUESTIONS

1 How did early scientists try to explain
a fold mountains
b the jigsaw-fit of the continents?
c What was wrong with their theories?

2 The jigsaw-fit of South America and Africa is very good in detail.
a Which features either side of the Atlantic Ocean match up in the reconstruction?
b Despite this, why did no-one believe Wegener's continental drift idea at first?

3a What are polar wandering curves?
b How does the fact that the curves are different for each continent support the fact that it was the continents that moved, rather than the pole?

4a Explain how the symmetrical magnetic pattern across the Mid-Atlantic Ridge supports the idea that the continents have drifted.
b How does this idea lead to an explanation of the formation of fold mountains?

5 What is the energy source that drives the convection currents in the mantle? (see 10.3)

10.6 *Explaining the past*

Plate tectonics has proved to be a tremendously powerful theory, as it not only explains what is happening today, but can also make sense of what has happened in the past.

Earth's great cycles

Churning convection currents in the mantle are constantly recycling oceanic crust. One complete cycle takes, on average, about 200 million years. Here is a 'typical' sequence.

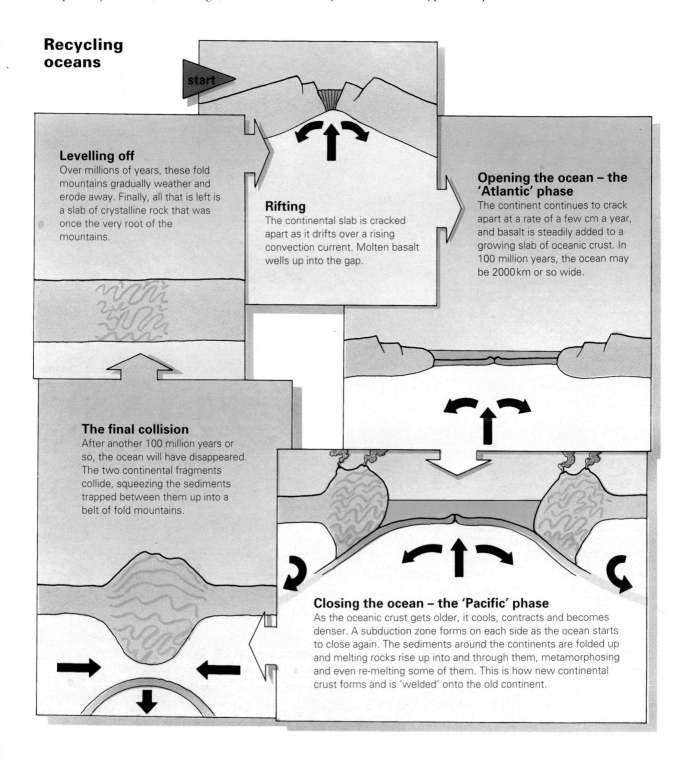

Recycling oceans

start

Levelling off
Over millions of years, these fold mountains gradually weather and erode away. Finally, all that is left is a slab of crystalline rock that was once the very root of the mountains.

Rifting
The continental slab is cracked apart as it drifts over a rising convection current. Molten basalt wells up into the gap.

Opening the ocean – the 'Atlantic' phase
The continent continues to crack apart at a rate of a few cm a year, and basalt is steadily added to a growing slab of oceanic crust. In 100 million years, the ocean may be 2000 km or so wide.

The final collision
After another 100 million years or so, the ocean will have disappeared. The two continental fragments collide, squeezing the sediments trapped between them up into a belt of fold mountains.

Closing the ocean – the 'Pacific' phase
As the oceanic crust gets older, it cools, contracts and becomes denser. A subduction zone forms on each side as the ocean starts to close again. The sediments around the continents are folded up and melting rocks rise up into and through them, metamorphosing and even re-melting some of them. This is how new continental crust forms and is 'welded' onto the old continent.

Growing continents

The continental slabs have built up like snowballs over Earth's history, new slabs being added with each cycle. This happens because the continental rocks have too low a density to sink back into the mantle with the oceanic crust.

Solving a puzzle

The rocks of Scotland and North Wales formed in a cycle like this, ending about 400 million years ago. This belt of rocks runs up into Norway, and also reappears across the Atlantic. Before plate tectonics, it always presented a great problem. The fossil trilobites that are found in Wales are very different from those found in Scotland, just a few hundred kilometres away. Yet the same pattern is found in north and south Newfoundland, several *thousand* kilometres away!

Part of the answer has already been explained. At that time, 'Scotland' and 'Wales' were separated by thousands of kilometres of deep ocean, which stopped the trilobites mixing. The second factor is that the Atlantic is a 'young' ocean, so it did not exist at that time, and 'Britain' and 'America' were joined.

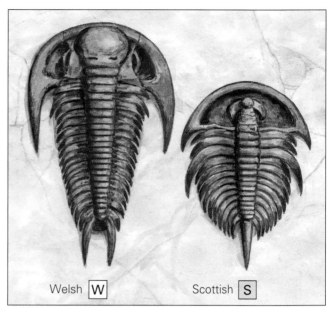

The trilobites of Wales and Scotland.

The pattern today.

To solve the puzzle you need to close the Atlantic ...

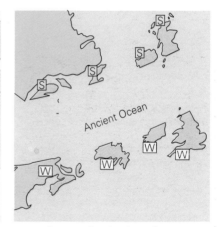

... and open the Ancient Ocean. Now it all makes sense!

QUESTIONS

1 The rock sequence in Wales shows the following pattern over about 200 million years.

a Some ancient metamorphic rocks were faulted and basalt lava formed.

b A sequence of clean sands and clays followed, without volcanic activity.

c The next sequence shows evidence of regular volcanic activity and mixed up sediments.

d Finally, the entire sequence was squeezed up to form fold mountains.
Use your understanding of plate tectonics to explain this sequence of events.

2 Explain how the 'trilobite puzzle' can be solved using plate tectonics.

10.7 *How time passes*

The Earth is in a state of constant, if very slow, change, and this has affected the atmosphere, the rocks of the crust and even life itself. If you try to compare the situation today with conditions when the Earth first formed, you will begin to understand just how immense the timescale of Earth history must be. Yet, even so, the idea of millions of years can be very difficult to grasp, so a model is helpful. In this scale model, the entire history of the Earth has been condensed into one year – that's one day for every 12.3 million years!

June = 2000 million years ago

Oxygen pollutes the environment, poisoning most early micro-organisms. These can only survive now in oxygen-free environments like stagnant ponds.

atmosphere of carbon dioxide, water, ammonia and methane

molten Earth

JUL

JUN

plants make oxygen

MAY

first simple plants

APR
no life
(no oxygen)

JAN

FEB

MAR
oldest rocks

January = 4500 million years ago

The **heat of formation** melted all the rocks. The oldest rocks date back to the end of February. For the first four months, the Earth was lifeless.

May = 3000 million years ago

Evidence is found of the first **life on Earth**. These were simple **plants** – just single cells. They made their food using the Sun's energy and gave off oxygen as a 'waste' product.

DEC   5th

10th

coal swamps

15th

20th

25th

mammals

limestone common

25th December = 65 million years ago

Early mouse-like **mammals** had been around with the dinosaurs but they only increased in numbers when the dinosaurs became extinct. In the week after Christmas, they came to dominate the land.

Mid December = 225 to 65 million years ago

This was the age of **dinosaurs** on land, while ammonites flourished in the sea. Atmospheric conditions like today – roughly 80% nitrogen, 20% oxygen plus small amounts of carbon dioxide.

Early December = 3000 million years ago

Life had now now moved onto land. Britain was covered by th **swamp forests** that later form our coal, locking up more carb

6pm

5pm   OF

noon

1pm   2pm   3pm   4pm

AFTERNOON

first humans (begin life in Africa)

Noon 31st December = 6 million years ago

The first of our ape ancestors to walk upright lived in the Rift valley of Africa.

Australopithecus walks upright

October = 1000 million years ago

In this 'safer' world, higher plants developed. **Green algae** appeared. It was like the stuff that grows on the sides of fish tanks. Scientists think that all higher life forms, (including us!) come from this.

oxygen in atmosphere; nitrogen instead of methane and ammonia

first green algae

August = 1500 million years ago

By now **oxygen** had begun to collect in the atmosphere. Some oxygen formed **ozone**, which stopped dangerous ultra-violet rays form reaching the surface.

November = 600 million years ago

The first animals appeared in the seas – **trilobites** and other strange shellfish. But there was still no life on land.

trilobites

Thick limestones form from shell remains, removing carbon dioxide from the atmosphere.

hard-shelled fossil-forming animals common

first fish

limestone common

Late November = 400 million years ago

The first fish had appeared in the seas – strange armour-plated creatures.

woolly mammoth

11.56pm December 31st = 30 thousand years ago

The first humans appeared and quickly spread throughout the world.

DECEMBER

ice age begins

human ancestors use tools and fire!

midnight = today

And what of history?

The processes of plate tectonics seem to have run at a fairly constant rate over Earth history, but the evolution of life seems to have become faster and faster. The dinosaurs lasted nearly a fortnight, but direct human ancestry is limited to the last day on this model. So what of recorded history? To this scale, the Romans conquered Britain at about 14 seconds before midnight, and 'modern' history (since 1945) can be crammed into the last half second of the year!

121

11.1 *Measure it!*

Much of what is now known about chemistry, in terms of atoms and compounds for example, grew out of the extensive experimental work of early chemists such as John Dalton. Today you will often use your understanding of scientific theories and models to work out what is happening. But these theories were developed only after many years of detailed observations and accurate measurements. It is such **empirical** data that forms the foundations of science.

The work of John Dalton

About 200 years ago, John Dalton was studying the way that elements combined to form compounds. In particular, he used accurate balances to work out what mass of each element was needed – their **combining masses**.

By careful experimentation he established that the simple compounds he made always contained elements in the same proportion. He called this the **Law of Constant Composition**. At the time there was much argument, but continued experimentation showed it to be correct, and today it is an accepted scientific fact.

You can see his Law of Constant Composition in action by studying common salt.

John Dalton ...

Composition of common salt		
Source	Sodium %	Chlorine%
from the sea	39.34	60.66
from Siberia	39.34	60.66
from Cheshire	39.34	60.66
made in the lab	39.34	60.66

... and his Law of Constant Composition.

Magnesium oxide

One of the simplest ways to show this law in action is to burn a metal such as magnesium in air. The mass rises during this experiment, as oxygen from the air is combining with the metal. If you find the mass before and after burning, you can find the proportion of magnesium to oxygen in the compound.

Here are some typical class results:

	John	Aisha	Kylie
mass of Mg	0.24g	0.3g	0.36g
mass of oxide	0.4g	0.5g	0.6g
mass of O	0.16g	0.2g	0.24g
Mg:O	0.24:0.16	0.3:0.2	0.36:0.24
simple ratio	3:2	3:2	3:2

From these figures, the law seems to hold true. If you started with 3g of magnesium, you would expect it to react with 2g of oxygen to give 5g of oxide.

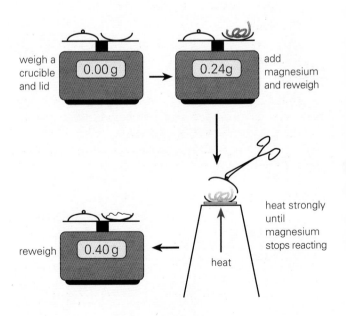

weigh a crucible and lid — 0.00 g

add magnesium and reweigh — 0.24g

heat strongly until magnesium stops reacting

heat

reweigh — 0.40 g

Magnesium burns in air to give magnesium oxide.

Different combinations

Dalton also showed that if two elements formed more than one compound, then the different ratios were simple mathematical multiples.

This is Dalton's second law. It may be demonstrated clearly using the two oxides of copper. You can reduce both of these oxides to copper using hydrogen, as copper is below hydrogen in the reactivity series.

If you find the mass of the oxide and then the mass of copper that is produced from this, you can work out how much oxygen there was. This tells you the original combining masses in the oxide.

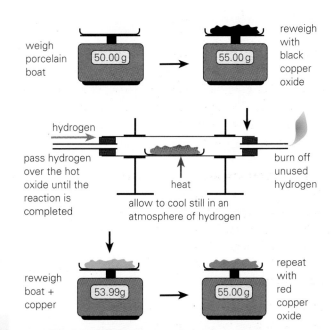

Finding the percentage of copper in copper oxide

Calculating the proportions

Here are some sample results from this experiment.

For black copper oxide

original mass of oxide:	5.00 g
final mass of copper:	3.99 g
therefore mass of oxygen =	1.01 g

ratio calculation:

3.99 g copper combines with 1.01 g oxygen
ratio Cu : O = 3.99 : 1.01
approximately **4 : 1 [8 : 2]**

For red copper oxide

original mass of oxide:	5.00 g
final mass of copper:	4.44 g
therefore mass of oxygen =	0.56 g

ratio calculation:

4.44 g copper combines with 0.56 g oxygen
ratio Cu : O = 4.44 : 0.56
approximately **8 : 1**

Comparing the two

Black copper oxide contains proportionally twice as much oxygen as red copper oxide. Their copper/oxygen ratios are clearly simple multiples by a factor of two, agreeing with Dalton's second law.

There is twice as much oxygen in black copper oxide as in red copper oxide.

QUESTIONS

1 Calcium metal burns in air to give calcium oxide. If 0.4 g of metal gave 0.56 g of oxide,

a how much oxygen combined with the metal

b what is the calcium : oxygen ratio

c how much oxygen would combine with 5 g of calcium

d how much metal would there be in 2.1 g of oxide?

2 Sulphur forms two different compounds with oxygen. In the first, 5 g of oxide contained 2.5 g of sulphur. In the second, 5 g of oxide contained 2 g of sulphur.

a What are the sulphur : oxygen mass ratios for the two compounds?

b Do the two oxides match Dalton's second law?

11.2 *Chemistry by numbers*

Relative atomic mass

Atoms are so very small that it would be cumbersome to talk about their tiny masses all the time. So their masses are usually just compared to each other. Hydrogen, the smallest atom, is 1 on this scale. A helium atom has four times the mass of a hydrogen atom, so it is 4. A carbon atom has twelve times the mass of a hydrogen atom, so it is 12, and so on. This is their relative atomic mass (A_r) (see 3.4). These figures have been calculated for all elements, and you can look them up in tables.

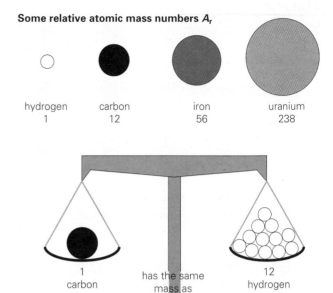

Some relative atomic mass numbers A_r

| hydrogen 1 | carbon 12 | iron 56 | uranium 238 |

Formula mass

Molecules are also very small, so it makes sense to compare their masses on the same scale. If you know the formula of a compound, you can add up the relative atomic masses of all the atoms that make it up to find its **formula mass** (M_r) (sometimes called relative molecular mass).

1 carbon atom   has the same mass as   12 hydrogen atoms

For example:

water:
formula H_2O (A_r H = 1, O=16)
formula mass (M_r) = $(2 \times 1) + 16$ = **18**

methane:
formula CH_4 (A_r H = 1, C = 12)
formula mass (M_r) = $12 + (4 \times 1)$ = **16**

carbon dioxide:
formula CO_2 (A_r C = 12, O=16)
formula mass (M_r) = $12 + (2 \times 16)$ = **44**

calcium carbonate:
formula $CaCO_3$ (A_r Ca = 40, C=12, O = 16)
formula mass (M_r) = $40 + 12 + (3 \times 16)$ = **100**

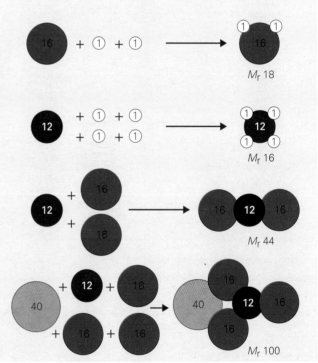

Finding the right formula

You can use relative atomic mass and formula mass alongside your findings from experiments to work out the formula of a compound.

For example, magnesium oxide is made from magnesium and oxygen atoms. But how many of each are there? To take some simple examples, it could be Mg_2O, MgO or MgO_2. If you know the relative atomic masses of magnesium (24) and oxygen (16), you can work out the metal/oxygen ratio by mass (the **simple mass ratio**) that each one would give.

Possible formulae

Mg_2O: M_r would be 64
magnesium:oxygen ratio would be $(2 \times 24) = 48:16$
simple mass ratio would be **3:1**

MgO: M_r would be 40
magnesium:oxygen ratio would be 24:16
simple mass ratio would be **3:2**

MgO_2: M_r would be 56
magnesium:oxygen ratio would be 24:32 (2×16)
simple mass ratio would be **3:4**

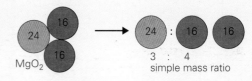

If you compare these 'theoretically possible' ratios to the ratio found by experiment in 11.1, you will see that the formula must be MgO, giving the simple 3:2 ratio.

Copper's two oxides

For red and black copper oxide you get two different experimental results, so clearly these compounds must have different formulae. Again, you can work out the formulae from the metal/oxygen mass ratios found by experiment, if you know the relative atomic mass of copper (64) and oxygen (16).

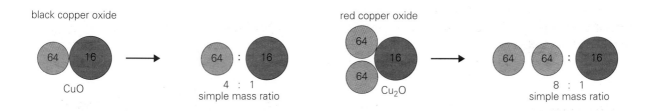

One atom of copper combining with one atom of oxygen would give a mass ratio of 64:16, or 4:1 in its simplest form. By experiment, black copper oxide gives a 4:1 copper/oxygen mass ratio. So the formula of black copper oxide must be CuO.

Two atoms of copper combining with one of oxygen would give a 128:16, or 8:1 copper/oxygen mass ratio. That is the ratio found by experiment for red copper oxide, which must therefore have the formula Cu_2O.

QUESTIONS

1 Using the A_r values given, calculate M_r for:
a aluminium oxide, Al_2O_3 (Al 27, O 16)
b magnesium carbonate, $MgCO_3$ (Mg 24, C 12)
c iron(II) sulphide, FeS (Fe 56, S 32)
d calcium oxide, CaO (Ca 40)
e sodium nitrate $NaNO_3$ (Na 23, N 14)

2 What is the sulphur/oxygen mass ratio in:
a sulphur dioxide, SO_2
b sulphur trioxide, SO_3?

3 By experiment, it is found that the copper/sulphur mass ratio in copper sulphide is 2:1. Is the formula of copper sulphide Cu_2S, CuS or CuS_2?

11.3 *How much reacts?*

Metals in ores

Calculations with the relative atomic and formula masses can be very useful. You can find the percentage of metal in different metal ores, for example. This information is important for mining and metal refining companies. For example, both haematite (Fe_2O_3) and pyrites (FeS_2) can be used as iron ores. Which one gives the most iron per tonne of ore?

To calculate the percentage of iron
(A_r values Fe = 56, O = 16)

haematite (Fe_2O_3):

$$M_r = (2 \times 56) + (3 \times 16) = 160$$

$$\text{iron} = (2 \times 56) = 112$$

$$\% \text{ iron} = \frac{112}{160} \times 100\% = \textbf{70\%}$$

pyrites (FeS_2):

$$M_r = 56 + (2 \times 32) = 120$$

$$\text{iron} = 56$$

$$\% \text{ iron} = \frac{56}{120} \times 100\% = \textbf{47\%}$$

haematite

pyrites

Which gives the most iron per tonne of ore?

Quicklime from limestone

You can use a similar method to find how much quicklime you could get from a tonne of limestone. Limestone is mostly calcium carbonate. When it is roasted in a kiln, carbon dioxide is driven off, leaving behind calcium oxide ('quicklime') which is used as a simple fertiliser, to neutralise acid soils and improve the soil texture.

Quicklime from limestone

$$\text{calcium carbonate} \xrightarrow{\text{heat}} \text{calcium oxide} + \text{carbon dioxide}$$

(A_r values: Ca = 40, C = 12, O = 16)

reaction: $\quad CaCO_3 \xrightarrow{\text{heat}} CaO \quad + \quad CO_2$

M_r: $\quad (40 + 12 + 3 \times 16) \longrightarrow (40 + 16) + (12 + 2 \times 16)$

$\qquad\qquad 100 \qquad\qquad\longrightarrow \quad 56 \qquad + \qquad 44$

%CaO: $\quad \dfrac{56}{100} \times 100\% = \textbf{56\%}$

You would get 560 kg of quicklime from every tonne of limestone.

Finding reacting masses

You can also use theoretical values to calculate the quantities required for industrial (or laboratory) reactions. This makes for efficient use of reactants, but may also be crucial to ensure that a reaction runs smoothly.

Iron and sulphur react when heated, to give iron sulphide. This reaction is often used in school laboratories to demonstrate the formation of a compound from elements (see 4.1). If the mixture is made up in the right proportions, a very clear reaction starts and an orange-red glow spreads through the mixture. How can you be sure that you have the 'right' mixture to start with?

Getting the mixture right

$$iron + sulphur \longrightarrow iron\ sulphide$$

as a balanced equation:

$$Fe + S \longrightarrow FeS$$

add the A_r and M_r values:

$$56 + 32 \longrightarrow 88$$

so the iron/sulphur mass ratio is:

$$56:32 \quad or \quad 7:4$$

The perfect thermit

The thermit reaction (see 6.3) is used as a demonstration of displacement. When it works well, aluminium pushes iron out of its oxide in a spectacular reaction, leaving a ball of nearly white-hot iron. But it is a notoriously difficult reaction to 'get right' and often just fizzles out. To be sure of success, you need the correct proportions of iron oxide and aluminium. This ratio can again be found by calculation.

$$iron\ oxide + aluminium \longrightarrow aluminium\ oxide + iron$$

Calculating the proportions that must be used for a perfect thermit reaction:

(A_r values: Fe = 56, O = 16, Al = 27)

as a balanced equation:

$$Fe_2O_3 + 2Al \longrightarrow Al_2O_3 + 2Fe$$

calculate M_r:

$$(2 \times 56 + 3 \times 16) + (2 \times 27) \longrightarrow \text{(product calculation not needed)}$$

$$160 + 54$$

working ratio of oxide/metal:

$$160 : 54$$

(approximately **3 : 1** by mass)

9g iron(III) oxide   3g aluminium powder

QUESTIONS

1   What is the percentage of lead in galena? (Galena is lead sulphide, PbS: Pb = 207, S = 32.)

2   What is the percentage of aluminium in bauxite? (Bauxite is aluminium oxide, Al_2O_3: Al = 27, O = 16.)

3   What mass of carbon dioxide is given off if 1 kg of limestone is roasted until it has completely broken down?

4   What mass of carbon dioxide is given off if 1 kg of limestone is completely dissolved in hydrochloric acid?

5   Aluminium will push copper from copper(II) oxide in a thermit reaction:
$$3CuO + 2Al \longrightarrow Al_2O_3 + 3Cu$$
In what proportion by mass should they be mixed? Show your working. (A_r of Cu = 64)

11.4 Introducing the mole

Scaling up

When you write an equation, you are describing the reaction between one set of particles. But the equation would also be true if you were to double the number of each type of particle present, or treble them, or multiply them by ten, a hundred, a million, or any number you choose to use – for the relative proportions would still remain constant. And, of course, in the actual reaction, countless billions of particles will be involved.

The reason that formula mass calculations work is that if you scale the A_r and M_r figures up to grams, the ratio of particles remains the same. To put it another way, if you take the M_r of any particle and weigh out that number of grams of the substance (the **formula mass in grams**), you will always have the same number of particles. This number is very large indeed. It is approximately **6×10^{23}** or six hundred thousand million million million!

1 mole of carbon = 12 g

1 mole of iron = 56 g

1 mole of water = 18 g

1 mole of calcium carbonate = 100 g

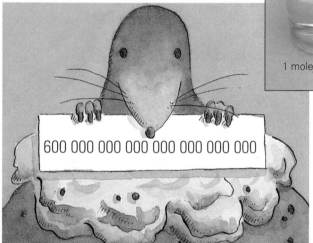

600 000 000 000 000 000 000 000

This number is used to define a standard unit of particles – the **mole**. You can have a mole of atoms, molecules, ions – even a mole of electrons. Whatever it is, if you have 6×10^{23} of them, you have a mole. In its simplest form, you have one mole if you have the atomic (or formula) mass in grams. But the mole can take on many other guises.

Be careful with your moles

In order to know the mass needed to give you one mole of something, you need to be clear about the particles involved. In many cases this is straightforward.

1 mole of magnesium *atoms*:
 A_r of Mg = 24, therefore 1 mole = 24 g

1 mole of carbon dioxide *molecules*:
 M_r of CO_2 = 12 + 2 × 16 = 44,
 therefore 1 mole of CO_2 = 44 g

But what about 1 mole of oxygen? You need to decide if you are referring to oxygen atoms or oxygen molecules:

 A_r of O = 16, so one mole of oxygen *atoms* = 16 g
 M_r of O_2 = 32, so one mole of *molecules* = 32 g

For the production of sulphur dioxide
(S = 32, O = 16)

	S	+	O_2	→	SO_2
so	32 g S	+	32 g O_2	→	64 g SO_2
or	6×10^{23} S	+	6×10^{23} O_2	→	6×10^{23} SO_2
or	1 mole S	+	1 mole O_2	→	1 mole SO_2

Working with gases

If you are looking at reactions involving solids or pure liquids (not solutions), you can easily find the *mass* of each reactant by weighing it. If you are looking at the way gases react, however, this is not so easy. With gases, it is much easier to measure the *volume*. But how does this link up with the idea of moles?

It's not easy to find the mass of a gas!

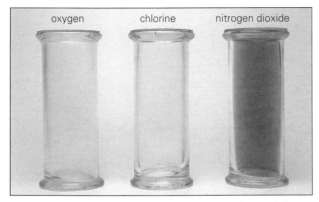

There are the same number of molecules in each jar.

A mole of gas

The number of particles in a mole is often called **Avogadro's number**, after the Italian scientist Amedeo Avogadro. Working with gases in 1811, he concluded that, given the same temperature and pressure, the same volume of any gas contains the same number of particles. Thus $1 \, dm^3$ (litre) of hydrogen contains as many particles as $1 \, dm^3$ of chlorine, or $1 \, dm^3$ of methane, and so on.

Conversely, if you have the same number of particles, you must have the same volume (all else being equal). Thus 1 mole of any gas will have the same volume – roughly **$24 \, dm^3$ (litres)** at atmospheric pressure and room temperature. This is very useful when performing calculations with reactions involving gases, as their volume is far easier to measure than their mass.

Different mass, same volume

This may, at first, seem odd. 1 mole of hydrogen (H_2) molecules has a mass of 2 g and a volume of $24 \, dm^3$ at room temperature and pressure. 1 mole of chlorine (Cl_2) molecules has a mass of 71 g – yet also has a volume of $24 \, dm^3$.

To see why this works, you need to think about the difference between solids, liquids and gases. In solids and liquids, the particles are close-packed, so the amount of space a given number of particles takes up depends on what type of particles they are. In a gas, however, the particles are widely spaced. Typically, a gas takes up about 1000 times the volume of the same particles as a solid or liquid. In this case, the volume is controlled by the number of particles and how fast they are moving, rather than what they are.

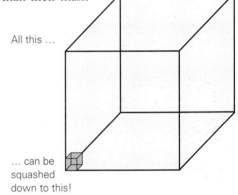

All this ...

... can be squashed down to this!

Avogadro's theory works because gas particles are small compared to the distances between them.

QUESTIONS

1 How many grams would you need for:
a a mole of CaO
b 2 moles of NaCl
c 0.1 mole of C_2H_5OH
d 0.5 mole of $FeSO_4$
e 10 moles of water
f 4 moles of ammonia?

2 How many moles are there in:
a 100 g of $CaCO_3$
b 120 g of sand (SiO_2)
c 115 g of PbI_2
d 127 g iodine (I_2)?
(Na =23, Si = 28, S=32, Pb = 207, I = 127)

3 What mass would give you one mole of:
a sulphur atoms
b sulphur molecules (S_8)?

4 At atmospheric pressure and room temperature, how many moles are there in:
a $6 \, dm^3$ of SO_2
b $24 \, dm^3$ of CH_4
c $1.2 \, dm^3$ of CO?

11.5 *Moles in solution*

1 mol dm⁻³ solutions

Although concentrations are often given in grams of solute per 100g of solvent, the mole can provide a more useful measure when dealing with reacting solutions. A **1 mol dm⁻³ solution** is defined as a solution containing 1 mole of solute in a total volume of $1\,dm^3$ (1 litre) of solution.

This system is often used for acid/alkali reactions. For example, the formula mass of sodium hydroxide (NaOH) is 40 (Na = 23 + O = 16 + H = 1). You could make a 1 mol dm⁻³ aqueous solution of sodium hydroxide, therefore, by dissolving 40g of sodium hydroxide (that is, 1 mole) in water up to a total volume of $1\,dm^3$.

However, a solution of the same concentration (or 'strength') could also be made from:

20 g NaOH (0.5 moles) in $0.5\,dm^3$ of solution

or

4g NaOH (0.1 mole) in 100ml of solution

and so on.

So when dealing with reacting solutions, you need to know both the *concentration* and *volume* before you can work out how many moles you have.

sodium hydroxide
1 mol dm⁻³ solution

40g of sodium hydroxide

1 dm³ (1 litre) of a 1 mol dm⁻³ solution contains 1 mole of solute particles.

For the simplest case

In the reaction between sodium hydroxide and hydrochloric acid, neutralisation occurs if the reactant particles are present in equal numbers:

$$NaOH + HCl \longrightarrow NaCl + H_2O$$
1 mole + 1 mole ⟶ 1 mole + 1 mole

So $1\,dm^3$ of 1 mol dm⁻³ sodium hydroxide would neutralise exactly $1\,dm^3$ of 1 mol dm⁻³ hydrochloric acid.

Neutralisation will always occur in this reaction if you have the same number of particles of acid and alkali. So if 1 mol dm⁻³ solutions are used, you will get neutralisation as long as you mix equal volumes of sodium hydroxide and hydrochloric acid.

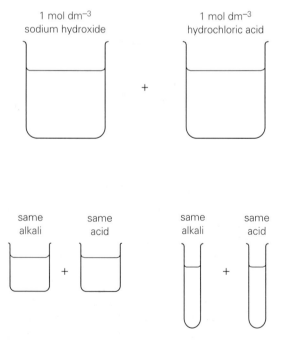

1 mol dm⁻³
sodium hydroxide
+
1 mol dm⁻³
hydrochloric acid

same alkali + same acid   same alkali + same acid

For the sodium hydroxide and hydrochloric acid reaction, equal volumes of 1 mol dm⁻³ solutions will always give neutralisation.

Check the equations

The picture is not quite so simple with sodium hydroxide and sulphuric acid. This time, you need two particles of alkali for every one of acid:

$$2NaOH + H_2SO_4 \longrightarrow Na_2SO_4 + 2H_2O$$
$$2 \text{ moles} + 1 \text{ mole} \longrightarrow 1 \text{ mole} + 2 \text{ moles}$$

So you would need 2 dm^3 of 1 mol dm^{-3} sodium hydroxide to neutralise 1 dm^3 of 1 mol dm^{-3} sulphuric acid.

Again, it is the ratio that counts. So, for 1 mol dm^{-3} solutions, you always need twice the volume of sodium hydroxide to neutralise sulphuric acid.

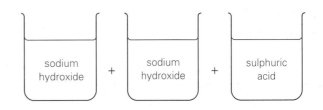

With 1 mol dm^{-3} solutions you will always need twice as much sodium hydroxide as sulphuric acid for neutralisation.

Different 'strengths'

You can, of course, make up solutions with different 'strengths'. For example, if you were to dissolve only 20 g of sodium hydroxide in water and make the solution up to 1 dm^3, you would get only 'half-strength' solution, or 0.5 mol dm^{-3}.

If you were to try to neutralise 1 mol dm^{-3} hydrochloric acid with this 'half-strength' solution, you would obviously need to use twice as much of it (twice the volume). If the hydrochloric acid was also half strength, however, the 'equal volumes' rule would still apply.

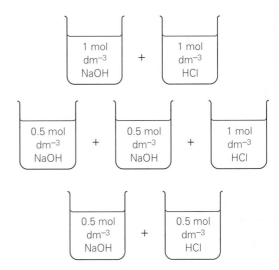

For a one-to-one reaction such as this, you will get neutralisation as long as you have the same number of particles reacting.

Working backwards

Sodium hydroxide solution is made by dissolving solid sodium hydroxide in water. But hydrochloric acid has hydrogen chloride gas dissolved in water, so how can you tell its concentration? The answer is to work backwards from its reaction with sodium hydroxide.

If you found that equal volumes of hydrochloric acid and sodium hydroxide were needed, then the acid must have the same concentration as the alkali. If twice as much acid was needed, then it must be only half as concentrated as the alkali, and so on.

QUESTIONS

1 What mass of solid is needed per dm^3 of aqueous solution to produce 1 mol dm^{-3} solutions of the following:
   a KOH (K = 39)
   b LiOH (Li = 7)
   c CaCl$_2$ (Ca = 40, Cl = 35.5)

2 What volume of 1 mol dm^{-3} NaOH would be needed to neutralise:
   a 25 cm^3 of 1 mol dm^{-3} hydrochloric acid
   b 25 cm^3 of 1 mol dm^{-3} sulphuric acid?

3a What strength solution would you get if you dissolved 4 g of sodium hydroxide and made it up to 1 dm^3 with water?
   b How much of this would you need to neutralise 100 cm^3 of 1 mol dm^{-3} sulphuric acid?

4 50 cm^3 of 'unknown strength' hydrochloric acid neutralised 100 cm^3 of 1 mol dm^{-3} sodium hydroxide. What was the strength of the acid?

11.6 *Moles in 'mixed' reactions*

'Mixed' reactions

Whenever you use the idea of moles in solution, you must always start with the balanced symbolic equation, to check the number of moles that are needed for the reaction. With sulphuric acid and magnesium oxide, for example:

$$MgO + H_2SO_4 \longrightarrow MgSO_4 + H_2O$$
$$1 \text{ mole} + 1 \text{ mole} \longrightarrow 1 \text{ mole} + 1 \text{ mole}$$

In this case, however, there is a difference. The sulphuric acid is in solution, but the magnesium oxide is an insoluble solid. But this is not a problem. It is perfectly possible to compare different 'versions' of the molar quantities. So:

1 mole of solid magnesium oxide = 24 + 16 = 40 g
1 mole of sulphuric acid = 1 dm³ of 1 mol dm⁻³ sulphuric acid.

As this is a one-to-one reaction, then you would need 40 g of magnesium oxide to neutralise 1 dm³ of 1 mol dm⁻³ sulphuric acid. But again, it is the *ratio* that is important, so 20 g would neutralise 500 cm³, 4 g would neutralise 100 cm³, and so on.

1 dm³ of 1 mol dm⁻³ sulphuric acid

40 g of magnesium oxide

The same number of particles are needed for neutralisation, whether liquid or solid.

Solutions and gases

You can also add gas volumes to your equations. For example, calcium carbonate dissolves in hydrochloric acid to give calcium chloride, water and carbon dioxide gas:

$$CaCO_3(s) + 2HCl(aq) \longrightarrow CaCl_2(aq) + H_2O(l) + CO_2(g)$$
$$1 \text{ mole} + 2 \text{ moles} \longrightarrow 1 \text{ mole} + 1 \text{ mole} + 1 \text{ mole}$$

(A_r values: Ca = 40, C = 12, O = 16, H = 1, Cl = 35.5)

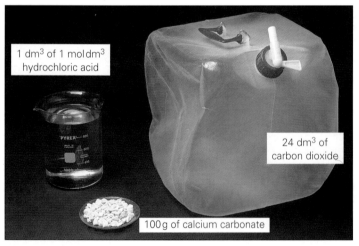

1 dm³ of 1 mol dm³ hydrochloric acid

24 dm³ of carbon dioxide

100 g of calcium carbonate

What you get for a mole!

The most appropriate way to look at molar quantities for solids is in terms of mass, while for solutions it is by volume and concentration. So in this case 100 g of calcium carbonate would react with 2 dm³ of 1 mol dm⁻³ hydrochloric acid.

With those amounts, 1 mole of carbon dioxide would be produced. In terms of its mass, this would be 44 g (12 + 2 × 16). But it is easier to measure the volume of a gas than its mass. By Avogadro's theory (see 11.4), that would be 24 dm³ of carbon dioxide at room temperature and atmospheric pressure.

Checking it out

How much hydrogen will be produced if a known mass of magnesium dissolves completely in sulphuric acid? From the balanced equation on the next page, 24 g of magnesium will give 2 g of hydrogen. But it is easier to think about the volume of a gas. As with carbon dioxide, 1 mole of hydrogen (H_2 molecules) will have a volume of 24 dm³ at room temperature and atmospheric pressure.

Checking the quantities

	magnesium	+	sulphuric acid	$\longrightarrow$	magnesium sulphate	+	hydrogen
word equation:							
balanced equation:	$Mg(s)$	+	$H_2SO_4(aq)$	$\longrightarrow$	$MgSO_4(aq)$	+	$H_2(g)$
$A_r\ M_r$:	24		98		120		2
moles:	1 mole		1 mole		1 mole		1 mole
most appropriate molar quantities:	24 g		1 dm³ of 1 mol dm⁻³ acid		120 g		24 dm³ gas
scaled down:	0.24 g		10 cm³		1.2 g		240 cm³

You can follow this reaction by dissolving different amounts of magnesium in sulphuric acid, and measuring the volume of the gas produced each time in a **gas syringe**. Use plenty of acid to make sure there is enough to dissolve the metal completely.

From the theory, you can predict how much hydrogen will be produced, and plot this on a graph. You can then plot your results on the same graph to see how they compare. You should find that the amount of hydrogen produced is always in the same ratio to the amount of magnesium used (it is proportional to the amount of magnesium).

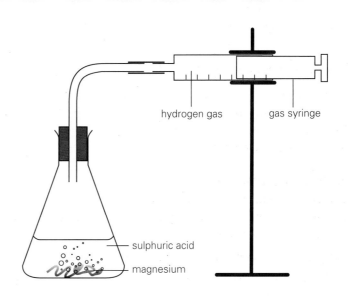

Different metals

If you repeat the same experiment with a different metal such as calcium, what masses of metal would you use to make it a fair test? If you used the same amounts as you did for magnesium, you would get only about half the volume of hydrogen produced, mass for mass. This is because the relative atomic mass for calcium is almost twice that of magnesium. So for a given mass, you get only just over half the number of atoms.

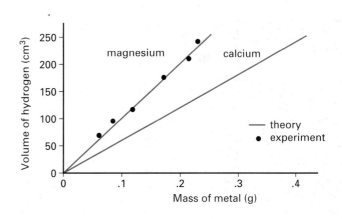

QUESTIONS

1 How many grams of calcium oxide would you need to neutralise 1 dm³ of 1 mol dm⁻³ sulphuric acid?

2 What volume of carbon dioxide would you get if you dissolved 50 g of limestone in an excess of acid?

3 What volume of hydrogen gas would you get if you dissolved 4 g of calcium metal in an excess of hydrochloric acid?

4 What volume of 1 mol dm⁻³ hydrochloric acid would you need to dissolve 2.4 g of magnesium, leaving no unreacted acid?

11.7 *Electrolysis by the mole*

Electrolysis summary

You have come across electrolysis in different contexts already (see 4.3, 5.3 and 6.5). Here is a summary.

- Electrolysis takes place when electrodes are placed in aqueous solutions of ionic substances, or molten ionic substances.

- Positive ions (cations) move towards the cathode.

- Negative ions (anions) move towards the anode.

- Cations may collect electrons at the cathode and so have their net charge cancelled out – for example
$$Cu^{2+} + 2e^- \longrightarrow Cu$$

- Anions may lose electrons at the anode, and so lose their net charge – for example
$$2Cl^- - 2e^- \longrightarrow Cl_2$$

In the electrolysis of molten, simple ionic compounds such as lead bromide ($PbBr_2$), this means that the metal forms at the cathode, whilst the non-metal forms at the anode:

$$Pb^{2+} + 2e^- \text{ (from cathode)} \longrightarrow Pb$$

$$2Br^- - 2e^- \text{ (to anode)} \longrightarrow Br_2$$

This method is therefore used to obtain reactive metals such as aluminium and magnesium from their ores, and sodium and chlorine from salt.

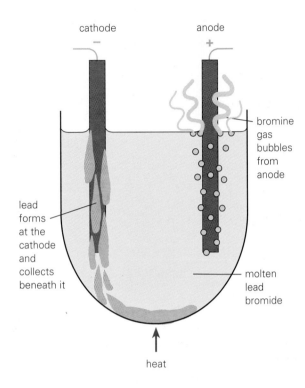

Electrolysis at its simplest: lead and bromine form from molten lead bromide.

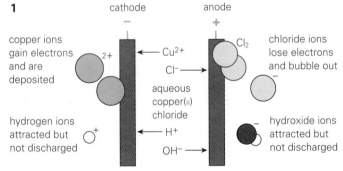

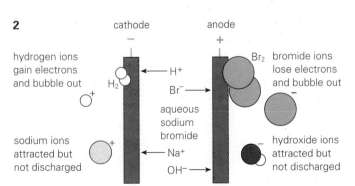

The reactivity series again

In solution in water, however, the position is complicated by the presence of hydrogen and hydroxide ions (H^+ and OH^-) which come from the ionisation of the water itself. This means that in aqueous solution, there is always a choice of ions to be discharged. At the cathode, the choice is between the (usually metallic) cation and hydrogen. The rule is that the metal will be deposited only if it is *below* hydrogen in the reactivity series (see 6.2). If it is more reactive, then hydrogen will be formed. So at the cathode in diagram 1:

$$Cu^{2+} + 2e^- \text{ (from cathode)} \longrightarrow Cu$$

but in diagram 2:

$$2H^+ + 2e^- \text{ (from cathode)} \longrightarrow H_2$$

Which cation will be discharged from solution? You need to know your reactivity series!

Faraday's work

You may have come across the name of Michael Faraday in your work on electromagnetism in physics, but he was also responsible for some of the pioneering work on electrolysis. Faraday showed that the amount of metal deposited at the cathode of a simple electrolytic cell, for example, depended on the amount of charge that passed through the circuit.

This makes sense as, when electrolysing silver nitrate solution, for example, one charged particle (electron) is needed to turn each silver cation into a silver metal atom.

Moles of electrons

Faraday also made the link with what you now know as the mole. He found that for metals with single charges such as silver or sodium, it always took the same amount of charge to deposit 1 mole of metal. This figure (96 500 coulombs) represents 1 mole of electrons. He also found that, not surprisingly, metals with double-charged cations such as copper or lead needed twice the charge to deposit 1 mole of metal.

108 g of silver (A_r 108) at the cathode:

$$Ag^+ + e^- \longrightarrow Ag$$
(1 mole)   (1 mole)   (1 mole).

64 g of copper (A_r 64) at the cathode:

$$Cu^{2+} + 2e^- \longrightarrow Cu$$
(1 mole)   (2 moles)   (1 mole)

A fair split

In any electrolytic cell, the number of electrons gained at the cathode must be the same as the number lost at the anode. So if, for example, you produced 1 mole of metallic sodium atoms from molten salt, you would get 1 mole of chlorine *atoms* at the anode. (These atoms will, of course, combine to give 0.5 moles of chlorine *molecules*, Cl_2.) So:

at the cathode: $Na^+ + e^- \longrightarrow Na$

at the anode: $Cl^- - e^- \longrightarrow Cl$
$\quad\quad\quad (2Cl^- - 2e^- \longrightarrow Cl_2)$

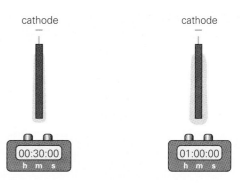

A current of 1 amp passes 1 coulomb of charge every second. So the longer the current flows, the greater the charge and the more metal is formed.

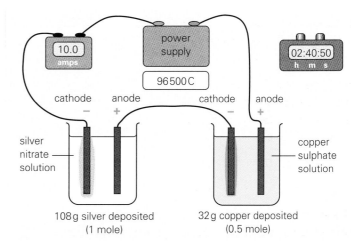

The same charge passes through both cells, but in 'mole' terms, you only get half as much copper.

QUESTIONS

1 Write separate cathode and anode equations for the electrolysis of molten bauxite (Al_2O_3).

2 What would form at the cathode if the following salts were electrolysed in solution:
   a $CaBr_2$ **c** NaF **e** KBr?
   b $Cu(NO_3)_2$ **d** $AgNO_3$

3 Explain why passing a charge of 96 500 C through the appropriate electrolytic cell deposits 108 g of silver but only 32 g of copper.

4 A sheet of steel set as the cathode in copper sulphate solution gained 0.64 g in mass while being copper-plated. What charge must have passed?

5 During the electrolysis of molten lead bromide, a charge was passed which released 1.6 g of bromine at the anode. What mass of lead formed at the cathode? (A_r Pb = 207, Br = 80).

135

SECTION B: QUESTIONS

1a The liquid in your stomach would turn pH paper red. What does this tell you?

b This sometimes causes acid indigestion. Various 'antacid' tablets may be taken to relieve this. What type of chemical must they contain?

c Some tablets contain magnesium hydroxide – your stomach contains hydrochloric acid. Write a word equation for the reaction.

2a **i** What ions are present in an aqueous solution of hydrochloric acid?

  ii Which are the cations and which the anions?

  iii Which are there most of (why is it an acid)?

b **i** What ions are present in an aqueous solution of potassium hydroxide?

  ii Which are the cations and which the anions?

  iii Which are there most of (why is it an alkali)?

c Write an *ionic* equation for the reaction that occurs if **a** and **b** are mixed.

3a When zinc metal is put in hydrochloric acid it effervesces (fizzes), giving off a colourless gas.

  i What is this gas?

  ii How could you test for it?

  iii How could you collect a sample of it in a gas jar?

  iv Write a word equation for the reaction.

  v What colour would pH paper turn in the acid?

  vi What colour would it change to if *excess* zinc was added to the acid? Why?

b Zinc oxide dissolves in hydrochloric acid, but does not fizz.

  i Write a word equation for this reaction.

  ii What type of *oxide* is zinc oxide?

  iii What does this tell you about the element zinc?

c When zinc dissolves in acid, the tube gets hot. What type of reaction is this?

4 A careless chemist was reacting metals with dilute sulphuric acid. Here are her incomplete notes:

Metal	Gas off?	Other changes
Zn	hydrogen	zinc dissolves - colourless sol.
Mg		Mg dissolves - colourless sol.
Fe	no gas	Iron dissolves - pale green sol.
Cu	no gas	

a Complete the blanks in the table.

b One entry is wrong. What is it/what should it be?

c How could you prove that the gas was hydrogen?

d What is the order of reactivity shown by this table?

e What would happen if a clean steel knife blade was dipped into copper sulphate solution?

f Write word and symbolic equations for this.

5a Aluminium is common in the crust, gold is very rare. Why was gold discovered thousands of years before aluminium?

b Which metals can be obtained by carbon displacement? Why is this?

c Which metals can only be obtained by electrolysis?

d All metals *could* be obtained by electrolysis. Why is displacement used wherever possible?

e How is it possible that such a reactive element as carbon is found uncombined in the rocks? (What form is it in and where did it come from – see 7.1).

6a Titanium is a strong, corrosion resistant, high melting point, low density metal. It is also very expensive to produce. Why is it used, rather than steel, to make high performance aircraft?

b Titanium can be used to produce a 'thermit' reaction with magnesium oxide, and zinc oxide, but not sodium oxide. What is the order of reactivity of these metals?

c Titanium is produced by reacting sodium metal with its chloride ($TiCl_4$). Write a balanced symbolic equation for this.

d Magnesium is also used for aircraft parts. Magnesium powder burns easily, but the magnesium parts do not usually catch fire after a plane crash. Why is this?

e Magnesium also reacts (albeit slowly) with water, giving off hydrogen. Write an equation for this.

f Magnesium reacts faster with hot water or steam. Why should water *not* be used on a magnesium fire?

7 The diagram shows chromium-plating apparatus.

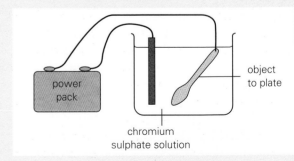

power pack

object to plate

chromium sulphate solution

a To which electrode is the object to be plated attached? Why is this electrode used?

b The electric current is carried through the wires by electrons. What carries it through the electrolyte?

c Plastic objects may be chromium-plated by first coating them with a thin layer of graphite. Why is this needed?

8a Steel cans are often recycled. Why is this done? Tin melts at 232°C and is moderately reactive. World reserves of tin could run out in 20 years. Iron melts at 1535°C, is more reactive than tin and reserves will last 200 years or more.

b Why would it be a good idea to recycle the tin?

c How might this be done from tin cans?

d Why can it not be dissolved off in acid?

9 The diagram shows some iron nails in tubes.

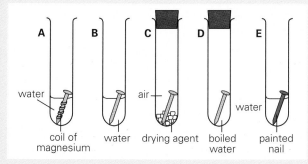

a In which tube(s) will the nail rust?

b Explain why the nail rusts in your answer to **a**. Why does it not rust in the other tubes?

c Another way to protect iron from rust is to zinc- or tin-plate it. Which of these methods gives the longer protection in situations where the protective coating is likely to be scratched? Explain your answer.

10a Describe how you would separate a sample of crude oil into its various fractions in the laboratory.

b A careless chemist performed this experiment, but muddled up his notes and fraction samples. He collected samples over the temperature ranges: 30–150°C , 150–250°C and 250–350°C. His three samples were (in muddled order!):
P was a viscous, yellow-brown liquid that would not catch fire with a splint.
Q was a clear, runny liquid that immediately caught fire when a lighted splint was brought near it.

R was slightly less runny than **Q**, and had a slight yellow tinge. It did not immediately catch fire with a lighted splint but, if a small piece of filter paper was used as a wick, it burnt with a yellow, smoky flame.
Link each sample to its temperature range, giving reasons for your answer.

c Batch processes like this are not suitable for large-scale industrial production. Describe how crude oil is split into its useful fractions industrially.

d List the properties and uses of the different fractions produced in this way.

11 The apparatus below tests the waste gases that are produced when a candle burns. The liquid in **B** is lime water.

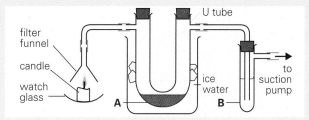

a What happens to the lime water during the course of the experiment?

b What waste gas does this show is present?

c Liquid **A** condenses in the tube during the experiment. What is this liquid?

d What test could you use to prove this?

12 The table shows the proportions of the four main fractions in crude oil from three different areas, with the typical demand for those fractions.

Source	'Light fraction'	Kerosine	Gas oil	'Heavy fraction'
Arabian	18%	12%	18%	52%
Iranian	21%	13%	20%	46%
North Sea	23%	15%	24%	38%
Demand	39%	11%	30%	20%

a From the figures, why do think that North Sea oil fetches a higher price than Arabian oil?

b How is the *supply* of each fraction made to meet the *demand*, so that nothing is wasted?

SECTION B: QUESTIONS

13 Ethene may be produced by heating paraffin as shown:

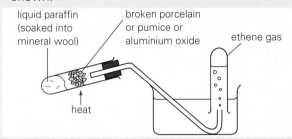

liquid paraffin (soaked into mineral wool)

broken porcelain or pumice or aluminium oxide

ethene gas

heat

a What name is given to this process?
b If paraffin contains dodecane ($C_{12}H_{26}$), what other product might form alongside ethene (C_2H_4)?
c **i** What test could you perform on the gas to check that it was an *unsaturated* hydrocarbon?
   ii What type of reaction does this test show?
   iii Write an equation for the reaction.
d Ethene may be made to undergo a *substitution* reaction with chlorine, to form chloroethene.
   i What other compound forms?
   ii Write a symbolic equation for the reaction.
e The old name for chloroethene was vinyl chloride. Draw a structural diagram to show how three chloroethene molecules might polymerise to form part of a polyvinyl chloride (PVC) molecule.

14 Polymers form very long chain molecules that have strong covalent bonds within them, but only weak forces between them. Because of this, most polymers become soft when they are heated and can easily be moulded. They are called 'thermoplastics'. A few polymers form strong covalent bonds between the long chains when they are first heated. They are called 'thermosetting' plastics. The diagram shows three possible arrangements for polymer chains:

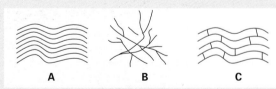

A   **B**   **C**

A straight chain molecules lie close together in a regular, crystalline way
B branching chains form a loose, open tangle
C permanent cross-links form between the chains, fixing them together
a Bakelite is a rigid, thermosetting polymer.
   i Which structure (**A**, **B** or **C**) best represents this?
   ii How does this help to explain its properties?

b Low density polythene is a thermoplastic which may be melted and reshaped. It has low strength and a low melting point.
   i Which structure (**A**, **B** or **C**) best represents this?
   ii How does this help to explain its properties?
c High density polythene is also a thermoplastic, but this has a higher melting point and is much stronger.
   i Which structure (**A**, **B** or **C**) best represents this?
   ii How does this help to explain its properties?

15 Petrol contains a mixture of hydrocarbons typified by octane (C_8H_{18}). The composition of gases formed in a car engine (by volume) is:
   water 49.5%   nitrogen monoxide 0.4%
   carbon dioxide 44%   others 0.1%
   carbon monoxide 6%

a Explain, with the help of equations, why the two main compounds are carbon dioxide and water.
b Where does the oxygen needed for this reaction come from?
c Why is some carbon monoxide gas produced as well as carbon dioxide?
d The fuel/air mixture fed to the engine is controlled by the carburettor. This may be adjusted to give a *lean* (less fuel) or a *rich* (more fuel) mixture. When the engine is cold, the mixture needs to be richer. What effect is this likely to have on the proportion of carbon monoxide in the exhaust?
e It is very dangerous to keep a car engine running in a closed garage. Explain why.
f Petrol does not contain nitrogen compounds, so how does the nitrogen monoxide form?
g Exhaust gases from vehicles pollute the atmosphere. Explain how this causes local problems in cities and adds to the wider problems of atmospheric pollution.

16 The table below shows how the pattern of fuel use in the UK has varied since 1950.

Date	Coal %	Oil %	Natural gas %	Nuclear %	Hydro-electric %
1950	89.6	10.0			0.4
1955	85.4	14.2			0.4
1960	74.0	25.4			0.6
1965	61.8	35.0	0.4	2.0	0.7
1970	46.6	44.6	5.3	0.8	2.7
1975	36.9	42.0	17.1	3.3	0.6
1980	36.7	37.0	21.6	4.1	0.6
1985	32.2	35.2	25.2	6.8	0.6

a **i** Plot a graph of these figures to show the trend.
  ii Try to extrapolate the graph lines to predict usage 5 and 10 years beyond the data given.
  iii How reliable are your projected figures?
b In the 1960s and early 1970s, gas and oil were discovered in the sedimentary rocks under the North Sea.

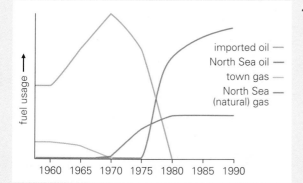

  i When did North Sea oil first come ashore?
  ii When did Britain become self-sufficient in oil?
  iii When did natural gas overtake town gas as the dominant form of gas in use?

c Town gas was made from coal gas, which was produced by the destructive distillation of coal. The composition of coal gas is approximately:
hydrogen (H_2) 50%   carbon monoxide (CO) 10%
methane (CH_4) 30%   other gases 10%
Natural gas is almost pure methane.
Suggest one safety advantage that arose from the changeover to natural gas.

17 The diagram shows a simplified version of the carbon cycle.

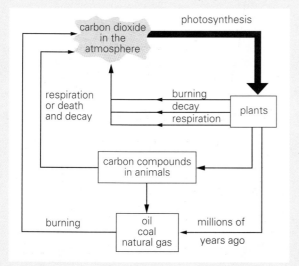

It is estimated that 30 000 km² of rain forest is burnt or cut down every year in order to grow crops or graze cattle.
a Give two effects that this has on the carbon cycle.
b What effect does this have on the global climate?

18 The percentage of carbon dioxide in the atmosphere 400 million years ago was much higher than today. From 350 million years ago, the proportion began to drop towards present levels, which were reached about 70 million years ago. Since then the figure has remained fairly constant. The period from 350–70 million years ago saw the widespread deposition of limestone and chalk in the sea, plus the evolution and spread of land plants.
a What was the origin of the carbon dioxide in the atmosphere?
b Explain how the evolution of land plants would have helped to reduce the carbon dioxide levels in the atmosphere.
c Only a tiny fraction of plant material is ever fossilised (as coal, for example). What happens to most plant remains when they die?
d Explain how the formation of limestone and chalk also helped to reduce these levels.
e Under what conditions might the trapped carbon be *released* from the limestone? (Natural cycle or human intervention.)
f What do the high carbon dioxide levels suggest about the global climate 400 million years ago?

19 The diagram shows part of a cliff face.

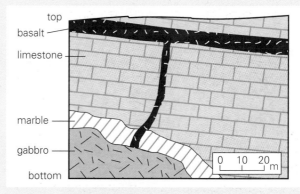

a Which two rocks formed from magma?
b The crystals of the gabbro are larger (5 mm) than those of the basalt. Explain why this is.
c What type of rock is limestone?

d A fossil coral was found in the limestone. In what environment did this limestone form?

e i What type of rock is marble?

ii Explain how it formed from the limestone.

f Which came first, the limestone or the basalt? Explain your answer.

g The gabbro formed deep within the Earth's crust.

i What has happened to expose it here?

ii What has happened to all the rock that has been removed?

20 The field sketch shows a river flowing out across a beach, with low cliffs at the back. The cliffs fizz when tested with acid and contain fossil ammonites and corals. On the beach are some large angular blocks that also fizz with acid and contain fossils. Most of the upper part of the beach is made of rounded pebbles, some of granite. When the tide goes out, there is sand at the water's edge. Up stream, the river passes through a moorland area with outcrops of granite.

a What are the rocks of the cliff made from?

b What age are these rocks, Palaeozoic or Mesozoic? How can you tell?

c What are the angular blocks on the beach made from? Where have they come from?

d Where have the granite pebbles come from?

e Why are the granite pebbles so well rounded compared to the angular blocks?

f The sand is made of quartz. Where did the quartz in this sand come from?

g What processes freed the quartz to make sand?

h i The river is quite muddy. How did this mud (clay) originally form?

ii There is no clay on the beach. Where does all the clay go?

21 The diagram shows a cross-section through three crustal plates.

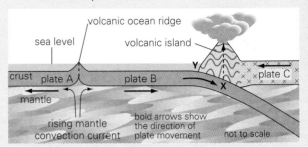

a Where does the magma which forms the oceanic ridge come from?

b Explain why the igneous rock close to the ridge is younger than that further away on plates A and B. The descending plate melts at **X** to form magma. This rises to form the volcanic island.

c Explain why the magma at **X** starts to rise.

d A deep ocean trench forms at **Z**. Why is the ocean so much deeper here?

22 This diagram shows where the main continental blocks were 200 million years ago.

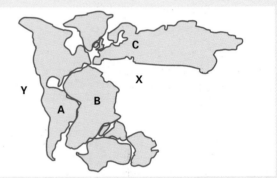

a What name is given to the process that has moved them to their positions today?

b What feature formed between continents **A** (South America) and **B** (Africa) as they split apart?

c As **B** and **C** (Europe) moved together, sediments began to fill in ocean **X**. What happened to those sediments as **B** and **C** came together?

d If **A** and **B** are moving apart, what must be happening to ocean **Y** (the Pacific)?

23 Work out the formula mass (M_r) of:

a iron(II) sulphate ($FeSO_4$)

b glucose ($C_6H_{12}O_6$)

c lead nitrate ($Pb(NO_3)_2$)

d potassium iodide (KI)

e anhydrous copper sulphate ($CuSO_4$)

f hydrated copper sulphate ($CuSO_4 . 5H_2O$)

(Fe = 56, S = 32, O = 16, C = 12, H = 1, Pb = 207, K = 39, I = 127, N = 14, Cu = 64)

24 What is the percentage of:
 a lead in lead nitrate
 b iron in iron(II) sulphate
 c iodine in potassium iodide
 d copper in anhydrous copper sulphate
 e copper in hydrated copper sulphate?

25 Rutile is a natural oxide of titanium. 10 g of rutile produced 6 g of metallic titanium when it was reduced. What is the formula of rutile, Ti_2O, TiO or TiO_2? (Ti = 48, O = 16)

26 The main lead ore is a silvery mineral called galena, lead sulphide, PbS. (Pb = 207, S = 32)
 a Calculate the proportion of lead in pure galena.
 b Most samples of lead ore have galena mixed with other rocks and minerals. New ore samples are sent away to be assayed (to find out how much lead there is in the sample).
   i A sample was found to contain 70% lead. What proportion of the sample was galena?
   ii How much sulphur is in a tonne of this ore?
   iii What volume of sulphur dioxide gas would form if this were burnt in air? (Use standard conditions.)

27 Iron is usually extracted from one of its oxide ores – haematite (Fe_2O_3) or magnetite (Fe_3O_4).
 a Calculate the percentage of iron in each of these ores.
 b If you were running a company which produced iron, which ore would you buy if they cost the same per tonne? Explain your answer.
 c Which would you use if magnetite cost 10% more per tonne?

28 1 mol dm^{-3} sulphuric acid was reacted with a 25 cm^3 sample of sodium hydroxide solution of unknown strength drop by drop until neutralisation occurred.
 a How could you tell that neutralisation had occurred?
 b 12.5 cm^3 of acid were found to neutralise the alkali.
   i Write an equation for the reaction.
   ii How many moles of sulphuric acid are needed to neutralise 1 mole of sodium hydroxide?
   iii From this, work out the concentration in mol dm^{-3} of the 'unknown strength' sodium hydroxide solution.

29 If acid is added to calcium carbonate in an open container, the carbon dioxide formed escapes into the atmosphere. If this experiment is carried out on a digital balance, the mass of carbon dioxide lost can be read off directly. What mass loss would you expect if:
 a 1 g of calcium carbonate was completely dissolved in hydrochloric acid
 b 1 g of calcium carbonate reacted completely with sulphuric acid
 c 10 cm^3 of 1 mol dm^{-3} sulphuric acid was reacted with 10 g of calcium carbonate
 d 10 cm^3 of 1 mol dm^{-3} hydrochloric acid was reacted with 10 g of calcium carbonate?

30 Molten lead iodide can be electrolysed using carbon electrodes as shown.

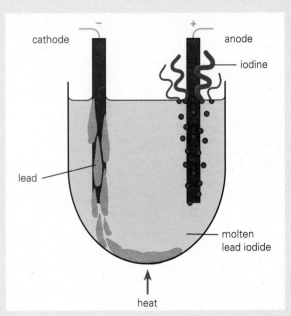

 a Copy and complete these 'half equations' for the reaction at the cathode and anode:
   at cathode: $Pb^{2+} + e^- \rightarrow Pb$
   at anode: $I^- - e^- \rightarrow I_2$
 b The formula of lead iodide is PbI_2. If 2.07 g of metallic lead was produced at the cathode, what mass of iodine was produced at the anode?
 c Molten lead chloride can also be electrolysed like this. Write 'half equations' for the reaction at the cathode and anode in this case.
 d If 120 cm^3 of chlorine gas was produced at the anode (adjusted volume for room temperature and atmospheric pressure), what mass of metallic lead was produced at the cathode?

12.1 *Looking for patterns*

Looking for patterns

When you first turned this page, the black and white picture probably appeared as a complete jumble. It is, in fact, dalmatians in the snow, and now that you know that, it probably looks obvious! The same problem faced the early chemists as they searched for patterns in the mass of information they were uncovering about the different elements. Thanks to them, you are now in the fortunate position of knowing what to look for!

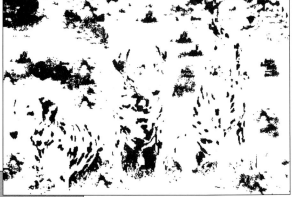

The alkali metal family

Ordering the elements

Some early chemists found that elements could be grouped in families – the soft, reactive, alkali metals (lithium, sodium and potassium) for example. They also found that, by experiment, it was possible to arrange the elements in order of increasing relative atomic mass. Once they did this, a pattern started to emerge.

The first 20

When the first 20 elements (by relative atomic mass) are listed in order, they show a repeating pattern. The chart shows clear repetition, particularly in the very reactive gas/unreactive gas/very reactive metal sequence that appears three times (element numbers 1/2/3, 9/10/11 and 17/18/19). The pattern *between* these is not quite so clear, though carbon and silicon are similar.

1	hydrogen	a very reactive gas
2	helium	an unreactive gas
3	lithium	a soft, very reactive metal
4	beryllium	a reactive metal
5	boron	solid non-metal
6	carbon	solid non-metal
7	nitrogen	non-metal
8	oxygen	reactive non-metal (gas)
9	fluorine	a very reactive gas
10	neon	an unreactive gas
11	sodium	a soft, very reactive metal
12	magnesium	a reactive metal
13	aluminium	a reactive metal
14	silicon	solid non-metal
15	phosphorus	non-metal
16	sulphur	reactive non-metal
17	chlorine	a very reactive gas
18	argon	an unreactive gas
19	potassium	a soft, very reactive metal
20	calcium	a reactive metal

Can you find the repeating pattern in this table of the first 20 elements?

Introducing the periodic table

If these 20 elements are arranged so that those with similar properties stack above one another, a simple repeating or **periodic** table is produced. This links in precisely with the way the electrons are arranged around the atoms of each element.

The numbered rows across the table are called **periods**. They are numbered using Arabic numerals (1, 2, 3, etc.). This number tells you how many shells of electrons the element has. The main vertical columns are called **groups**. They are numbered using Roman numerals (I, II, III, etc.). This number tells you how many electrons an element has in its outer shell.

Hydrogen is unique!

	Groups							VIII (0)	Periods
I	II	III	IV	V	VI	VII			
								H	
								He	1
Li	Be	B	C	N	O	F		Ne	2
Na	Mg	Al	Si	P	S	Cl		Ar	3
K	Ca								

A simple periodic table for the first 20 elements

For example, all the elements in period 2 have two shells. Lithium is in group I, so it has only one electron in its outer shell; carbon is in group IV, so it has four electrons in its outer shell; neon is in group VIII (sometimes called group 0), so it has eight electrons in its outer shell, which is therefore full (see 3.5). Hydrogen and helium stand alone, as the first shell can take only two electrons. But as helium's two electrons give it a stable 'full shell', it is usually put in with the other unreactive gases in group VIII (0).

The power of this table is the way it can be used to predict the chemical properties of elements, which are governed by this electron configuration.

Historical note

Though there had been earlier attempts to make sense of the repeating patterns visible in the properties of the elements, the forerunner of the modern periodic table was put forward by Dmitri Mendeléev in 1869. He introduced the idea of groups of similar elements, repeated in separate periods down the table. There were gaps, as not all of the elements were known. But he was able to use his table to predict the properties of these 'unknowns'. When some of the missing elements were later discovered, the accuracy of his predictions gave great support to his ideas.

Dmitri Mendeléev

QUESTIONS

1 Suggest two factors that made the interpretation of chemical patterns so difficult for the early chemists.

2 Overall, there are far more metallic elements than non-metallic elements. Is this true of the first 20?

3 How are metals and non-metals grouped in the simple version of the periodic table?

4 What proportion of the first 20 elements are gases at room temperature?

5 Why is helium put in with group VIII (0), even though it has only two electrons in its shell?

6 In the full periodic table, krypton is below argon. Predict its properties.

7 Mendeléev had many elements 'missing' from his table. How did he use these 'gaps' to support his ideas, as new elements were discovered?

12.2 The periodic table

The modern version of the **periodic table** puts the elements in order of increasing atomic number (Z) (see 3.5). Here is the pattern for the first 89 elements. The simple pattern of vertical groups and horizontal periods is wedged apart by the block of transition metals. The additional blocks that wedge in after elements 57 and 89 have been left out, including element 92, uranium. Each element has two numbers shown. The smaller is the atomic number. The larger is the relative atomic mass (A_r) (see 3.5).

Example:

relative atomic mass (A_r)

atomic number (Z)

238	
92	**U**
uranium	

Metals are found on the left of the table. They become more reactive towards the bottom left.

Groups I and II contain reactive metals. They conduct heat and electricity but they tend to be soft and have low melting and boiling points, so are not 'typical' metals in terms of these physical properties.

Group I is often called the **alkali metals** (see 12.4), as they form strongly alkaline, soluble hydroxides such as sodium hydroxide (**caustic soda**). They become more reactive and have lower melting and boiling points down the group.

Group II is called the **alkaline earth metals**. The group number tells you how many electrons there are in the outer shell, which is the same as the valency number (see 3.3).

Hydrogen is unique – it is a very reactive non-metal but, sometimes, its chemistry is more like that of a metal!

	I	II									
1							1 **H** 1 hydrogen				
2	7 **Li** 3 lithium	9 **Be** 4 beryllium									
3	23 **Na** 11 sodium	24 **Mg** 12 magnesium									
4	39 **K** 19 potassium	40 **Ca** 20 calcium	45 **Sc** 21	48 **Ti** 22 titanium	51 **V** 23	52 **Cr** 24 chromium	55 **Mn** 25 manganese	56 **Fe** 26 iron	59 **Co** 27 cobalt		
5	85.5 **Rb** 37 rubidium	88 **Sr** 38 strontium	89 **Y** 39	91 **Zr** 40	93 **Nb** 41	96 **Mo** 42	99 **Tc** 43	101 **Ru** 44	103 **Rh** 45		
6	133 **Cs** 55	137 **Ba** 56 barium	139 **La** 57	178.5 **Hf** 72	181 **Ta** 73	184 **W** 74	186 **Re** 75	190 **Os** 76	192 **Ir** 77		
7	223 **Fr** 87	226 **Ra** 88	227 **Ac** 89								

A block of rarer metals wedges in after element 57. They are all very similar and of no particular interest. A second group appears after element 89. Many, such as uranium, are unstable and radioactive and, from 93 onwards, do not occur naturally on Earth.

The **transition metals** (see 12.7) wedge in between groups II and III. They contain the 'typical' metals in common use, such as iron and copper. These metals have high melting and boiling points, and are much harder and denser than those of groups I and II. The salts of many transition metals are coloured and their oxides are insoluble. Many can have different numbers of electrons in their outer shells, so they have variable valencies, forming two or more families of salts.

Groups III, IV and V have less clear-cut properties. They are non-metals at the top, but grade into metals at higher periods. The boundary between metals and non-metals steps down to the right. Elements on the boundary show intermediate properties.

Group IV contains elements with a valency of 4 that form long and complex molecules. Carbon chemistry forms the basis of all living things, while silicon compounds build most rocks.

Group VI contains reactive non-metals, including the very reactive (and life-giving) gas oxygen and the yellow solid, sulphur. Both have a valency of 2, as the six electrons in their outer shell mean that they are 'two short' of a full outer shell.

Non-metals are found on the right of the table. They become more reactive towards the top right of group VII.

III	IV	V	VI	VII	VIII (0)
					4 **He** 2 helium
11 **B** 5 boron	12 **C** 6 carbon	14 **N** 7 nitrogen	16 **O** 8 oxygen	19 **F** 9 fluorine	20 **Ne** 10 neon
27 **Al** 13 aluminium	28 **Si** 14 silicon	31 **P** 15 phosphorus	32 **S** 16 sulphur	35.5 **Cl** 17 chlorine	40 **Ar** 18 argon
59 **Ni** 28 nickel / 64 **Cu** 29 copper / 65 **Zn** 30 zinc	70 **Ga** 31	72.5 **Ge** 32	75 **As** 33	79 **Se** 34	80 **Br** 35 bromine / 84 **Kr** 36 krypton
106 **Pd** 46 / 108 **Ag** 47 silver / 112 **Cd** 48	115 **In** 49	119 **Sn** 50 tin	122 **Sb** 51	128 **Te** 52	127 **I** 53 iodine / 131 **Xe** 54 xenon
195 **Pt** 78 / 197 **Au** 79 gold / 201 **Hg** 80 mercury	204 **Tl** 81	207 **Pb** 82 lead	209 **Bi** 83	210 **Po** 84	210 **At** 85 astatine / 222 **Rn** 86 radon

Group VII, also known as the **halogens** (see 12.5), contains coloured non-metals. They have a valency of 1, as the seven electrons in their outer shell mean that they are 'one short' of a full outer shell. Fluorine and chlorine are poisonous gases, bromine is a brown, fuming liquid and iodine an almost-black solid with a purple vapour.

Group VIII (often called **group 0**) contains the completely unreactive **noble gases** (see 12.3).

QUESTIONS

Using the information from the periodic table:

1 Are the following elements metals or non-metals: lithium (3), nitrogen (6), calcium (20), titanium (22), palladium (46), iodine (53), francium (87)?

2 Which is likely to be more reactive:
 a sodium (11) or caesium (55)
 b bromine (35) or iodine (53)
 c oxygen (8) or sulphur (16)?

3 Describe the likely chemical properties of:
 a xenon (54)   **d** astatine (85)
 b strontium (38)   **e** rubidium (37)
 c cobalt (27)   **f** fluorine (9)

4 To which group (or block) are the following elements likely to belong?
 a X is a silver-grey solid that conducts heat and electricity. It is very hard and will not melt in a Bunsen flame. Its salts are green.
 b Y is a silvery solid that tarnishes in air. It dissolves in water to give a strongly alkaline solution. The formula of its chloride is YCl_2.
 c Z is a brown liquid that dissolves in water to give an acidic solution. It forms a colourless salt with sodium of formula NaZ.

5 Tellurium (52) and iodine (53) are out of position compared to their relative atomic masses. Find another pair of elements that have been switched 'out of relative mass order' in the table above.

12.3 *The noble gases*

Discovering the noble gases

Air contains approximately one fifth (20%) of reactive oxygen and four fifths (80%) of 'unreactive' nitrogen. But what was unsuspected until 100 years ago was that, hidden within the nitrogen, there was about 1% of truly unreactive gas.

In 1892, scientists discovered that nitrogen from the air was denser than nitrogen produced experimentally. Nitrogen reacts with hot magnesium, but when this reaction was performed with the 'nitrogen' from the air, about 1% would not react. That 1% was identified as other gases, which became known as the noble gases because they were so unreactive.

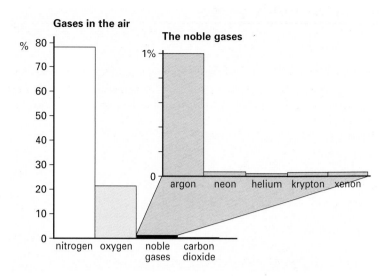

The noble gases make up 1% of the air – but most of that is argon.

Why are they unreactive?

The noble gases are all found in group VIII (0) of the periodic table. This means that they all have full outer electron shells. This gives the atoms great stability, so they will not form chemical bonds at all.

Because of this, the noble gases always exist as single atoms – they are **monatomic gases**. This is unlike the other gases in the atmosphere, which form molecules.

VIII (0)

4 **He** 2	
20 **Ne** 10	
32 **Ar** 18	
84 **Kr** 36	

neon   argon

Full electron shells give the noble gas atoms great stability.

Separating the gases

The gases in air can be removed chemically, one by one, to leave the noble gases. But a physical separation process is cheaper. The method used is similar to that used for the fractional distillation of crude oil (see 7.2). The difference is that the air must be compressed and cooled to liquefy it first. The gases then boil off at different temperatures and can be collected. The industrial plant therefore ends up as a cross between a refrigerator and a fractionating tower! After separation, the gases are recompressed, liquefied and bottled in strong steel cylinders.

Gas	Boiling point	
	K	**°C**
oxygen	90	-183
argon	87	-186
nitrogen	77	-196

Fractionating tower for air.

Using the noble gases

You may think that noble gases do not have much use, but sometimes their very lack of reactivity is just what is required.

Argon is the cheapest of the gases to produce, and this is used inside ordinary lightbulbs, to stop the filament from burning. It is also used to give an unreactive atmosphere for welding, which could be dangerous in air.

Helium, being rarer, is more expensive, but has the additional property of a very low density compared to air. This, coupled with its unreactive nature, makes it a suitable, safe alternative to hydrogen for airships and balloons.

Unlike nitrogen, helium is not very soluble in water, even under pressure. This makes it an excellent substitute for nitrogen in the gas mixture that deep-sea divers breathe. If you use it, it reduces the risk of the 'bends' on surfacing, but does have the side effect of making you sound like Mickey Mouse when you talk!

Helium also has the lowest boiling point (4 K), and liquid helium is now used to cool the giant electromagnets of brain scanners (for example) down to temperatures approaching absolute zero. This make the coils 'superconduct', and the huge currents generate powerful magnetic fields.

Neon is most commonly used for another property. It glows if an electrical discharge is passed through it. These discharge tubes can be coloured, making them ideal for flashy neon signs!

Krypton and **xenon** can also be used this way, as well as in lasers. Xenon is sometimes used in high-powered lighthouse lamps, as it is such a poor conductor of heat.

QUESTIONS

1 What clue lead to the discovery of the noble gases?

2 Plot out the electron configurations for the noble gases, to confirm their full outer shells. (Atomic numbers: $_2$He, $_{10}$Ne, $_{18}$Ar).

3 Nitrogen and oxygen form *diatomic* molecules, but argon is *monatomic*. Explain these two terms.

4a What proportion of the air is argon?
 b Describe how argon is obtained from the air.

5a What would happen to a lightbulb when it was switched on if it were filled with air rather than argon?
 b Why is argon used in lightbulbs rather than helium?

6 Why is helium used:
 a instead of hydrogen in airships
 b instead of nitrogen in the oxygen mix for divers
 c in some electromagnet coils?

7 Why were the noble gases such 'late' discoveries?

12.4 *The alkali metals*

What do they have in common?

The alkali metals form group I of the periodic table. Like all metals, they are good conductors of heat and electricity, but unlike most metals they are very soft and can be cut easily with a knife. They also have exceptionally low densities for metals, and **lithium**, **sodium** and **potassium** are less dense than water.

They are all very reactive, combining with the oxygen in the air so rapidly that they have to be stored under oil. They also react violently with water, giving off hydrogen gas and forming a strongly alkaline solution. This is why the group is called the alkali metals. For example:

sodium + water $\longrightarrow$ sodium hydroxide + hydrogen

$$2Na + 2H_2O \longrightarrow 2NaOH + H_2$$

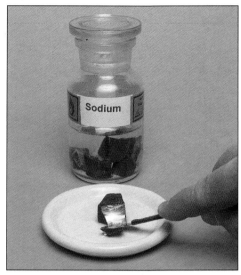

Sodium is a typical alkali metal – very reactive, very soft.

How do they vary?

There is a gradual change in properties as you go down group I, from lithium to francium. Physically, they get softer and their melting and boiling points get lower. This is shown in the physical data given for lithium, sodium and potassium.

Alkali metal	Density (g/cm³)	mp (°C)	bp (°C)	Hardness
Lithium	0.53	180	1330	soft
Sodium	0.97	98	890	very soft
Potassium	0.86	63.7	774	very soft

Physical properties of the alkali metals

Lithium fizzes rapidly in cold water and hydrogen gas is given off.

Chemically, the alkali metals get more and more reactive down the group. You can see this if you put *tiny* pieces of the metal into a trough full of water.

Lithium reacts by fizzing and giving off hydrogen gas. Sodium is more reactive, fizzing rapidly. So much heat is given off that the sodium melts into a silver ball which whizzes around the surface of the water as it reacts. Potassium reacts more violently.

Rubidium, caesium and francium are so dangerously reactive that you will not find them in a school laboratory.

Potassium reacts so violently and so much heat is given off that the hydrogen formed catches fire spontaneously.

Which is which?

The alkali metals all react to form ionic compounds (see 4.2), such as sodium chloride or sodium oxide. These are usually colourless, crystalline solids which dissolve in water. As these salts all look very much the same, it can be difficult to tell them apart.

Alkali metals all burn easily in air, giving a coloured flame. Each metal has its own distinct flame colour. The same colour also shows up if salts of the metals are heated, and this **flame test** can be used to spot which alkali metal is present in a salt. Flame tests are carried out by picking up a little of the salt on a piece of platinum wire dipped in hydrochloric acid, and holding this in a medium Bunsen flame. Lithium gives a bright red flame. Sodium gives a yellow–orange flame. Potassium gives a pale lilac flame.

The alkali metal salts all tend to look the same!

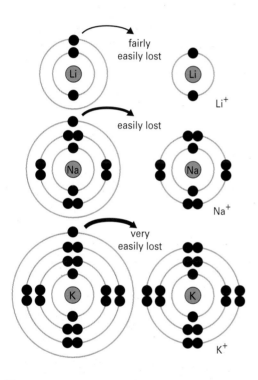

The alkali metals form single-charged cations.

Why are they so reactive?

The alkali metals all have just one electron in the outer shell of their atoms (see 3.5). These 'lone' electrons are easily lost. If this happens, the atoms are no longer electrically neutral – they become ions. The easier it is for this to happen, the more reactive the metal is.

Alkali metal ions are left with a single positive charge. These positive cations combine with non-metallic anions to form **ionic compounds** such as common salt, NaCl (Na^+Cl^-), and sodium oxide Na_2O ($Na^+_2O^{2-}$).

Going down

Electrons are held in position by the force of attraction from the positive nucleus at the centre of the atom. The further an electron is away from the nucleus, the weaker this force, so the outer electron of a big atom will be less tightly held than that of a small atom. The inner electron shells also have a shielding effect, further reducing the attraction.

Going down the group, the atoms of the alkali metals are getting bigger and bigger, with more electron shells, so their outer electrons are becoming easier and easier to 'lose'. This is why the alkali metals are more reactive down the group.

QUESTIONS

1a What physical properties do the alkali metals have in common with metals in general?
b What physical properties are rather more unusual?

2a Why are the metals in group I called the alkali metals?
b Write a word equation for the reaction of potassium and water.
c Write a balanced symbolic equation for the reaction of potassium and water.

3a What is the best way to tell group I metal salts apart?
b How would you do this test and what would you look for?

4 Why does sodium form an Na^+ cation?

5 Explain, with the help of electron-shell diagrams, why potassium is more reactive than lithium.

12.5 The halogens

What are they?

The halogens are coloured, pungent-smelling, reactive non-metallic elements – but smelling them is not a good idea, as they are poisonous and cause damage to the lungs. **Fluorine** and **chlorine** are gases at room temperature. They form covalent diatomic molecules (F_2 and Cl_2). Unlike the alkali metals, the melting and boiling points of the halogens get higher *down* the group. **Bromine** is a liquid and **iodine** a solid, but both are easily vaporised.

fluorine   chlorine   bromine   iodine

The halogens have coloured, diatomic vapours.

The halogens react with metals to form salts (*halogen* comes from the Greek for 'salt-formers'). These salts are called metal **halides**. They are generally very stable, typical ionic solids such as sodium chloride:

$$\text{sodium} + \text{chlorine} \longrightarrow \text{sodium chloride}$$
$$2Na + Cl_2 \longrightarrow 2NaCl$$

The halogens all react with hydrogen to form hydrogen halides.
For example, with chlorine:

$$\overset{\text{sunlight}}{\text{chlorine} + \text{hydrogen} \longrightarrow \text{hydrogen chloride}}$$
$$Cl_2 + H_2 \longrightarrow 2HCl$$

Hydrogen halides such as hydrogen chloride are very soluble in water. When they dissolve, they ionise to give acidic solutions, because of the H^+ ions which form.

You can see the reactivity order of the halogens from the reaction with hydrogen – fluorine is the most reactive and iodine the least. The halogens become more reactive *up* the group, which again works the opposite way to the alkali metals.

Halogen	Appearance	bp (°C)	Reaction with hydrogen
Fluorine	pale yellow-green gas	–118	explodes when mixed
Chlorine	green gas	–35	mixture explodes in sunlight
Bromine	red-brown liquid	59	mixture reacts if heated
Iodine	purple-black solid	184	partial reaction only

Some physical and chemical trends in the halogens

Displacement and solution

As with metals, non-metals can act as 'chemical bullies', displacing less reactive ones from their compounds. You can see this clearly with the halogens if they are dissolved in a solvent such as tetrachloroethene, where they show their characteristic colours: chlorine/green, bromine/red-brown and iodine/purple. If chlorine solution is added to aqueous potassium bromide solution and the mixture shaken, the green colour is replaced by brown as chlorine displaces bromine from its compound. The same process is used to extract bromine from sea water.

$$\begin{array}{cccccc} \text{chlorine} & + & \text{potassium} & \longrightarrow & \text{bromine} & + & \text{potassium} \\ \text{(green)} & & \text{bromide} & & \text{(red-brown)} & & \text{chloride} \\ Cl_2(sol) & + & 2KBr(aq) & \longrightarrow & Br_2(sol) & + & 2KCl(aq) \end{array}$$

Fluorine would displace chlorine from a chloride, and bromine would displace iodine from an iodide in a similar way.

Cl_2 (sol)   KBr (aq) Br_2 (sol)

Br_2 (sol)   KI (aq) I_2 (sol)

Displacement in the halogens.

Never mix these two!

Chlorine and bleach

Chlorine is used extensively to kill bacteria – in the swimming baths but also in your water supply. Household bleach is made by dissolving chlorine in sodium hydroxide solution, and is often used to kill germs in the toilet – but be careful. Other toilet cleaners contain acid to dissolve the limescale. If you mix these with bleach you will produce large amounts of chlorine gas – enough to kill you!

Iodine is also used to kill germs, but is milder in its action – iodine solution used to be put onto cuts and grazes to prevent infection. Fluorine compounds are put into toothpaste and drinking water to help strengthen teeth against acid attack. Silver halides are used in black and white photography. Silver bromide breaks down in the light to give grains of silver metal. These grains form a negative image, appearing black where there was light. Old hospital X-ray photographs can be recycled to get the silver back.

Why are they so reactive?

The halogens all have seven electrons in the outer shell of their atoms (see 3.5). That's just one short of a full shell. The shell can be filled if the atom gains an extra electron. This turns the once-neutral atom into an anion with a single negative charge. The easier it is for this to happen, the more reactive is the halogen.

Going up

Extra electrons are captured by the force of attraction from the positive nucleus of the atom. The further an electron is away from the nucleus, the weaker this force (made weaker still by the shielding effect of the inner electron shells). A big atom will find it less easy to capture an electron than a small atom.

Going up the group, the atoms of the halogens are getting smaller and smaller, so it is increasingly easy for them to capture an extra electron and become an ion. So the halogens are more reactive *up* the group, where the atoms are smaller. This is why the reactivity trend in the halogens works in the opposite direction to that in the alkali metals.

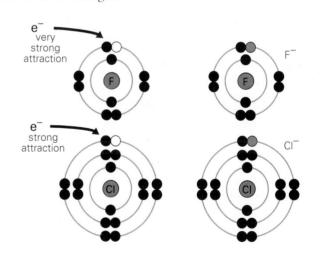

Smaller halogen atoms are more reactive than big ones.

QUESTIONS

1 Draw a simple bubble diagram of the particles in chlorine gas.

2 Hydrochloric acid is made industrially by burning hydrogen in chlorine. This produces hydrogen chloride gas, which dissolves in water to form hydrochloric acid. Write word and balanced symbolic equations for this reaction.

3a What would happen if chlorine gas was bubbled through potassium iodide solution?

b Write word and symbolic equations for this reaction.

4 Why is chlorine such a useful gas, despite the fact that it is so poisonous?

5a How do halogen atoms form ions?

b Why is it easier for small atoms to do this than large ones?

c Why do halogens get more reactive up the group, the opposite trend to the alkali metals?

12.6 *Chemicals from the sea*

Two thirds of the world's surface is covered by sea or ocean, to an average depth of 6 km or so. It is an aqueous solution containing 36 parts per thousand of dissolved salts. Most of this is common salt, sodium chloride, with lesser amounts of other group I and II metal salts, such as magnesium and potassium chlorides and calcium sulphate.

Getting out the salt

Salt is essential to our diet. All around the world, shallow parts of the coast are often blocked off and the sea water is allowed to evaporate naturally in the hot sun in **salt pans** (see 2.4). The salt is then scraped up and this **sea salt** is especially prized for cooking as it contains *all* of the dissolved elements, including some trace elements that are essential to our diet.

Sea water contains 2.8% sodium chloride and 1% other salts.

The Great Salt Lake in Utah is slowly evaporating away, leaving the salt behind.

This can also happen naturally on a much larger scale when inland, shallow seas such as the Great Salt Lake of Utah, USA evaporate away.

A similar inland sea covered the area that is now Great Britain about 250 million years ago, when the climate was much hotter. This formed thick deposits of **rock salt**, which are now buried by younger rocks. These are mined in places, and the impure rock salt is put directly onto roads in the winter to melt the ice. Elsewhere, water is pumped underground. This dissolves the salt, and the resultant brine is pumped back to the surface for purification.

Getting out the elements

Common salt forms cube-shaped crystals where the sodium cations and chlorine anions are held tightly in place by electrostatic forces – it is a typical ionic solid (see 4.3). If you melt salt, however, the ions become free to move so the molten salt will conduct electricity. Sodium metal and chlorine gas can be produced from molten salt like this by electrolysis.

$$Na^+ + e^- \text{ (from cathode)} \longrightarrow Na$$

$$2Cl^- - 2e^- \text{ (to anode)} \longrightarrow Cl_2$$

The electrolysis of brine

Sodium and chloride ions are also free to move in solution in water, so brine can be electrolysed too. This is a cheaper method, as no energy is needed to melt the salt, but it is complicated by the fact that there are four ions present, as ionised water is also involved.

$$NaCl + H_2O \longrightarrow Na^+ + Cl^- + H^+ + OH^-$$

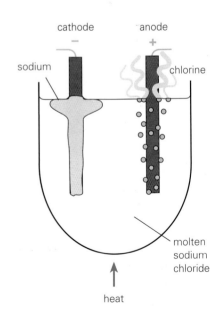

If an electric current is passed through this, chlorine gas is given off at the anode as before, but hydrogen gas is given off at the cathode rather than sodium metal. This is because sodium is above hydrogen in the reactivity series, and so stays in solution as an ion in preference to the hydrogen. (See 11.7 and 12.4 – think about what happens if you *put* sodium metal into water.) Sodium hydroxide is left behind in solution.

You can test for these products. A tube full of hydrogen gas will 'pop' with a lighted splint; chlorine gas will turn damp pH paper red and then bleach it; sodium hydroxide solution turns pH paper dark blue.

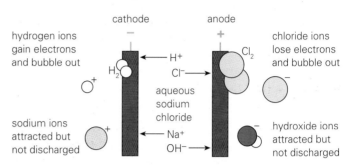

The electrolysis of brine leaves sodium cations (Na⁺) and hydroxide anions (OH⁻) in solution.

The chlor-alkali industry

The electrolysis of brine is an important industrial process (the **chlor–alkali** process) as it provides three important chemicals for industry.

- **Chlorine** is an important sterilising agent either directly or as bleach. It also has the ability to remove the colour from coloured materials by reacting with the dyes. Bleach is often used, therefore, as a whitener in washing powders. Industrially, it is also used to make the plastic PVC.

- **Sodium hydroxide** (caustic soda) is a very strong alkali that is often used to remove grease from ovens. It is also used to make soap, paper and ceramics.

- **Hydrogen** is also a very important industrial chemical with a wide range of uses, from reforming fuels after cracking (see 7.5) to the hydrogenation of unsaturated vegetable oils to make fats for margarine or chocolate. It is also used to make ammonia for fertilisers.

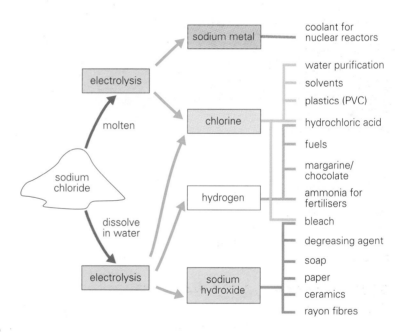

Some of the important products that can be made, starting with brine as the raw material.

QUESTIONS

1a Why is the Great Salt Lake in Utah getting smaller?

b What happens to the dissolved salt?

c How did the rock salt beds found underground in Britain form?

2a How can you get metallic sodium from salt?

b Why can't you get metallic sodium from brine in this way?

3 In your practical science class, you may well have been asked to make sodium chloride by neutralising sodium hydroxide with hydrochloric acid. Describe how both of these reactants may originally have been made, starting from sodium chloride in brine. Use word and symbolic equations wherever possible.

4 Salts of sodium and calcium are released when rocks such as granite are weathered. Why do you think the sea is salty?

12.7 The transition metals

After calcium, the simple pattern of the periodic table is interrupted by a block of ten metals with similar properties. These are the transition metals. In general, transition metals are hard and dense, have high melting points and are less reactive that the metals in groups I and II. In everyday terms, these are the 'typical' metals that you will see in use around you – from the cast iron of manhole covers to the copper used for water pipes.

The transition metals tend to have two 'loose' electrons left in the outer shell, which in general gives them a valency of 2 (see 3.3). But there are many exceptions, and some metals can vary their valency. Iron, for example, can have a valency of 2 or 3 – shown as Fe(II) or Fe(III).

potassium permanganate
$KMnO_4$

copper(II) sulphate
$CuSO_4$

The transition metals form ionic salts, many of which have characteristic colours.

Property	Manganese	Iron	Copper	Zinc
Symbol	Mn	Fe	Cu	Zn
Atomic number (Z)	25	26	29	30
mp °C	1220	1535	1083	420
Density g/cm³	7.20	7.86	8.92	7.14
Valencies	2, 4, 7	2, 3	1, 2	2
Coloured ions	Mn^{2+} pink MnO_4^- purple	Fe^{2+} green Fe^{3+} brown	Cu^{2+} blue Cu^+ white	Zn^{2+} white

Some properties of four 'first row' transition metals.

The two faces of iron

If you dissolve iron in hydrochloric acid, hydrogen gas is given off and a green solution of iron(II) chloride is produced:

$$Fe + 2HCl \longrightarrow FeCl_2 + H_2$$

If, on the other hand, you heat iron wool and then plunge it into a jar of chlorine gas, the iron glows and brown iron(III) chloride is produced:

$$2Fe + 3Cl_2 \longrightarrow 2FeCl_3$$

The physical properties of iron are described in 6.6.

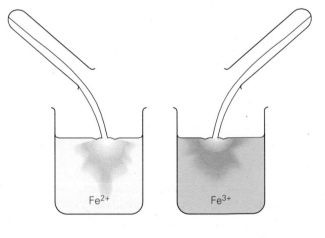

Iron(II) ions (Fe^{2+}) give a green colour, while iron(III) ions (Fe^{3+}) give brown. You can use sodium hydroxide to test for these ions in solution.

Fe^{2+}

Fe^{3+}

$$Fe^{2+} + 2OH^- \longrightarrow Fe(OH)_2$$

$$Fe^{3+} + 3OH^- \longrightarrow Fe(OH)_3$$

Testing for water with anhydrous copper sulphate.

Copper

Copper is unusual in that it has a pinky-brown colour as opposed to the silver-grey of most metals. It is soft, bendable and is easily shaped. It is an excellent conductor of electricity so it is used for electrical wiring.

You are probably very familiar with the blue colour of its salts from copper(II) sulphate. It is worth remembering, however, that this blue colour appears only with water – either in solution, or with water locked up in the crystal structure as **water of crystallisation**. If copper sulphate crystals are heated gently, they turn into white, powdery **anhydrous** copper sulphate. This reaction is reversible and, if water is added, the blue colour returns. This is used as a test for water.

$$
\begin{array}{ccc}
\text{hydrated} & & \text{anhydrous} \\
\text{copper sulphate} \underset{\text{recombines}}{\overset{\text{heat}}{\rightleftharpoons}} & \text{copper sulphate} & + \text{ water} \\
\text{(blue)} & \text{(white)} &
\end{array}
$$

$$CuSO_4.5H_2O \rightleftharpoons CuSO_4 + 5H_2O$$

Manganese and zinc

Manganese is used in steel alloys, as well as being the metal in 'alkaline' batteries such as the original Duracell. Zinc is used for 'galvanising' steel to protect it from rust (see 6.7), and also forms the outer casing (cathode) of the old-style 'dry' cells and batteries.

Transition metal catalysts

Transition metals or their oxides are also used as **catalysts** to speed up chemical reactions (see 13.4). Manganese dioxide acts as a catalyst to break down hydrogen peroxide to water and oxygen in the laboratory. In industry, iron is the catalyst used to make ammonia from nitrogen and hydrogen in the Haber process (see 8.5 and 15.3).

Zinc and manganese are used to make different types of batteries.

Hydrogen peroxide breaks down to water and oxygen rapidly when manganese dioxide is added.

QUESTIONS

1 In what ways are the transition metals 'typical' metals?

2 What ions could be responsible for the following colours in salts:
 a blue **d** purple
 b green **e** brown?
 c pink

3 Copper has two oxides, copper(I) oxide and copper(II) oxide. Write their formulae.

4 Cobalt is another transition metal. Cobalt chloride forms pink crystals from solution in water. These turn to a blue powder if heated gently. This powder turns back to pink in time, unless it is kept very dry. What might be happening here?

5 Why is iron important to the fertiliser industry?

12.8 *More about redox*

Redox and electron transfer

Zinc can displace copper from its oxide in a simple thermit reaction. This can also be viewed as a redox reaction (see 6.3), as the zinc becomes oxidised, while the copper is reduced.

If you look at the electron movement in diagram 1, you will see that the zinc has lost electrons, while the copper has gained them. So oxidation is associated with electron loss, while reduction is associated with a gain in electrons. This is sometimes a more useful way of thinking about oxidation and reduction than simple gain or loss of oxygen.

In this example, the oxygen has not changed. But if you burn zinc in air, as in diagram 2, the oxygen gains electrons and so is reduced, while the zinc loses electrons and so is oxidised.

OIL-RIG might help you to remember which is which –
Oxidation Is Loss - Reduction Is Gain

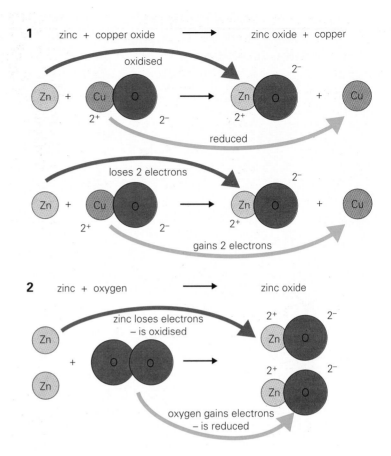

Oxidation numbers

As you know from 12.7, iron has two families of salts, those with Fe^{2+} ions (usually green) and those with Fe^{3+} ions (generally rusty brown). If green iron sulphate solution is left standing, it steadily turns brown as the Fe^{2+} ions change to Fe^{3+} ions. This involves losing an electron and so is an oxidation reaction.

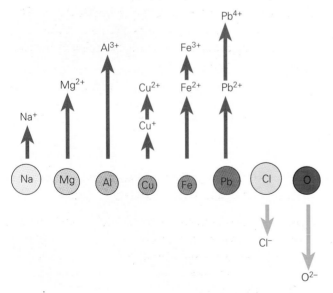

The oxidation and reduction numbers of some common ions

Compared to neutral iron, Fe^{2+} ions have lost two electrons and Fe^{3+} ions have lost three. They are therefore given **oxidation numbers** of 2 and 3 respectively – shown as iron(II) and iron(III). These numbers are then quoted to show which family of compounds are being described – green iron(II) sulphate, for example. This number, of course, also tells you the valency of the metal, so you can work out the formula:

iron(II) sulphate $=$ $FeSO_4$

iron(III)sulphate $=$ $Fe_2(SO_4)_3$

Anions can also be fitted to this pattern. A chloride ion has *gained* one electron compared with an atom, so is given an oxidation number of –1 (that is, if you like, a reduction number), while oxide ions have gained two electrons and so are -2.

Oxidising and reducing agents

Anything that takes electrons is an **oxidising agent**, while anything that loses electrons is a **reducing agent**. But do not forget that oxidation and reduction go together, so oxidising agents are themselves reduced, while reducing agents are themselves oxidised. (Confused? Just remember OIL-RIG!)

Some redox reactions involve colour changes, and these can be used to test for oxidising or reducing agents. The first breathalysers relied on the reduction of yellow chromate(VI) (CrO_4^{2-}) ions to green chromium (Cr^{3+}) ions by alcohol in the breath.

'Just blow into the bag, ladies ...'

Redox and reactivity

Metals are reducing agents, as they supply electrons when they ionise. The higher the metal is in the reactivity series, the more easily it loses its electron(s) and so the more powerful a reducing agent it is. In this way, reactive metals reduce (displace) less reactive ones:

$$Zn \longrightarrow Zn^{2+} + 2e^-$$
$$Pb^{2+} + 2e \longrightarrow Pb$$

Similarly, non-metals are oxidising agents as they take electrons when they ionise. The more reactive a non-metal is, again the stronger an oxidising agent it is, and so it can cause displacement:

$$Cl_2 + 2e^- \longrightarrow 2Cl^-$$
$$2Br^- \longrightarrow Br_2 + 2e^-$$

Redox and electrolysis

Electrolysis can also be thought of in redox terms. The metal cation is reduced as it gains electrons at the cathode, while the anion is oxidised as it loses electrons to the anode. For molten salt:

$$Na^+ + e^- \longrightarrow Na \text{ (reduction)}$$
$$2Cl^- - 2e^- \longrightarrow Cl_2 \text{ (oxidation)}$$

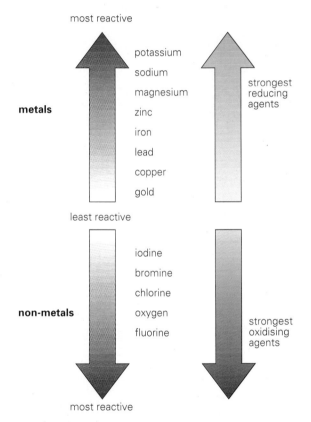

Redox and the reactivity series

QUESTIONS

1   Describe the following reactions in redox electron transfer terms:
   a chlorine displacing bromine from KBr
   b iron burning in chlorine gas to form $FeCl_3$
   c the Al/Fe_2O_3 thermit reaction (see 6.3)
   d iron rusting (to Fe_2O_3).

2   In redox terms, why does iron dipped in copper sulphate solution become copper-plated?

3a Copy and complete these 'half equations' for the electrolysis of bauxite:
   $Al^{3+} + e^- \longrightarrow Al$ (metal)
   $O^{2-} - e^- \longrightarrow O_2$
   b Explain this reaction in redox terms.

157

13.1 *Rates of reaction*

How fast?

You already have some idea of the speed of a reaction – the reactivity series of metals may be found, in part, by seeing how rapidly different metals react with acid, for example. Greater extremes may be seen in cars. In a petrol engine, the fuel/air mixture reacts in an almost instantaneous explosion, whilst the iron/air mixture on the bodywork may take several years to turn it to rust.

Reaction rates are very important in industry. If a reaction runs too quickly, it might get out of control and cause an explosion. But if it runs too slowly, this will make the process very inefficient and will raise production costs. Reaction rates need to be controlled, but before you can do that you need to be able to measure them.

Millions of mini explosions for every speck of rust!

How can you measure it?

To find how fast a reaction is going, you first need to be able to time something. In the case of a metal dissolving in an acid, you can time how long it takes for all the metal to dissolve.

You could set up an experiment, for example, where samples of different metals are dissolved in a large amount of acid. You need a large amount of acid to make sure that all the metal will react. And you would need to use the same amounts of each metal in order to make it a fair test. The table shows the time taken to dissolve 0.1 g samples of different metals in an excess of strong acid.

Remember that the *longer* it takes for the reaction to occur, the *slower* the reaction is. To find the speed (or **rate**) of the reaction, you can divide the mass lost (g) by the time it took (s). This would give you a reaction rate in terms of grams per second (g/s).

$$\frac{\text{mass (g)}}{\text{time (s)}} = \text{rate of reaction (g/s)}$$

What can you measure?

To time a reaction, you need some way of following either the loss of the reacting chemicals (reactants) or the increase in the products of the reaction. The method used will depend on the particular reaction.

With magnesium and sulphuric acid, for example:

$$\underset{\text{reactants}}{Mg(s) + H_2SO_4(aq)} \longrightarrow \underset{\text{products}}{MgSO_4(aq) + H_2(g)}$$

Here, the solid metal (reactant) disappears as it dissolves, while bubbles of hydrogen gas form (product). So the 'end point' of the reaction can be when 'bubbles stop forming' as an alternative to 'when all the metal has gone'.

Metal (0.1 g)	Time to dissolve (s)
calcium	13
magnesium	24
zinc	90
iron	120

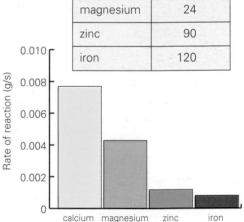

The rate at which 0.1 g samples of different metals dissolve in an excess of strong acid is calculated from the the table as a mass loss per second.

It is possible to measure the volume of the gas as it is produced. This is most simply done by connecting the apparatus to a gas syringe. As the gas is formed, it forces the barrel back against atmospheric pressure, giving a true volume for the given room temperature and pressure conditions.

Using this simple method you can find how long it takes to produce a particular volume of gas. You can then work out the rate of reaction in terms of cm³ of gas per second.

Alternatively, you can take readings every few seconds and plot a graph of the volume of hydrogen formed against the time. Graphs like this clearly show that the reaction slows down as it approaches the 'end point', as the reactants get 'used up'.

Changing mass?

If the gas is allowed to escape, the total mass of the reactants and other products would fall. You can follow this mass loss using a balance.

If you leave the equipment on a top-pan balance and take readings at regular time intervals, you can see how the rate changes with time, as with the gas syringe method.

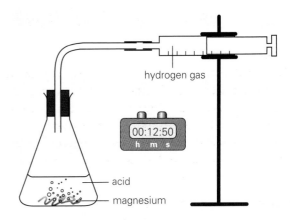

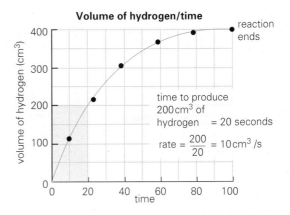

The information from the 'gas syringe' experiment can be analysed by plotting a graph.

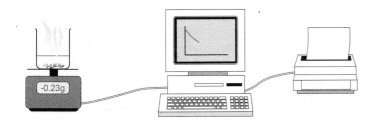

Data logging can do the 'number crunching' for you, but you will need to analyse the results!

QUESTIONS

1   Suggest a simple way to detect the end-point of the following reactions:
 a magnesium ribbon burning in air
 b sodium hydrogencarbonate and tartaric acid solutions reacting.

2   The reaction of zinc in hydrochloric acid was monitored continuously on a top-pan balance that was not 'zeroed' at the start. The following readings were taken:

time (s)	0	20	40	60	80
mass (g)	150.23	149.27	148.75	148.49	148.37

 a Plot a graph of mass *loss* against time.
 b Describe how the rate of reaction varies.
 c You could compare different metals by using the same mass. Is this a fair test? (See 11.6.)

3   The limestone/acid reaction was monitored using a gas syringe:

time(s)	0	30	60	90	120	150	180	210
vol(cm³)	0	45	84	115	140	150	155	158

 a Plot a volume/time graph.
 b Is the reaction near its end point?
 c How do you know?

13.2 *Speed it up*

What controls the rate of any given chemical reaction?

Surface area

Caster sugar dissolves faster than granulated sugar because it has a larger **surface area** (see 1.4). Solution can occur only at the surface of the solid, and this is also true for chemical reactions between solids and liquids. If you drop a large marble chip into acid it will fizz steadily – but add an equivalent amount in powdered form and it is likely to foam up out of the beaker.

All else being equal, you would expect the reaction rate to double if the surface area were doubled, and so on. Powdering a crystal may increase the surface area by a factor of many thousand, so it is not surprising that you see such a marked increase in the rate of reaction.

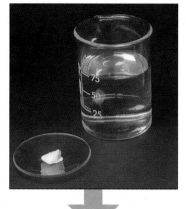

The same mass of marble – but a much faster reaction when powdered!

weak acid | medium acid | strong acid

Concentration

You can see the effect of concentration on rate of reaction very simply by dropping marble chips into beakers of acid of increasing strength. You should not be surprised to find that stronger acid gives a faster reaction. What is the explanation?

Before two particles can react, they must meet! If the acid is at low concentrations, the acid particles will be widely spread in the water, and the number of collisions between them and the marble chips will be limited. At higher concentrations, however, the chances of a collision between the acid particles and the marble chips are greatly increased.

Pressure

In reactions involving gases, the equivalent factor to this is pressure. All else being equal, the greater the pressure, the greater the number of particles in a given space and so the greater the chance of collision.

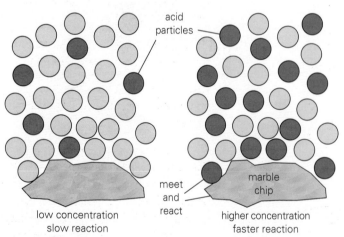

acid particles

meet and react

marble chip

low concentration slow reaction

higher concentration faster reaction

The greater the concentration, the faster the reaction.

Temperature effects

If you think a reaction is going too slowly in the school laboratory, the first thing you would probably do is heat it up. It is a common experience in chemistry that heating makes things happen faster. Meat cooks faster in a hotter oven, but you keep milk cool in the fridge to stop it going 'off'.

What might surprise you is just how *much* an increase in temperature affects the rate of reaction. The 'rule of thumb' for most reactions is that the **rate doubles for every 10°C** rise in temperature.

These bottles of milk are the same age. Which do you think was left in a warm room, and which was left in the fridge?

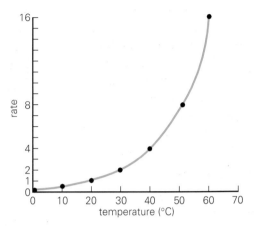

A typical rate/temperature graph
(Remember: rate = $\frac{1}{time}$)

What type of collision?

To understand why this happens, you need to think about what is going on at particle level. As you have seen, the reactant particles must collide, otherwise they cannot possibly 'change partners'. But that on its own is not enough – if it were, most chemical reactions would be almost instantaneous. They must also collide with enough energy to break the existing bonds.

The minimum collision energy required for any given reaction is called its **activation energy**. At any given temperature, collisions of many different types will occur, from the maximum energy 'head-on' to gentler glancing blows. But temperature will also have an effect, as the higher the temperature, the higher the average speed of the particles.

Clearly, the faster a particle is moving, the more kinetic energy it has and so the more chance it has of reaching the activation energy threshold in collision. If the temperature is raised, the average speed increases, so a larger proportion of the particles have a chance to react.

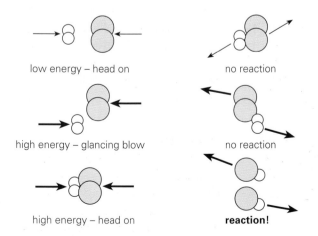

low energy – head on

no reaction

high energy – glancing blow

no reaction

high energy – head on

reaction!

You need the right kind of collision before you get a reaction.

QUESTIONS

1 Why is it that delicate carvings on churches seem to suffer more from the effects of acid rain than the large building blocks of the same stone?

2 Why do iron filings on a sparkler burn whilst the iron wire on which they are glued does not?

3 In 1970 flour dust caused an explosion in a biscuit factory. How could this happen?

4 Explain why reaction rate increases with concentration.

5 Why doesn't every collision between reactant particles cause a reaction?

6 Explain why it is that increasing the temperature has such a great effect on reaction rate.

7 Limestone buildings are made from calcium carbonate, and these slowly weather away due to the reaction with acid in the rain. What factors might control the rate of weathering? Design an experiment to test out your ideas.

13.3 *Case studies*

Marble chips in acid

Marble (or limestone) chips are a natural form of calcium carbonate.
If they are dropped into hydrochloric acid, they dissolve giving off carbon dioxide gas.

$$\underset{\text{reactants}}{CaCO_3 \ + \ 2HCl} \ \longrightarrow \ \underset{\text{products}}{CaCl_2 \ + \ H_2O \ + \ CO_2}$$

This reaction can be used to investigate the effects of surface area, concentration and temperature on the rates of reaction. It *can* be followed by simply timing how long it takes for the chips to dissolve. A more accurate method is to follow the production of carbon dioxide continuously, either directly with a gas syringe, or by the mass loss on a top-pan balance (see 13.1). To make this a fair test, of course, everything apart from the factor being investigated should remain exactly the same.

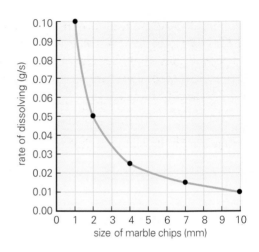

Reaction rate varies with chip size.

Surface area

You cannot get an absolute surface area figure for marble chips. But if you crush some marble chips and carefully sieve the product, you get three to five different grain sizes. If you weigh out equal masses of these (1 g for example) the surface area will increase from the largest pieces to the smallest. As a rule of thumb, for the same mass, if the average diameter doubles, the total surface area is halved.

Concentration

Using marble chips of a standard size, you could dissolve samples in an excess of acid of different concentrations. The simplest way to vary the concentration is to start with a set volume of strong 'bench' acid , and dilute this to larger and larger volumes using distilled water. You should find that the rate will halve if the total volume is doubled.

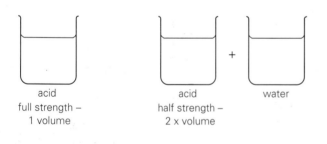

acid
full strength –
1 volume

+

acid
half strength –
2 x volume

water

Temperature

You can try a similar experiment using the same amounts of marble chips and acid. But this time you can heat the acid to different temperatures. You should get a curved graph, with the temperature doubling every 10°C or so (see 13.2).

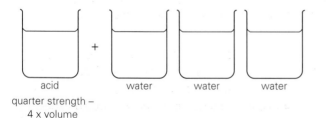

acid
quarter strength –
4 x volume

+

water

water

water

Diluting the acid – you would need about 50 cm³ of 1 mol dm⁻³ acid for 1 g of marble, to be sure you had more than enough to dissolve it.

The 'thiosulphate' reaction

If you mix a clear solution of sodium thiosulphate with hydrochloric acid, a reaction occurs and a creamy-yellow precipitate of sulphur (one of the products) is produced.

reactants   products

$$Na_2S_2O_3 + 2HCl \longrightarrow 2NaCl + SO_2 + S + H_2O$$

The sulphur does not start to form immediately, but begins to appear after a short time, turning the mixture cloudy. You cannot tell precisely when this reaction had stopped, but you could time how long it takes for a pencil-cross viewed through the liquid to 'disappear'.

This experiment can be used to investigate the effects of concentration and temperature on rate of reaction.

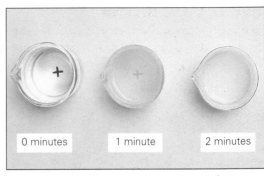

Going ... going ... gone! The thiosulphate/acid reaction turns the solution cloudy.

Concentration

You can use different dilutions of hydrochloric acid. You can mix these in turn with a fixed amount of sodium thiosulphate solution, and then record the time taken for the cross to disappear. (If you used $25\,cm^3$ of $1\,mol\,dm^{-3}$ thiosulphate solution, you would need to use $50\,cm^3$ of acid, diluted down as before.)

You could display the results in different ways, but if the total volume of acid is plotted against time taken, a clear relationship is shown.

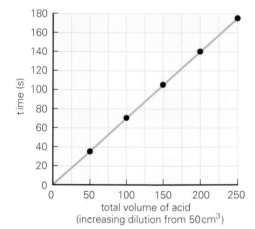

As the acid becomes more diluted, so the time taken by the reaction increases

Temperature

This experiment is also easy to follow at different temperatures. All you need to do is to heat the acid to a higher temperature each time before adding a fixed amount of thiosulphate solution. You can measure the reaction temperature with a thermometer once the reactants have been mixed and the stop-clock started.

This reaction should again show a clear relationship between the reaction rate and temperature. But this time the graph will look different, as time rather than rate is being plotted against temperature.

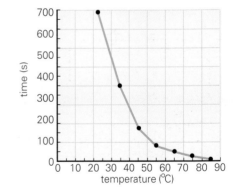

The time taken drops as the temperature increases.

QUESTIONS

1 A 2 cm cube can be broken up into 8 × 1 cm cubes.
 a What is the surface area of a 2 cm cube?
 b What is the total surface area of 8 × 1 cm cubes? Do these results agree with the 'rule of thumb' mentioned above?

2 If you had a 'mass loss over time' graph for the marble chips in acid experiment, how could you get the reaction rate from it? (See 13.1)
3a Sketch the shape of graph you would expect if you plotted reaction rate against temperature.
 b Compare this to the time against temperature graph for the thiosulphate/acid reaction. Explain the difference.

13.4 *Catalysts*

Hydrogen peroxide

Hydrogen peroxide is an unstable compound of hydrogen and oxygen. Left on its own, it will slowly break down into water and oxygen gas. This process is speeded up by light, so hydrogen peroxide is usually stored in brown glass bottles.

Hydrogen peroxide can be used to investigate the changes in rates of reaction brought about by concentration and temperature. The reactions can be followed by measuring the volume of oxygen produced with a gas syringe, or the mass loss with a balance, as before (see 13.1). As you might expect, the rate of reaction increases with concentration or temperature. But hydrogen peroxide may also be used to investigate a different way to increase reaction rates.

Hydrogen peroxide has to be stored in brown glass bottles to stop light speeding up its decay.

Everlasting activity!

If you drop a spatula of manganese dioxide into hydrogen peroxide, it starts to fizz rapidly as oxygen is given off. Nothing particularly surprising in that, you might think – just another chemical reaction in progress. But if you were to filter the mixture afterwards, you might be surprised to find that the residue was unaltered manganese dioxide. And, what is more, if you repeated the experiment with a known mass of manganese dioxide, you would find that none of this was lost during the reaction.

The reaction that occurs is the simple breakdown of hydrogen peroxide to water and oxygen, which would have occurred slowly on its own. The manganese dioxide has simply speeded up this reaction without itself being altered. It has acted as a catalyst in a process called **catalysis**.

$$2H_2O_2 \quad \xrightarrow{\text{MnO}_2 \text{ catalyst}} \quad 2H_2O \ + \ O_2$$

In fact, many other metals or metal oxides will speed up this particular reaction. But they must be finely powdered, as catalysts work best when they have as large a surface area as possible.

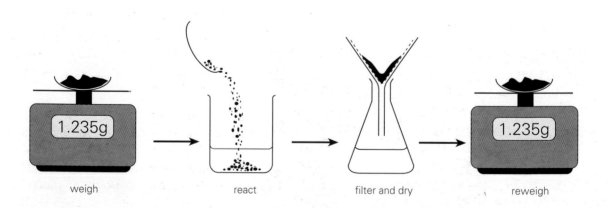

weigh   react   filter and dry   reweigh

Manganese dioxide speeds up the breakdown of hydrogen peroxide, but remains unchanged itself.

What do they do?

Catalysts are very important in industry, as they allow reactions to take place more efficiently and at lower temperatures. This, of course, saves money! Transition metals or their oxides are often used as catalysts – iron is used to make ammonia in the Haber process, while vanadium oxide is used to make sulphuric acid.

Catalysts appear to lower the activation energy needed for the reaction. Most reactions need this kick-start of energy to get them going, as existing bonds need to be broken before new ones can form. This is the activation energy hump (see 14.2). The larger this hump, the more difficult it is to get a reaction to progress. Catalysts help to flatten the hump!

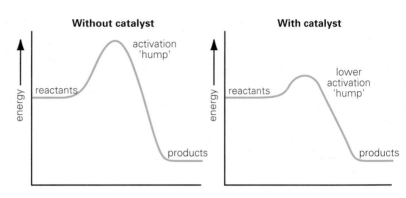

Catalysts lower the activation energy needed to get the reaction going.

Catalyst problems

Although catalysts are not used up in the main reaction, they may become involved in reactions with impurities. This interferes with the catalytic process and so catalysts can slowly lose their effectiveness. If this happens, the catalyst is said to have been poisoned, and it must be replaced.

In order to reduce pollution from car exhausts, modern cars are often fitted with catalytic converters (see 8.6). Car exhaust gases contain carbon and nitrogen monoxides, both of which help to form city smog. But if these are passed over a suitable catalyst, they combine to form carbon dioxide and nitrogen.

$$2CO + 2NO \xrightarrow{\text{catalyst}} 2CO_2 + N_2$$

Unfortunately, 'old-style' petrol contains lead compounds, which come out in the exhaust. These pollute the environment, but they also poison the catalyst and stop it working. So cars fitted with catalytic converters must use unleaded fuel only.

This is a good thing, as it reduces pollution even further. But if the petrol tank is ever accidentally filled with leaded petrol, the catalytic converter would be permanently poisoned, which would be a very expensive mistake!

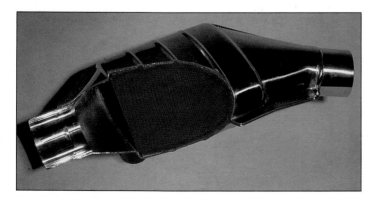

Catalytic converters reduce pollution ... as long as they have not been poisoned.

QUESTIONS

1 Chemicals such as magnesium destroy hydrogen peroxide by themselves reacting with the 'extra' oxygen. How is this different from catalysis?

2 Describe in simple terms **a** what catalysts do and **b** how they are able to do it.

3 The effect of catalysis depends in part on how finely divided the catalyst is. How does this suggest that catalysis occurs on the surface of the catalyst?

4 Copper(II) oxide also causes the breakdown of hydrogen peroxide, with the liberation of oxygen. Design an experiment to see whether or not this is a catalytic reaction. How could your experiment be adapted to compare the effectiveness of copper(II) oxide and managnese dioxide as catalysts?

13.5 *Biological catalysts*

Enzymes

If you added a drop of blood or some chopped liver to hydrogen peroxide the effect is even more dramatic than adding manganese dioxide. This is because of the presence of an organic, protein-based catalyst called catalase. These organic catalysts are called **enzymes**, and their action can be very powerful. Most life processes, such as digestion and respiration, depend on the enzyme action which goes on in living cells.

Enzymes appear to work by having molecules which fit jigsaw-fashion with the reacting chemicals. Because organic molecules such as proteins and sugars have such complex shapes, any given enzyme will lock onto only one particular reactant: it is specific in its effect. This makes it possible to have many different enzymes in action at the same time, each targeting and controlling its own reaction, without upsetting the others. You could not exist without this ability, for each cell in your body uses hundreds of different enzymes.

Chopped liver catalysis in action!

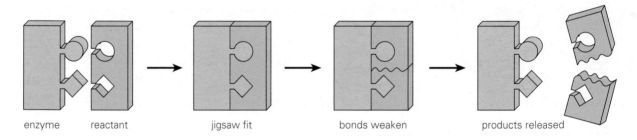

enzyme   reactant   jigsaw fit   bonds weaken   products released

Each enzyme fits just one reactant, like jigsaw pieces, so many enzymes can work independently.

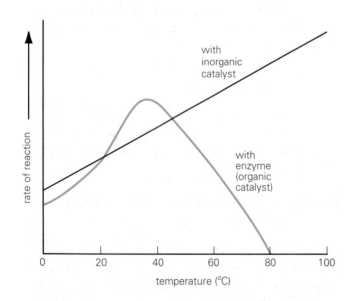

Enzyme action peaks at 37°C – that's body temperature!

So what's different?

From 0°C up to about 40°C, enzymes act like inorganic catalysts in that reaction rates double with every 10°C rise. However, above this temperature the reaction starts to tail off and, by about 80°C, stops altogether.

This is because enzymes are proteins and proteins break down (become cooked!) at these higher temperatures. It should not surprise you that the best temperature for enzyme action corresponds closely to your body temperature. This is called the **optimum temperature**.

Enzymes may also be put to good use in industry. They have been used for centuries to make cheese and yogurt, bread, wine and beer. Nowadays protein destroying enzymes are used in biological washing powders, whilst others are used to predigest baby food!

Fermentation

Sugars are energy foods – body fuels. You react glucose with the oxygen you breathe to make carbon dioxide, water and the energy you need for life. But some organisms such as **yeast** (a simple fungus) are able to use their special enzymes to get energy from sugars without oxygen, by the process of **fermentation**. If living yeast cells are put into a sugary solution and this is kept at about 37°C, they start to grow and divide rapidly, turning the sugar into **alcohol** and producing lots of carbon dioxide.

$$\text{sugar} \xrightarrow[\text{yeast enzymes}]{\text{fermentation}} \text{alcohol} + \text{carbon dioxide}$$

This process has been used for centuries. Sometimes it is the alcohol that is of interest, making drinks such as beer and wine. But if the yeast is mixed with flour dough, the carbon dioxide gets trapped as tiny bubbles, making the dough 'rise'. This makes light-textured bread when it is baked.

Fermentation has been used for centuries to make wine, beer and bread.

Cheese and yogurt

Some bacteria get their energy in a similar way from the sugar in milk (lactose), producing lactic acid rather than alcohol. This makes the milk curdle to form cheese or yogurt. You can buy some yogurts still with the live bacteria in them. If you want to make your own yogurt, all you need to do is mix a little of this 'live' yogurt into some milk and leave it in a warm place. The bacteria will grow best at around 37°C, and their enzymes will get to work on the milk – providing the bacteria with food and energy and you with an endless supply of yogurt.

Some people love a bowl of bacteria for breakfast every day!

Stopping enzymes working

Below about 40°C, enzymes behave in a similar way to inorganic catalysts. So if you cool living things down, their enzyme action becomes less and less effective, and they eventually die. Bacteria are not quite so drastically affected, but their life processes slow down as the chemical reaction rate slows – halving every 10°C fall in temperature. Bacteria cause decay as they use enzymes to break down the food. Chilling slows this down, and so slows their breeding rate. This is why food keeps much longer in the fridge.

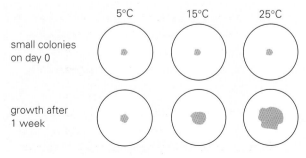

Bacteria cultured on agar grow at a much slower rate if kept chilled.

QUESTIONS

1a In what ways are enzymes similar to inorganic catalysts? In what ways are they different?

  b Why is it that enzyme action drops away so rapidly above 40°C?

2 Suggest a reason why your body temperature is maintained at 37°C.

3 Why do think that industry is so interested in the action of enzymes (what advantages might there be in running reactions at lower temperatures)?

4 Describe the two main uses of fermentation.

5 Why should milk be kept at 37°C to make home-made yogurt?

6 Fresh milk will last eight days in the fridge (5°C).
  a Approximately how long would you expect it to last at room temperature (25°C)?
  b How long would it last on a hot summer's day?

13.6 Organic vs inorganic catalysts

What is alcohol?

The term alcohol is usually used to describe **ethanol** (ethyl alcohol), which is the 'active' ingredient in wines, beers and spirits. **Absolute** (100%) **alcohol** is used in industry in vast quantities as an industrial solvent for varnishes, inks, paints and glues. It is particularly useful as it is miscible (see 2.5) with both oils and water. It also evaporates quickly, and so is used in perfumes and after-shave colognes.

For home use, it is mixed with water (10%) and poisonous methanol (5%) to stop people drinking it. This **methylated spirit** is often dyed mauve and given a bitter taste, to make doubly sure that people do not drink it. In the form of **surgical spirit**, it is used as an antiseptic for cleansing and hardening the skin.

It is made by two different methods, one of which has been used for thousands of years, while the other is a modern industrial process.

Alcohol has a wide range of uses.

The brewery versus the refinery?

Fermentation ...

As you have seen (13.5), yeast can break sugars down into alcohol and carbon dioxide. This process is used to make beer and wine. But fermentation can only produce a weak solution of alcohol in water (up to 6% for beer, 12% for wine). Fractional distillation (see 2.5) is needed to concentrate it further. Spirits such as whiskey or vodka may be up to 40% alcohol. Further distillation can lead to the production of 96% alcohol, which is far too strong for human consumption, but is needed for industrial solvents.

... or the hydrolysis of ethene

Ethene is produced in bulk during catalytic cracking (see 7.5). Much of this is then made to undergo an addition reaction with water (by passing it with steam over a phosphoric acid catalyst at 300°C) to make ethanol. This process of 'adding water' to the molecule is called **hydrolysis**. Vast quantities of ethanol are produced for industry in this way.

$$\text{ethene} + \text{steam} \xrightarrow[\text{catalyst at 300°C}]{\text{phosphoric acid}} \text{ethanol}$$

$$C_2H_4 + H_2O \longrightarrow C_2H_5OH$$

Which method is best?

	Fermentation	Hydrolysis of ethene
Type of process	This is a **batch process**: fixed amounts of sugary solution (grape juice for wine, malted barley mash for beer) are fermented at a time. The weak solution of alcohol must then be distilled.	This is a **continuous process**. Ethene and steam may be fed constantly over the heated catalyst, and the product condensed and piped out.
Speed of production	Fermentation is a slow process: beers or wines may take weeks to ferment, while even mashes produced specifically for distillation take days.	Catalytic hydrolysis is a very rapid chemical reaction – conversion takes place as fast as the reactants can be pumped through the system.
Quantity of product	This is limited by the size and number of fermentation vats.	Within the context of a large refinery complex, the amount of alcohol produced can be tailored to meet demand.
Quality of product	The percentage concentration of alcohol may be low, but the emphasis here is usually on the impurities – and the flavour they impart!	Absolute alcohol may be produced with ease – impurities are usually added later to stop people drinking it!
Nature of the raw material	Sugar (or starch) is produced as a result of photosynthesis by plants. It is therefore a renewable resource.	Ethene is produced from fossil fuels. These are currently available in bulk, but are finite and will soon be completely used up.
Cost	The use of batch processing and the long timescale makes this relatively expensive.	The continuous processing and current low price of oil make this relatively cheap.

For the future?

Ethanol burns in air with a clean flame and has a boiling point within the range of petrol hydrocarbons. With a little adjustment, ordinary petrol engines may be made to run on it. Brazil is a country with little crude oil of its own and is unable to support high import levels. It does, however, have a large land area, where sugar cane grows well. The Brazilian government therefore decided to increase sugar production, ferment the excess and distil it to produce ethanol as an alternative fuel for transport. This is now well underway, and the aim is to halve the imports of crude oil by the year 2000.

Filling up with alcohol in Brazil.

QUESTIONS

1 Explain how ethanol is made by 'adding water' to ethene.

2 Why is industrial alcohol commonly mixed with an unpleasant tasting poison, before being sold as 'methylated spirits'?

3 Ethanol for drinking is produced by fermentation, while most industrial ethanol is produced from ethene. Explain the advantages and disadvantages of the chosen method in each case.

14.1 *Energy changes*

Give it out

It is not always easy to tell when a chemical reaction has occurred. For example, if you mix cold, dilute hydrochloric acid and sodium hydroxide solutions, you will not *see* any obvious change. Two colourless liquids just mix to form another colourless liquid. But if you hold the tube you will *feel* that something has happened – it will have got warmer.

Chemical changes are often accompanied by changes in temperature. In this case, **energy** has been given out in the form of heat during neutralisation. Chemical reactions that give out heat energy like this are called **exothermic** reactions.

$$\text{acid} + \text{alkali} \longrightarrow \text{salt} + \text{water} + \boxed{\text{energy}}$$

$$\text{e.g. HCl} + \text{NaOH} \longrightarrow \text{NaCl} + \text{H}_2\text{O} + \boxed{\text{energy}}$$

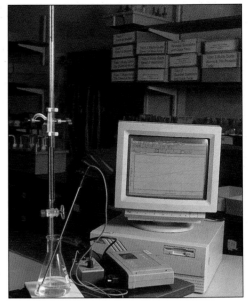

You could follow the rise in temperature during neutralisation with a temperature sensor connected to a computer.

Going on their own

Many chemical reactions are exothermic – particularly those that start reacting as soon as the reactants are mixed. For example:

● Metals **displacing** other metals from their salts:

$$\text{e.g. } \begin{array}{c}\text{zinc}\\\text{metal}\end{array} + \begin{array}{c}\text{copper}\\\text{sulphate}\end{array} \longrightarrow \begin{array}{c}\text{zinc}\\\text{sulphate}\end{array} + \begin{array}{c}\text{copper}\\\text{metal}\end{array} + \boxed{\text{energy}}$$

$$\text{Zn} + \text{CuSO}_4 \longrightarrow \text{ZnSO}_4 + \text{Cu} + \boxed{\text{energy}}$$

● Metals **corroding**:

$$\text{e.g. calcium} + \text{oxygen} \longrightarrow \text{calcium oxide} + \boxed{\text{energy}}$$

$$2\text{Ca} + \text{O}_2 \longrightarrow 2\text{CaO} + \boxed{\text{energy}}$$

● Metals **dissolving** in acids:

$$\text{metal} + \text{acid} \longrightarrow \text{salt} + \text{hydrogen} + \boxed{\text{energy}}$$

$$\text{e.g. Mg} + \text{H}_2\text{SO}_4 \longrightarrow \text{MgSO}_4 + \text{H}_2 + \boxed{\text{energy}}$$

Fresh calcium turnings soon corrode if exposed to air.

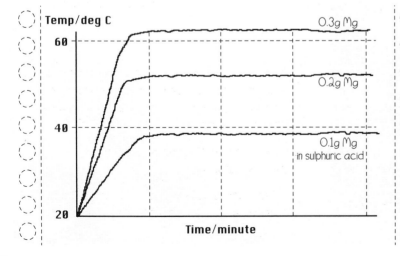

These data-logging graphs show that the more metal you add, the bigger the temperature rise (as long as you have excess acid).

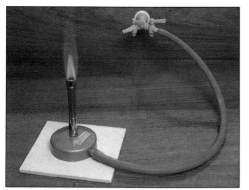

Fuels need a kick-start to burn, but their combustion reactions are strongly exothermic.

Kick-starts

Iron corrodes more slowly than calcium – it rusts – but this is still an exothermic reaction. If you heat small pieces of iron however, they oxidise rapidly, giving out so much heat that they glow white hot. So you may need to give sparklers a 'kick-start' of energy, but once the reaction is going it provides plenty more of its own. Fuels also need a kick-start like this but, once alight, the combustion reaction is very exothermic. In fact, for fuels, you are not usually bothered about the chemical products of the reaction, it is the heat energy output that you're after.

fuel + oxygen $\longrightarrow$ waste gases + energy

e.g. CH_4 + $2O_2$ $\longrightarrow$ CO_2 + $2H_2O$ + energy

Take it in

If you mix solutions of sodium hydrogencarbonate (sodium bicarbonate) and citric acid you will see a few bubbles produced as carbon dioxide is formed. But you will also feel a drop in temperature. This reaction has taken energy in as it occurred, cooling the surroundings in the process.

sodium hydrogen-carbonate + citric acid + energy $\longrightarrow$ sodium citrate + carbon dioxide + water

No ice needed for this cold drink!

Reactions like this are **endothermic**. It is fairly rare for endothermic reactions to 'go on their own' like this. You usually need to pump energy into them to make them work. For example, the production of aluminium by electrolysis is an endothermic reaction:

aluminium oxide + electrical energy $\longrightarrow$ aluminium + oxygen

One of the most important endothermic reactions of all is photosynthesis (see 7.1). Plants use the energy from sunlight to build complex chemicals such as glucose from carbon dioxide and water:

carbon dioxide + water + sunlight energy $\longrightarrow$ glucose + oxygen

$6CO_2$ + $6H_2O$ $\longrightarrow$ $C_6H_{12}O_6$ + $6O_2$

The sun drives this important endothermic reaction.

QUESTIONS

1 Apart from the temperature rise, how else could you tell that there has been a chemical reaction when hydrochloric acid and sodium hydroxide are mixed?

2a From the 'data-log' graph, work out the maximum temperature rise when the different amounts of magnesium were dissolved in acid.
 b Plot a graph of mass against temperature rise. Is there a relationship?

3 Most endothermic reactions need to have energy actively put in to make them work. What is unusual about the sodium hydrogencarbonate/ citric acid reaction?

4a What provides the energy input for photosynthesis?

 b Respiration is the reverse of photosynthesis. Is it an exothermic or an endothermic reaction?

14.2 *Making and breaking bonds*

Breaking bonds ...

The water molecules in ice are held together by interparticle force bonds. In order to break these bonds, you have to put in heat energy. If you heat ice to melt it, the temperature stays constant while it is melting, as all the energy goes into breaking the force bonds (see 1.2).

Similarly, energy is needed to break the chemical bonds *within* a molecule. For example, you have to put electrical energy in to tear water apart by electrolysis.

Both these processes are endothermic. You are putting energy into the system to make the change.

... and making bonds

When water freezes, the interparticle bonds are being remade. When this happens, you get back again the same amount of energy that was needed to break the bonds for melting. Energy is *lost* to the surroundings without a drop in temperature (see 1.2).

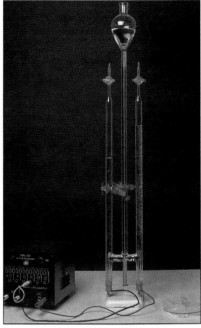

You need to break bonds to melt ice or electrolyse water – so both are endothermic.

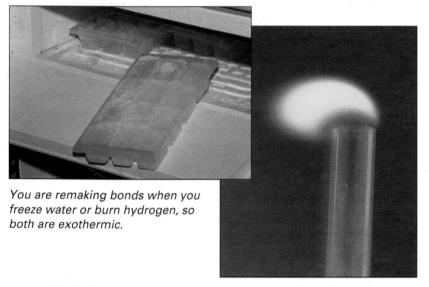

You are remaking bonds when you freeze water or burn hydrogen, so both are exothermic.

Similarly, when hydrogen and oxygen combine chemically, energy is given out as the chemical bonds *within* the water molecule snap back together. You get the same amount of energy out as you put in to break the bonds in the first place.

Both these processes are therefore exothermic. You get energy out of the system as the change is made.

Endothermic/exothermic

So whenever bonds (of whatever type) are broken, it is an endothermic process, and whenever bonds are formed it is exothermic. But in most chemical reactions, some bonds have to be broken before the new bonds can be made. For example, when hydrogen and oxygen molecules react, the bonds within the molecules must break before the oxygen–hydrogen bonds can be formed. This is why many reactions need a 'kick-start' of energy, to break a few bonds and so get the reaction started. Once going, exothermic reactions provide enough energy of their own to keep the reaction going.

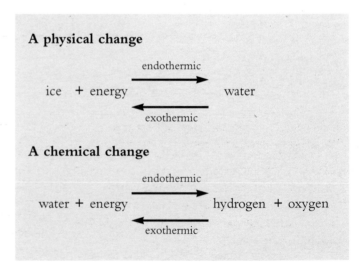

A physical change

ice + energy ⟶ (endothermic) ⟶ water

water ⟵ (exothermic) ⟵

A chemical change

water + energy ⟶ (endothermic) ⟶ hydrogen + oxygen

hydrogen + oxygen ⟵ (exothermic) ⟵

Energy profiles

So hydrogen and oxygen molecules need a kick start of energy to break the existing bonds before they will combine to form water in an exothermic reaction. To understand this, consider a boulder lying in a hollow on a hillside. The boulder has stored, gravitational **potential energy** – if it were on a simple slope it would roll to the bottom of the valley, changing its stored energy to kinetic energy as it fell. Because it is in a hollow, however, work must first be done on it (more energy must be put in) in order to push it up and over the lip of the hollow. It would only then be free too move and, once it came to a halt, the excess energy would be converted to heat.

Boulder on a hillside

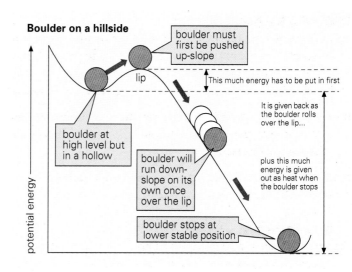

Similarly, molecules of hydrogen and oxygen contain stored **chemical energy**. As elements, they have higher energy levels overall than water molecules. Given the chance, the reaction would 'roll down' the energy slope, giving out its energy as the new bonds formed. But first it needs a 'kick' of energy to break the bonds and push it up over the energy lip. The energy needed to do this is called the **activation energy**.

Hydrogen reacting with oxygen

In endothermic reactions, of course, the energy profile is reversed and it is an uphill push all the way from reactants to product. The change in energy level is often shown by the symbol *delta H* (ΔH).

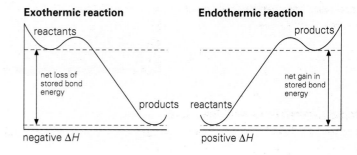

QUESTIONS

1 In what way is:
a melting ice similar to electrolysing water
b freezing water similar to burning hydrogen?

2a Explain why most chemical reactions have both an endothermic and an exothermic part.
b If a reaction is exothermic overall, what does it tell you about the bonds that have been broken and remade?

3 Why are exothermic reactions easier to achieve than endothermic ones?

4 What provides the activation energy for an exothermic reaction once it has started?

5a Use the 'boulder on a slope' model to explain the process of photosynthesis.
b Is ΔH positive or negative for this reaction?

14.3 *How much energy?*

Measuring heat output

It is not possible to measure the amount of heat energy produced directly. The standard method is to look at the effect that energy has on the temperature of a known volume of water. It takes 420 J to raise 100 cm³ (100 g) of water through 1°C.

So, for example, you could compare the energy output from different fuels by using them to heat a beaker containing 100 cm³ of water, and measuring the temperature change. If you weighed the burner before and after the experiment, you could then calculate the energy output per gram of each type of fuel.

Of course, you would have to take care to ensure that all the heat energy goes into the water, and that energy losses are minimised by insulation! Even so, the values obtained in the school laboratory are always rather low compared to those from more sophisticated experiments. The *relative* energy outputs for different fuels can be seen, however.

Example: burner mass:

before	253.75 g
after	252.25 g
fuel used	1.5 g

water temperature:

after	60°C
before	27°C
change	33°C

energy input $= 33 \times 420 = 13.86\,\text{kJ}$
energy/gram of fuel $= 13.86/1.5 = $ **9.24 kJ**

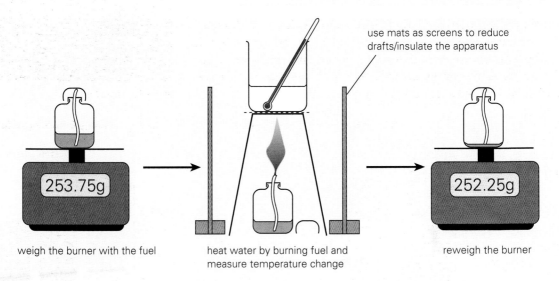

use mats as screens to reduce drafts/insulate the apparatus

weigh the burner with the fuel | heat water by burning fuel and measure temperature change | reweigh the burner

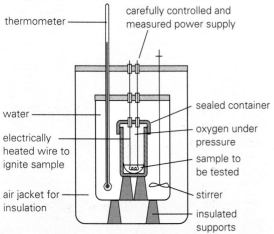

thermometer — carefully controlled and measured power supply

water

electrically heated wire to ignite sample

air jacket for insulation

sealed container

oxygen under pressure

sample to be tested

stirrer

insulated supports

Simple school laboratory apparatus

More sophisticated apparatus for the accurate determination of energy output from fuels

Fuel	Formula	Rise in temp. (°C)	Calculated energy input (kJ/g)	(Accepted value kJ/g for fuel)
ethanol	(C_2H_5OH)	22	9.24	(30)
propanol	(C_3H_7OH)	26	10.92	(33.5)
butanol	(C_4H_9OH)	28	11.76	(36)
pentanol	$(C_5H_{11}OH)$	29	12.81	(38)

Typical school laboratory results for the heating effect of 1g of different fuels on 100g of water

Value for money?

This kind of information is very important in industry, as different fuels are sold in different ways which are often difficult to compare. Energy costs affect profitability, so you need to know exactly what you are getting from your fuel. It is also a useful comparison for household users – which would be cheaper, gas or coal powered central heating?

Fuel	How bought	MJ equivalent	MJ per £
coal	£140 per tonne	30000 MJ/tonne	215
fuel oil	14p per litre (dm^3)	36.4 MJ/litre	260
gas	15p per m^3 (1.4p per kWh)	38.9 MJ/m^3 (3.6 MJ/kWh)	257 (257)
electricity	7p per kWh	3.6 MJ/kWh	51

Comparative costs of domestic fuels (1995 prices for household use)

Energy from food

Energy calculations have also been done for the energy content of foods, and most food labels now contain such information.

As the energy requirements for the chemistry of life have also been established, it is possible to match the energy content of the food you eat to your daily energy needs. This does, of course, depend in part on how active you are.

Your main energy foods are carbohydrates and fats (or oils), though proteins may also be used in this way, as well as for growth and repair. The carbon and hydrogen in these compounds react with the oxygen you breathe to form carbon dioxide and water. This process of respiration is the same chemical process as combustion.

NUTRITION INFORMATION		
Typical values	Amount per 100g	Amount per serving (210g)
Energy	312kJ/75kcal	655kJ/158kcal
Protein	4.7g	9.9g
Carbohydrate	13.6g	28.6g
(of which sugars)	(6.0g)	(12.6g)
Fat	0.2g	0.4g
(of which saturates)	(Trace)	(0.1g)
Fibre	3.7g	7.8g
Sodium	0.5g	1.0g

A typical food label

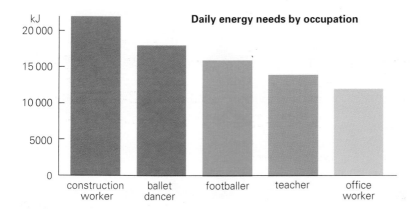

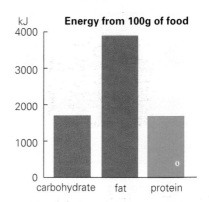

QUESTIONS

1a List as many reasons as you can think of why the 'school laboratory' experiment to find the energy output from fuels gives such low results compared to the accepted figures.
b Try to explain how the 'sophisticated' version overcomes these problems.

2a Which fuel is currently best value for money in simple energy terms?

b Would this be obvious from the ways in which costs are usually shown on fuel bills?
c Why is electricity so much more expensive?

3 Much of the energy in the food you eat goes towards keeping you body temperature at 37°C. If you had to spend a long time out in the cold, why might eating greasy chips be good for you?

4 Why do footballers need more energy than office workers?

14.4 *Energy by the mole*

Standard heats of reaction

In 14.3 the heat energy of different fuels was compared by gram. Sometimes it is more useful to compare the heat output in terms of moles. In a neutralisation reaction, the heat energy given out by the production of 1 mole of salt could be found by mixing appropriate quantities of acid and alkali in an insulated beaker.

If you compare the standard **heats of reaction** for several acid/alkali neutralisations, you will see that the figures are virtually identical. This is because the fundamental reaction is the same in each case:

$$H^+ \ + \ OH^- \ \longrightarrow \ H_2O \ + \ \boxed{energy}$$

The values in the table show the energy given out by the formation of 1 mole of water from the ions.

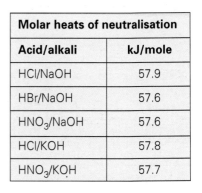

Molar heats of neutralisation	
Acid/alkali	kJ/mole
HCl/NaOH	57.9
HBr/NaOH	57.6
HNO_3/NaOH	57.6
HCl/KOH	57.8
HNO_3/KOH	57.7

Fuel by the mole

The **heat of combustion** of fuels may also be compared by the mole. For hydrocarbons, there appears to be a clear link between this figure and the number of C–H bonds present in the molecule. This should come as no surprise as, if you go back to the energy profile diagrams in 14.2, you will see that the heat of reaction depends in part on how much energy is needed to break the existing bonds.

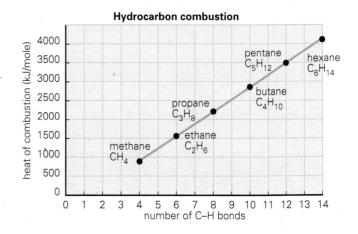

Hydrocarbon combustion

Breaking and making bonds

The difference between the energy needed to break existing bonds and that required to make new ones is often shown by the symbol ΔH. Exothermic reactions may need a kick-start of energy to get them going, but overall they give out more energy than they use. This energy is lost to the surroundings, so we say that there is a net loss of stored bond energy. This is shown as negative ΔH. So for burning carbon:

$$C \ + \ O_2 \ \longrightarrow \ CO_2 \qquad -\Delta H \ (-393 \text{kJ/mole})$$

For endothermic reactions, there is a net gain of stored bond energy, so ΔH is positive. So for photosynthesis:

$$6CO_2 \ + \ 6H_2O \ \longrightarrow \ C_6H_{12}O_6 \ + \ 6O_2 \qquad +\Delta H \ (+2802 \text{ kJ/mole})$$

Energy by the bond

By studying a range of reactions, the energy needed to make or break any bond has been established. You can use these **bond energies** to predict whether any given reaction will be endothermic or exothermic. It is worth noting that a 'bond' can mean a range of things here, from covalent or ionic bonding, through to the weak forces between covalent molecules.

The same ideas may also be applied to physical as well as chemical reactions. Melting and boiling are both endothermic processes, as energy must be put in to break the interparticle forces. The relatively high figures for water (mp 0°C, bp 100°C) reflect the high energy needed to overcome the unusually strong forces between water molecules.

Selected bond energies (kJ/mole)			
H—H	436	O=O	496
C—C	348	C=C	612
N≡N	944	C=O	743
H—C	412	H—O	463
Cl—Cl	242	Br—Br	193
H—Cl	431	H—Br	366

Remember – energy *in* to break a bond, energy *out* when a bond is made.

Example 1: Burning hydrogen in air to form water

<table>
<tr><td></td><td>reactants</td><td>products</td><td></td></tr>
<tr><td></td><td>$2H_2 + O_2$</td><td>$\longrightarrow$ $2H_2O$</td><td>ΔH</td></tr>
</table>

energy **in** to break bonds in reactants	energy **out** as bonds are made in products	net energy change
$2 \times (H–H) + (O=O)$	$4 \times (O–H)$	
$= 2 \times (436) + 496$	$= 4 \times (463)$	1368 kJ in
$= 1368$ kJ	$= 1852$ kJ	1852 kJ out

the reaction is exothermic: $\Delta H = -484$ kJ
         (-242 kJ/mole H_2O)

Example 2: Why does the energy per mole rise steadily with the alkanes?

Each alkane in sequence has an extra CH_2 plus an extra C–C bond; so, as a part-equation for the 'extra' bit:

$$CH_2 + 1\tfrac{1}{2}[O_2] \longrightarrow CO_2 + H_2O \qquad \Delta H$$

energy **in** to break bonds in reactants	energy **out** as bonds are made in products	net energy change
$1 \times (C–C) + 2 \times (C–H) + 1\tfrac{1}{2}(O=O)$	$2 \times (C=O) + 2 \times (OH)$	
$= 348 + 824 + 744$	$= 1486 + 926$	1916 kJ in
$= 1916$ kJ	$= 2412$ kJ	2412 kJ out

the reaction is exothermic: $\Delta H = -496$ kJ
         (per CH_2 group
           per mole)

QUESTIONS

1 In an experiment, 200 cm³ of 1 mol dm⁻³ nitric acid were used to neutralise 200 cm³ of 1 mol dm⁻³ sodium hydroxide. The temperature rose by 6°C. It takes 420 J to raise 100 cm³ of water or dilute acid through 1°C.

a Calculate the total amount of heat energy generated by this reaction.

b Calculate what it would have been if 1 dm³ of each of the same acid and alkali were used.

2a If you were buying fuel, which value do you think would be of more use to you, energy per gram or energy per mole? Why?

b Use the graph to work out approximate energy/gram figures for methane, butane and hexane. (You will need to work out their formula masses.)

3a Calculate and compare the ΔH values for:
   i $H_2 + Cl_2 \longrightarrow 2HCl$
   ii $H_2 + Br_2 \longrightarrow 2HBr$
Are the reactions endothermic or exothermic?

b Calculate the ΔH for the following combustion reactions:
   i $C_2H_6 + 3\tfrac{1}{2}O_2 \longrightarrow 2CO_2 + 3H_2O$
   ii $C_2H_4 + 3O_2 \longrightarrow 2CO_2 + 2H_2O$
Which fuel (ethane or ethene) gives more energy per gram?

4 Suggest a reason why nitrogen in the atmosphere appears to be so unreactive.

15.1 *Reactions in balance*

There and back again

So far you have looked at chemical reactions as one way processes:

reactants   ⟶   products

This is indeed the case in many instances. For example, if you burn wood you cannot easily get the wood and oxygen back from the carbon dioxide and water produced.

But you are also familiar with many reversible processes. Water turns to ice if cooled, but melts back to water when heated. This physical reversibility is mirrored by some chemical reactions, too. The test for water is an example:

anhydrous
copper sulphate + water
(white)   ⇄   hydrated
copper sulphate
(blue)

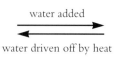

water added
water driven off by heat

Most chemical reactions are 'one-way' ...

... but some are reversible.

Heat it/cool it

If you heat ammonium chloride, it turns directly from a solid to a gas (it **sublimes**), only to reappear as a white solid at the cool end of the tube. But in this case it is not a simple physical change. Instead, it is another reversible chemical change:

ammonium chloride ⇄ hydrogen + ammonia chloride

heat / cool

$NH_4Cl(s) \rightleftharpoons HCl(g) + NH_3(g)$

Likewise, calcium carbonate breaks down to calcium oxide and carbon dioxide when heated, but these chemicals slowly recombine when cold (in a similar reaction to the way mortar sets):

calcium carbonate ⇄ calcium oxide + carbon dioxide

heat / cool

$CaCO_3 \rightleftharpoons CaO + CO_2$

The link with these two examples is temperature. Heating drives the reaction to the right, but the reaction reverses as it cools down.

Ammonium chloride breaks up when heated, only to reform at the cool end of the tube.

Open and closed systems

You can think of reversible reactions in terms of the **forward reaction** and the **back reaction**.

$$A + B \xrightleftharpoons[\text{back reaction}]{\text{forward reaction}} C + D$$

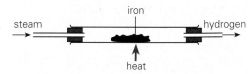

steam passed over hot iron – iron oxide forms
if hydrogen is removed

The reaction direction is often controlled by temperature, as in the examples above, but other factors can come into play.

If you pass steam over heated iron, the iron is oxidised to iron oxide and the steam is reduced. This is the forward reaction. But if the hydrogen produced is now pushed back over the hot iron oxide, the reaction is reversed and the oxide is reduced. This is the back reaction.

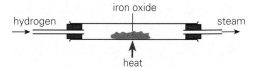

hydrogen passed over iron oxide – iron is
reformed if the steam is removed

$$\text{iron} + \text{steam} \xrightleftharpoons[\text{back reaction}]{\text{forward reaction}} \text{iron oxide} + \text{hydrogen}$$

This experiment works (it reaches one end point or the other) only because one of the products is removed from the reaction site each time: it is an **open system**. But if iron and steam were to be heated in a **closed system** (such as in a sealed, pressure-proof container), the reaction would stick part-way, with all four molecules present. It would reach **equilibrium** (shown in equations by the symbol ⇌):

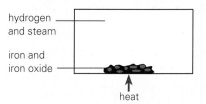

all four particles exist in a closed system

$$3Fe + 4H_2O \rightleftharpoons Fe_3O_4 + 4H_2$$

Dynamic equilibrium on the escalators.

Dynamic equilibrium

You might think that at equilibrium the reaction has stopped, but that is not the case. Some iron and steam particles are still reacting to give iron oxide and hydrogen, but they are compensated for by other iron oxide and hydrogen particles reacting to give iron and steam again.

This is called **dynamic equilibrium**. It might help you to understand it if you think about the escalators in a large shop. If the rate at which people go up is the same as the rate that people go down, the number of people on each floor will remain the same!

QUESTIONS

1a Describe the sublimation of ammonium chloride in terms of the forward and back reactions.

 b What factor controls the direction in which this reaction moves?

2 Iron and steam react to reach equilibrium in a closed container. Explain how the reaction may be made to move to completion, first one way and then the other, by opening the container and changing the experimental conditions.

3 Write your own explanation of dynamic equilibrium using a different analogy (such as cars on a motorway, for example).

15.2 *Shifting the balance*

Finding the balance point

If you mix equal volumes of hydrogen and iodine gases at a temperature of 400°C or so, they slowly react to give hydrogen iodide gas. The reaction stops, however, when about 80% of the possible product has formed. This balance point does not change, however long the reaction is left.

Again, the position is not static – it is simply that, at equilibrium, the number of hydrogen and iodine molecules combining to form hydrogen iodide is balanced out by the number of hydrogen iodide molecules breaking down, in a dynamic equilibrium. To understand this, you need to think about the concentrations of the particles, for reaction rate is dependant (in part) on concentration (see 13.2).

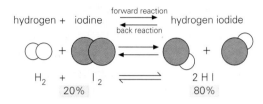

Equilibrium is reached at 400°C.

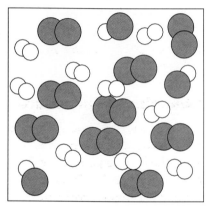

Initially, the concentration of reactant particles is high, whilst that of the product particles is low, so the forward reaction runs faster.

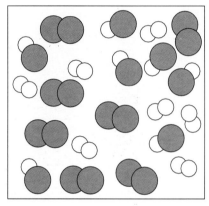

As the reaction progresses, however, the reactant concentration falls as the product concentration rises.

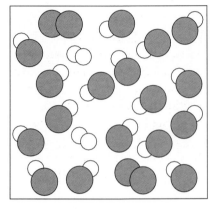

When the rates of the forward and backward reactions become equal and opposite, dynamic equilibrium is reached and the reaction appears to stop.

It is interesting to note that the same balance point is reached if the reaction is run in reverse (that is, starting with pure hydrogen iodide). Also, although catalysts speed up the reaction, they do not affect the equilibrium position – you just get there sooner!

In industry, reactions that stop half way can be very annoying. Fortunately, the position at which the reaction stops can be altered.

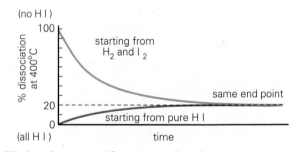

Equilibrium is reached from both directions.

Shifting the balance point

You have already seen how this can happen in open systems, where the product particles are removed before the back reaction can occur. But a similar effect can be obtained by tinkering with the conditions in closed systems. The basic rule is that if you upset the equilibrium by changing the conditions, the reaction will move to counteract the change. This is known as **Le Chatelier's principle**, after its discoverer.

Changing concentration

Bromine dissolved in water partially ionises as shown, but enough bromine is left at equilibrium to leave the characteristic yellow-brown colour.

$$Br_2(aq) + H_2O \underset{acid}{\overset{alkali}{\rightleftharpoons}} 2H^+ + Br^- + OBr^-$$
(yellow-brown)   (all colourless ions)

If alkali is added to this, the solution becomes colourless, showing that ionisation is complete. This is because the H^+ ions have reacted with the OH^- ions from the alkali, taking them out of the equation and so stopping the back reaction. The reaction has therefore continued to move to the right to counteract this loss. If acid is added, however, the increased concentration of H^+ ions speeds up the back reaction, and the colour of bromine reappears.

Changing pressure

If gases are involved, changing the pressure has a similar effect to changing the concentration of the reactants in solution. For example, calcium carbonate heated in a closed system will reach equilibrium as the pressure from the carbon dioxide formed increases, speeding up the back reaction.

$$CaCO_3 \underset{pressure}{\overset{heat}{\rightleftharpoons}} CaO + CO_2$$

The higher the gas pressure, the more the balance point is driven back to the left. That is why limestone can be metamorphosed to marble (see 9.5). At the surface, it would simply decompose when heated. But buried deep in the mountain roots, the enormous pressures stop the decomposition.

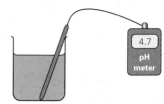
bromine dissolved in water...

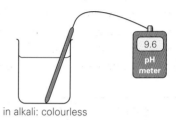
in acid: yellow-brown

in alkali: colourless

Acids and alkalis can shift the balance point.

Michaelangelo could not have made this marble statue without the Le Chatelier's principle!

Changing temperature

Heating increases the *rate* at which reactions occur, but it can also affect the balance point if the reaction is reversible. If the forward reaction is exothermic, giving out heat energy, then the back reaction must be endothermic, taking energy in. If you add *extra* heat energy, Le Chatelier's principle states that the system will change to counteract this effect. It will do this by shifting the balance in favour of the back reaction, which will then absorb the extra heat energy.

QUESTIONS

1 In two parallel experiments, gases were heated with a suitable catalyst to 400°C. In the first, equal volumes of hydrogen and iodine gas were mixed at the start, whilst in the second, hydrogen iodide gas was the sole reactant. Comment on the *final* composition of gases in the two experiments.

2 In an open system, one of the products is removed and so the forward reaction goes to completion. Is this in agreement with Le Chatelier's principle?

3 Explain why bromine dissolved in water is brown when acidified, but becomes colourless if excess alkali is added.

4 How is it that limestone can recrystallise to marble when heated during metamorphism, yet breaks down to calcium oxide when heated in the laboratory?

15.3 *The Haber process*

Nitrogen for fertilisers

Plants need nitrogen to grow well. Unfortunately, the vast amount of nitrogen in the atmosphere is mostly unavailable to plants (see 8.5). As populations grew, so did the need for artificial fertilisers. By the turn of this century, the race was on to find a way to tap the rich source of nitrogen in the atmosphere for fertilisers.

Early attempts to combine nitrogen with hydrogen directly to form ammonia were not successful. The reaction was far too slow and reached equilibrium when only a tiny amount of ammonia was produced – enough to turn damp litmus paper blue, but that was all! In 1904, a German chemist called Fritz Haber started a long study of the problem, which eventually led to a Nobel prize in 1918. Can you follow the logic of his work?

nitrogen	+	hydrogen	$\rightleftharpoons$	ammonia
N_2	+	$3H_2$	$\rightleftharpoons$	$2NH_3$

A simple equation for a complex process!

Fritz Haber – the father of fertiliser!

Problems	Haber's solutions
The reaction is very slow.	Run the reaction at a much higher temperature. Each increase of 10°C should double the rate of reaction. Even so, a temperature of 1000°C or more would be needed to speed this up to a reasonable rate. Higher temperatures are more expensive to maintain.
The reaction reaches equilibrium before full conversion to ammonia is achieved.	Looking at the reaction, four molecules of reactant are changed to two molecules of product. In gases at a given temperature and pressure, this would mean that the volume would be halved (see 11.4). Using Le Chatelier's principle, if the pressure is increased the equilibrium position should move to the right in order to counter the change. In fact, very high pressures were needed, and high pressure working is expensive and potentially dangerous.
As the reaction is exothermic, raising the temperature pushes the equilibrium point back to the left, countering the effect of increased pressure! Equilibrium is therefore reached rapidly, but the yield is low.	Use a catalyst to give an increased rate at lower temperatures. In this case, iron proved effective.

Eventually a working compromise between the advantages of a hot, fast reaction and the yield benefits of a cool, high pressure environment was reached. But Haber needed one last trick to make the process economically viable.

The final trick ...

In the Haber process, the final trick exploits the fact that ammonia is easily liquefied. The nitrogen/hydrogen mixture is recycled through the reaction vessel many times but, after each pass, the gases are cooled and the relatively small percentage of liquid ammonia is removed. This effectively makes the reaction part of an open system and reaction continues with each pass. Thus, as part of a continuous process, total conversion is eventually achieved.

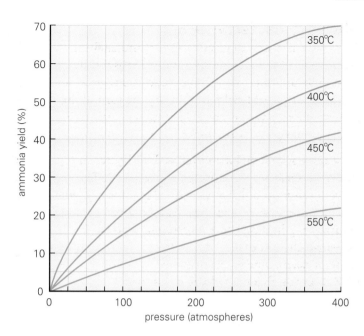

How yield varies with temperature and pressure. A typical Haber plant might run at 400°C and 250 atmospheres pressure.

A modern Haber plant

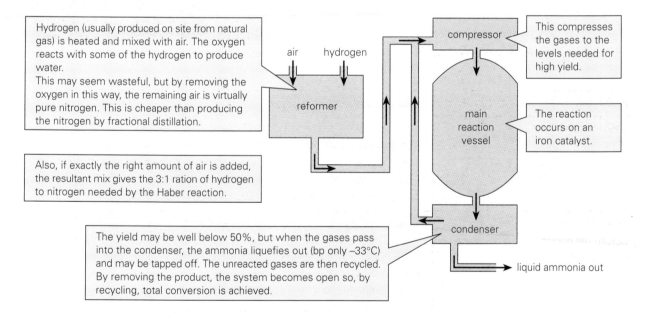

Hydrogen (usually produced on site from natural gas) is heated and mixed with air. The oxygen reacts with some of the hydrogen to produce water.
This may seem wasteful, but by removing the oxygen in this way, the remaining air is virtually pure nitrogen. This is cheaper than producing the nitrogen by fractional distillation.

Also, if exactly the right amount of air is added, the resultant mix gives the 3:1 ration of hydrogen to nitrogen needed by the Haber reaction.

This compresses the gases to the levels needed for high yield.

The reaction occurs on an iron catalyst.

The yield may be well below 50%, but when the gases pass into the condenser, the ammonia liquefies out (bp only –33°C) and may be tapped off. The unreacted gases are then recycled. By removing the product, the system becomes open so, by recycling, total conversion is achieved.

liquid ammonia out

QUESTIONS

1 From the graph, how do **a** temperature and **b** pressure affect the yield of ammonia?

2 From the graph, what is the yield under 250 atmospheres pressure at **a** 350°C and **b** 450°C?

3 Why is hydrogen mixed with air and not pure nitrogen at the start of the process?

4a Le Chatelier's principle alone suggests that this reaction should take place at very high pressures and low temperatures. Why is this combination *not* used?

b Explain how an economically viable yield of ammonia is achieved.

5 The reaction vessel is made form strong iron. What other important part does iron play in the Haber process?

183

SECTION C: QUESTIONS

1 The table below gives the melting and boiling points (in °C) of the first 38 elements:

No	element	mp	bp	No	element	mp	bp
1	H	−259	−253	20	Ca	839	1484
2	He	−272	−269	21	Sc	1541	2831
3	Li	181	1342	22	Ti	1660	3287
4	Be	1278	2477	23	V	1890	3380
5	B	2300	2550	24	Cr	1857	2670
6	C	3652	4827	25	Mn	1244	1962
7	N	−210	−196	26	Fe	1535	2750
8	O	−218	−183	27	Co	1495	2870
9	F	−220	−188	28	Ni	1455	2730
10	Ne	−248	−246	29	Cu	1083	2567
11	Na	98	883	30	Zn	420	907
12	Mg	649	1107	31	Ga	30	2400
13	Al	660	2467	32	Ge	937	2830
14	Si	1410	2355	33	As	sublimes	340
15	P	44	280	34	Se	217	685
16	S	119	445	35	Br	−7	59
17	Cl	−101	−35	36	Kr	−157	−152
18	Ar	−189	−186	37	Rb	39	686
19	K	63	760	38	Sr	769	1384

a By hand or using a computer, plot out graphs of melting point and boiling point against atomic number.

b How many of these are **i** gases and **ii** liquids at room temperature?

c i What do you notice about the melting and boiling points of elements 2,10,18 and 36?

  ii What group do these elements belong to?

  iii Why are their melting and boiling points like this?

d i What do you notice about the melting and boiling points of elements 6,14 and 32?

  ii What group do these elements belong to?

  iii Why are their melting and boiling points like this?

e i Plot a separate graph of the melting points of the group I metals and comment on the trend.

  ii How do the chemical properties of these metals vary along this line?

  iii The next group I metal is caesium (Cs, at. No. 55). Predict its melting point and chemical properties.

f i Plot a separate graph of the melting points of the halogens and comment on the trend.

  ii How do the chemical properties of these elements vary along this line?

  iii The next halogen is iodine (I, at. No. 53). Predict its melting point and chemical properties.

g Supersonic aircraft suffer great frictional heating. Suggest one advantage of titanium over aluminium in their construction.

2 The diagrams below show zinc reacting with dilute sulphuric acid in different situations.

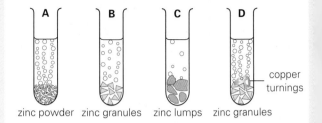

zinc powder zinc granules zinc lumps zinc granules

a Describe the reaction that is occurring.

b What test could be used to identify the gas?

c For A–C, comment on the rate of reaction. Explain why this effect occurs.

d i Comment on the rate of reaction shown in D.

  ii What is the purpose of the copper here? (Copper does not react with the acid.)

e The graph below shows how the total volume of gas given off varied with time in a more refined version of experiment B (zinc granules).

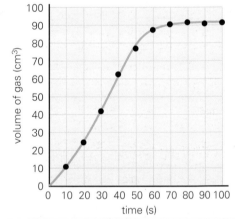

  i Describe how the volume of hydrogen could have been measured in this experiment.

  ii When was the *rate* of reaction highest?

  iii Suggest *two* reasons why the reaction slowed down after 50 seconds.

  iv Suggest a possible reason for the slightly slower start to the reaction.

f Make a sketch of the graph and draw the curves you would expect to see if it was repeated, using the same volume and strength of acid and the same mass of zinc, with **i** zinc dust and **ii** coarse granulated zinc.

g What volume of gas would you expect to be formed (at room temperature and atmospheric pressure) if 0.65 g of zinc was completely dissolved in excess sulphuric acid? (At. no. of Zn is 65.)

3 You can process black and white films at home using a developer solution to bring out the picture. This is usually bought in a concentrated form and is diluted down before use. The time needed for the chemical process to work depends on both the concentration and the temperature, and may be worked out using this graph:

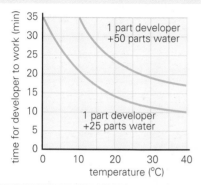

a What effect does *temperature* have on the time taken to develop the film? Explain your answer in terms of kinetic theory.

b What effect does *dilution* have on the time taken to develop the film? Explain your answer.

c How long should it take to develop a film at room temperature (27°C) if the developer has been diluted 1:25 with water?

4 Two fuel gases that were generally used before natural gas became common were *producer gas* and *water gas*. For producer gas, air was blown through red hot coke to make carbon monoxide (like the first stage of a blast furnace) in an exothermic reaction:

$$2C + O_2 \rightarrow 2CO \ (\Delta H \ -220\,J/mole)$$

For water gas, steam was passed through white-hot coke, to produce carbon monoxide and hydrogen.

$$C + H_2O \rightarrow CO + H_2 \ (\Delta H \ +130\,J/mole)$$

After just three minutes, the temperature of the coke drops and the reaction stops. Volume for volume, water gas is twice as good a fuel as producer gas (which is about 60% nitrogen).

a Explain why the coke cooled down when water gas was produced. (What sort of reaction is it?)

b The common industrial practice was to give alternate blasts of air and steam through the coke, to make producer gas and water gas in turn. Why was this done, given that water gas was a better fuel?

c Where did the nitrogen come from in producer gas?

d Water gas burns as shown:

$$CO + \tfrac{1}{2}O_2 \rightarrow CO_2 \ (\Delta H \ -283\,J/mole)$$
$$H_2 + \tfrac{1}{2}O_2 \rightarrow H_2O \ (\Delta H \ -242\,J/mole)$$

i In what way is carbon monoxide a better fuel than hydrogen?

ii Why is it not more commonly used?

iii Given your answer to **i**, why is it that water gas is *twice as good a fuel* as producer gas?

e Natural gas (methane) burns in air:

$$CH_4 + 2O_2 \rightarrow CO_2 + 2H_2O$$

i How many C—H and O=O bonds break?

ii How many C=O and O—H bonds are formed?

iii Use the bond energy figures in 14.4 to calculate the energy needed to *break* all of these bonds, and the energy given out when the new bonds are *made*.

iv From **iii** work out the overall energy change in this reaction (ΔH).

v Which is the better fuel?

5 During the industrial preparation of sulphuric acid from sulphur, sulphur dioxide has to be oxidised to sulphur trioxide. But this is a slow, reversible reaction:

$$2SO_2(g) + O_2(g) \ \underset{\text{vanadium oxide}}{\rightleftharpoons} \ 2SO_3(g)$$

a i What is the simplest way to speed up the reaction?

ii As this reaction is exothermic, which way will the balance point move if it is heated?

iii What do you think the vanadium oxide is used for?

b i How does the volume change from reactants to product?

ii Suggest a way to increase the yield of sulphur trioxide.

c i The yield of sulphur trioxide drops from 98% at 400°C to 90% at 500°C, 70% at 600°C and 40% at 700°C. Plot a graph for these figures.

ii The reaction starts at 400°C, but the temperature rises as the exothermic reaction progresses. Why do the reactants have to be cooled and recycled?

INDEX